attackpanic

YOUR GUIDE ON HOW TO OVERCOME
PANIC ATTACKS, SOCIAL PHOBIA,
AGORAPHOBIA, AND HEAL YOURSELF OF
HIGH ANXIETY (GAD, OCD, PTSD)—FOREVER

SECOND EDITION

SHAUN GRANT

Copyright © 2022 Shaun Grant.

All rights reserved. No part of this book may be reproduced, stored, or transmitted by any means—whether auditory, graphic, mechanical, or electronic—without written permission of both publisher and author, except in the case of brief excerpts used in critical articles and reviews. Unauthorized reproduction of any part of this work is illegal and is punishable by law.

ISBN: 979-8-88640-388-6 (sc)
ISBN: 979-8-88640-389-3 (hc)
ISBN: 979-8-88640-390-9 (e)

Because of the dynamic nature of the Internet, any web addresses or links contained in this book may have changed since publication and may no longer be valid. The views expressed in this work are solely those of the author and do not necessarily reflect the views of the publisher, and the publisher hereby disclaims any responsibility for them.

One Galleria Blvd., Suite 1900, Metairie, LA 70001
1-888-421-2397

CONTENTS

Dedication ix
Preface xi

PART 1
PREPARE YOURSELF

Chapter 1   My Story 3

Chapter 2   Introduction 15
How to Use This Book..18
   Building Blocks™ 1 (BB1). Understanding Anxiety Conditions......18
   Building Blocks™ 2 (BB2). Your Only Technique—*Attitude*..........19
   Building Blocks™ 3 (BB3). Destroy Panic Attacks and Phobias......19
   Building Blocks™ 4 (BB4). Removing High Anxiety
   (GAD, OCD, PTSD) 20
Medical Examination 23

Chapter 3   Getting Started 24

Chapter 4   The Right Mindset...................................... 29
Your 'Why'..30
No Compromises 31
Practice and Perseverance 31
Setbacks 32
One Foot in Front of the Other...33
How long will it take for me to heal myself?..............................34

PART 2
THE BUILDING BLOCKS™

**Chapter 5   Building Blocks™ 1 (BB1) Understanding
                Anxiety Conditions**.................................. 39
The Truth - So What's Really Going On? 39

What Is Anxiety?	41
The Emergency Response	42
The Brain	43
The Amygdala	44
Operant Conditioning	44
The Learning Process	45
The Nervous System	48
The Formation of Anxiety	52
The Formation of Panic attacks	56
The Formation of Phobias	58
Coping Strategies and Safety Crutches	60
Returning To A Healthy Balance	62
Case Study 1: Student D	67
Generalised Anxiety Disorder (GAD)	69
Does Medication help with GAD?	71
Obsessive Compulsive Disorder (OCD)	74
Post-Traumatic Stress Disorder (PTSD)	78
Case Study 1: Student D	80
Case Study 2: Student E	89
Panic Attacks	91
The Panic Cycle	95
Anxiety Related Phobias	96
Agoraphobia	97
Specific Phobia	98
Social Phobia	99
Medication	105
Johann Hari – Lost Connection	107
What Are You really Afraid Of?	108
Just Sensations	110
Analogy - Abseiling The Auckland Sky Tower	111
Anticipatory Anxiety: Frightened About Being Frightened	113
What's really The Answer?	115
Is Therapy And Counselling The Answer?	115
Summary of Building Blocks™ 1 (BB1)	118

Chapter 6 Building Blocks™ 2 (BB2) Your Only Technique - Attitude 120

Your Current Resistant Attitude 121
Non-Resistant Attitude 125
Your Best teacher - You 128
Turning Point.. 130
The Power Of The Subconscious Mind 131
   Then what happens? 133
   How does it do that? 133
   Example—Anxiety Conditions 134
   So who's in charge? 136
   Analogy 1... 136
   Analogy 2... 137
   Where Do Thoughts Come From?.. 138
   So what determines what thoughts you consciously observe?... 138
Cause and Effect of Thought 139
   What does this mean?.. 140
Case Study 142
Conscious Choice Maker.. 143
Imagination.. 147
Visualisation... 149
What Does All This Have To Do With My Anxiety Condition?... 150
Meaning/Interpretation... 151
Analogy - Threatening Dog 152
Acceptance 153
Habituation.. 154
Your Why 156
Meaningful Vision of the Future 157
Belief... 158
Trust 158
Exposure 158
Commitment 159
Practice and Perseverance 160
Deep Breathing 161
Deep Breathing Exercise... 162
Summary of Building Blocks™ 2 163

Chapter 7 Building Blocks™ 3 (BB3) Destroy Panic Attacks and Phobias 166

The Panic Attack Eliminator..168
Prepare Yourself For Success..168
   The Panic Attack Eliminator explained 170
   Important.. 174
   Important..177
Unwavering Trust..178
Look for More 179
Will I have more panic attacks? 180
Case Study—My Last Panic Attack..180
Summary of The Panic Attack Eliminator 183
The Mantra - Bringing it all together 183
Keeping a Journal - Your Feedback Loop 186
Breathe...189
Student Case Studies 190
   Student C..190
   Student D 198

Chapter 8 Building Blocks™ 4 (BB4) Removing High Anxiety (GAD, OCD, PTSD) 200

Get Off Drugs As Soon As You Can 201
The Six Golden Rules 201
Golden Rule 1: Acceptance 201
How to Implement Golden Rule 1 203
Mirror Work 205
The Correct Use Of Acceptance 206
Incorrect use of Acceptance..207
   Conditions/proviso's 207
   Wanting them to stop 208
   Expectation leads to disappointment 208
   A Quick Recap 210
Correct use of Acceptance 211
The Ten Minute Exercise 213
Your Mantra..218

Summary 219
Golden Rule 2: Gratitude 221
How to Implement Rule 2 223
Golden Rule 3: Finding Meaning 225
How to Implement Rule 3 228
Golden Rule 4, Diversion/Distraction 229
   Laugh Therapy 231
How to Implement Rule 4 233
Golden Rule 5, Stop Worrying - Eliminating Intrusive
Thoughts (Anticipatory Anxiety) 233
How to Implement Rule 5 236
   RULE 5 Mantra 236
   The Problem Solving Process – Interrupting the anxious
      feedback loop 236
Golden Rule 6, Relax 240
   Meditation 241
   Guided Visualisation Exercises 241
   Self-Hypnosis/Hypnotherapy 241
   Deep Breathing 242
   Nature 242
How to Implement Rule 6 242
Summary of The Golden Rules (BB4) 243
   1 x Golden Rule Per Day 244
   How to start 244

Chapter 9 Taking Action 246
How to Get Started 246
   BB3: Dealing with Panic Attacks and Phobias 246
   BB4: Removing the underlying anxiety condition (GAD,
      PTSD, OCD) – Implementing the Golden Rules 248
The Daily Planner 251
My Daily Planner 253
   Breathe 256
   Chime Watch 256
   Your only Job 256

    When Will I get Better? 258
    Use Only One Method 260
Dealing With Family & Friends 261
    The wrong Support 261
    The Right Support 262
    Be ok with bringing it out into the open 262
    Who gives a shit! 263
    Tell your Friends and family what's going on 263
    Give them instructions 264

Chapter 10 Final Thoughts 265

Chapter 11 Further Reading 268

DEDICATION

This book is dedicated to my four children, Finn, Paige-Huia, Tane and Gussy—who were the sole reason for me to finally take action and heal myself and also the inspiration I needed to write both the first and second edition of this book. You are the motivation of my life; you are the meaningful vision of my future. Thank you, I love you so much.

To Nikki, the mother of Finn and Paige-Huia, who endured the worst years of my life and supported me unconditionally and continues to be a close friend and a great mother. Thank you for being there for me; it can't have been easy. I love you.

To my wife, Raylene, you are the most amazing, beautiful, loving, loyal, generous, and supportive woman I have ever known. I want to be just like you when I grow up! What a ride the last 13 years have been with you. I am so blessed to have you in my life, to have you as my wife. Your belief in me and the support and generosity you have afforded me over the last 13 years made it possible for me to not only complete this enormous project, but you also empowered and enabled me to dedicate the last 13 years to helping anxiety sufferers all over the world find healing and peace. You are the reason this is book is a reality. Thank you, I love you so much.

PREFACE

Tuesday 23rd August 2022: Since first publishing attackpanic back in 2013, I have had the privilege and honour of helping thousands of sufferers from all around the world, from all walks of life heal themselves from various anxiety conditions including panic attacks, agoraphobia, social phobia, driving phobias, GAD, OCD, PTSD, to fear of sleeping bags, breathing (imagine that!), and even drinking water, not only through this book, but also my online course and my four week personal coaching programme.

I have learned a great deal over the past nine years through all of the highs and lows, successes and failures while working closely with sufferers through my coaching programme. I have studied and reviewed the latest books, programmes and scientific discoveries promoting so called 'break throughs', 'magic bullets' or some other claimed 'quick fix' to ending anxiety conditions (spoiler alert, there aren't any!).

I have taken the most important insights and lessons learned and incorporated them into this revised and updated edition in the form of new tools and approaches that will help you to adopt and embrace the healing principles outlined within the Building Blocks™. Some of these tools include The Problem Solving Process, The Journal, The Daily Planner, more real-life case studies and much more.

One unintended positive consequence over the last nine years was the benefit that non-sufferers reported from reading and implementing the healing principles contained within the Building Blocks™ of the attackpanic programme of healing which you are about to learn about.

These principles don't just help anxiety sufferers remove their underlying anxiety condition, but they can also help non-Sufferers find peace, joy and a meaningful vision of the future.

Irrespective of where you are in your own journey of life, whether things are going well right now, or whether you have found yourself in a real pickle, good old fashioned attitudes and mindsets like unconditional love and acceptance, gratitude, forgiveness, present moment awareness and the ability to step back and consciously choose how you want to respond in any given moment can benefit anyone who embraces them.

I wish I could offer you some 'new' break through, a recently discovered 'magic bullet' here in this revised edition that will end your sufferer overnight, I really do! I know exactly what you are going through, I have been where you are. I have seen so much pain and suffering I would love nothing better than to say 'hey, go here, take this, do this, do that and all your suffering will miraculously disappear and you will once again live an unrestricted, unlimited, full and happy life.

But I can't because that 'magic bullet' or 'quick fix' doesn't exist for anxiety sufferers, it didn't exist nine years ago when I first published attackpanic, and it certainly doesn't now. But thankfully you don't need a quick fix to heal yourself, you just need to find the determination to follow the attackpanic programme and be willing to do whatever you have to do to be well again.

'It's not things that upset us, it's our judgement about things.'

(Epictetus)

****

After fifteen years of suffering and over six years of research and trial and error, I finally healed myself of social phobia, agoraphobia, and generalised anxiety disorder (GAD). I healed myself using a programme of healing that I developed. Although my programme, specifically my

Building Blocks™ are unique, the principles contained within them are not. These principles are well proven and taught by all successful teachers and programmes. In fact, all ex-sufferers have healed themselves through these principles, whether by accident, whether they were aware of it or not, or through a teacher.

After I was healed, I found myself working with other sufferers. In the beginning, people were referred to me through friends. Then, through word of mouth, I began getting referrals from doctors from the New Zealand Defence Force who had patients that were struggling with varying degrees of high anxiety, from GAD, PTSD, OCD, right through to panic attacks and phobias such as social and driving-related phobias, and who were not responding to conventional treatment, intervention, and therapy. And that's pretty much how attackpanic was born. That was nearly 13 years ago now!

It turns out that the way I explained things, the way I simplified the truth and perceived complexities surrounding anxiety-related disorders, resulted in their own healing. The information wasn't necessarily new to them, but it just seemed to make sense through the way in which I communicated. I was then encouraged to write this book.

This is probably not the first book or programme you will have invested in. In most cases, I am the last resort for sufferers. If this is the case, you will probably know just as much as I do when it comes to the anatomy and psychology of anxiety-related disorders. Reading my book will not make you smarter, but it will make you better.

If, for some extraordinary reason, this is the first book you have ever read about anxiety disorders, then you are one of the lucky ones. I am about to save you lots money and years of searching for an answer to your suffering. All you need to do is build your belief and trust that what is contained in these pages is all you will ever need to understand, believe, do, and be to heal yourself.

When I first started writing this book nearly 13 years ago, a large area of my first draft detailed extensive strategies, techniques, and safety crutches to help you cope with your panic and anxiety. Those sufferers that I worked with were usually familiar with most of the strategies and techniques and had used them with varying levels of success during their suffering.

Coping strategies and techniques are aptly named as they help you to 'cope', not heal. If they healed you, you wouldn't need them any more, and you wouldn't be reading this book. Coping strategies and safety crutches like avoidance for example might very well provide you with some form of relief, thereby making you feel better, but they will not make you better.

My job is to make you better, not show you how to cope, not to make you feel better. Coping strategies usually work only for a short period of time; sooner or later, they become redundant, and you will need to replace them with new and invariably more drastic strategies and techniques to help you 'cope', which will again be effective only temporarily. You do not need to cope with panic and anxiety, and using strategies and techniques to help you cope only perpetuates the anxiety cycle.

So I have removed all the stuff on coping strategies and techniques that will definitely help you cope, help you feel better (for a while anyway), but will not make you better.

As you will discover, panic and anxiety disorders are nothing more than a bad habit; for whatever reason, you have conditioned yourself to respond in perfectly normal situations with fear.

All habits develop through persistent exposure, action, and practice until that behaviour is accepted by the subconscious mind as perfectly normal. That's how you learn any skill, behavioural pattern, or discipline. This process of learning is called Operant Conditioning.

Panic and anxiety disorder is simply a bad habit, but what makes it worse is that it is a habit built on fear. To heal yourself of panic attacks and phobias, you will need to practice and persevere in a routine programme of healing, which will require you to expose yourself to the very thing which causes your panic: fear.

If you suffer from any of the high-anxiety disorders mentioned earlier, and you are willing to embrace my Building Blocks™ and commit to practising and persisting with the principles outlined in them, then you will heal yourself.

This book contains only the answers to end your suffering. It won't help you to 'cope' with your condition, because I am not going to teach you any coping strategies or techniques; if you are reading this book, you will already possess an arsenal of strategies and techniques to help you cope, from medication to exit strategies, to the ultimate and most potent coping strategy available: avoidance.

I know that this is a winning recipe because it worked for me, and over fifteen years, my case became extreme. It has worked for every single sufferer I have worked with over the last 13 years who has embraced this programme, and finally the principles in this book are the precise principles that every ex-sufferer and every successful teacher has adopted.

Take some comfort in the fact that I completely healed myself of inappropriate anxiety, social phobia, and agoraphobia, having suffered for so many years, sabotaging relationships and opportunities, and destroying businesses, careers, and fortunes along the way.

Ready? Let's get started.

PART 1

PREPARE YOURSELF

CHAPTER 1

MY STORY

My anxiety condition developed during my ten-year career in the New Zealand Police. I joined at the tender age of twenty in 1990, and before that point, I was a pretty normal (maybe a little bit cocky), fun loving and outgoing individual. I remember when I was growing up thinking I was ten foot tall and bullet proof and I used to do all sorts of stupid shit without any consideration to the consequences.

I was brought up in a large family with six other brothers and sisters. My mum was the bread winner and a hard worker all her life. My dad, yeah not so much. He was a bit useless to be fair, not a very nice man at all most of his life. Until his later years, all I remember about him was that he was a physically and verbally violent drunk, who never managed to work and provide for his family. He died of lung cancer at the age of sixty-nine. He was at home for the last week of his life, so I was able to make my peace with him.

I didn't miss out on great male role models, though. I had three elder brothers whom I looked up to, and they took good care of me, apart from the times when they would see how long *they* could hold my head under water—bless.

I am very grateful, however, with some of the lessons my dad taught me. He taught me exactly how *not* to treat your wife and children, and how destructive alcohol abuse, verbal and physical violence can be on a family nucleus. I now have four beautiful children, and neither their mothers nor I have ever laid a finger on them for any reason whatsoever, and they are the most respectful, loving, and well-behaved children you could ever wish for. I managed to break the cycle I guess, so thank you Dad.

There will be no argument that a career in the police is extremely dangerous at times and very stressful most of the time. Why and how I developed high anxiety when others around me may have not is not important and is irrelevant to the healing process, and therefore not even worth discussing—but I did, and that's just the way it is. At a very young age, I was exposed to some horrific scenes and many life-threatening situations.

My first posting out of the police college was in a small town called Levin, with a population of about 15,000. I was working as a uniform constable on section. There were three officers on each section.

On my very first nightshift, I was called to a motorcycle accident. The other two officers were busy, so I had to attend by myself. When I got there, the scene was sickening. The rider had lost control and crashed into a palm tree, but before he crashed into the tree, he lost his helmet (he was a gang member, and wearing the correct headgear wasn't cool). He was dead on my arrival. His head had swollen up like a basketball and picking him up and supporting his head was like trying to pick up a bag full of broken pottery. I had to deal with the whole incident myself!

I could continue with hundreds of stories like this one, along with others relating to physical attacks, constant threats to my life and family, child abuse and rape cases, homicides and suicides, but you get the picture—it's pretty traumatic and stressful.

So how did I deal with these stressful and traumatic events throughout my years in the police? Did I go to counselling and therapy? No, but I should have! Therapy and counselling at the time of a traumatic event is very effective as part of the grieving and healing process. But that's not how we 'rolled' back then. The way I dealt with it was through alcohol and overindulgent behaviour, lots of it! I was very social, and would drown my sorrows, usually in large groups along with colleagues.

Now this was very effective at masking the symptoms and sensations of anxiety, but it didn't do anything to reduce stress and anxiety levels. So over the years, the anxiety levels just kept creeping up higher and higher.

I didn't really know how to completely relax and recharge the batteries. My career in the police was full on. I laughed at any invitations made by the department for professional help.

I experienced my very first panic attack about 30 years ago, 1993 to be exact. I was a constable at the time and talking in front of a classroom full of children. At the time, I didn't know what was happening, but I started experiencing these very uncomfortable sensations building up. The more I focused on them, the more powerful they became. My heart began beating out of control, my hands were shaking, I felt dizzy, I was sweating, my throat was dry and I couldn't talk properly, I was stuttering, and my body felt numb and I felt really weird, like disorientated weird. I had this overwhelming urge to escape; I just wanted to get out of the classroom. But I couldn't go, so I just sat there, terrified and embarrassed at the same time. I don't know what it looked like, but it felt like I was losing control. There was nothing I could do about it though, it wasn't like I could just get up and leave (I would later develop coping strategies in the form of a suite of excuses of why I had to leave a room or meeting. I had a reason for every occasion!). It turns out that staying right there and not running was the best and only thing to do (I'll explain why later), as eventually, rather quickly in fact all the horrible sensations and thoughts all of a sudden went away, and I was back to normal.

I completed my talk without any problems and left. I remember thinking 'What the hell just happened there?' One minute I was freaking out, and then the next I'm good to go again. But at 23 years of age and because I had never experienced this before, I didn't have a clue and just shrugged my shoulders and boxed on.

As time went by, my anxiety levels crept up, and my behaviour became more and more anxious. I never gave my mind and body, the time and space to relax, calm down, and bring my anxiety levels back down to normal levels. At the time I had no idea of what was happening.

As the years went by in the police, I began experiencing the same type of panic attacks as mentioned above more often.

I distinctly remember one incident sometime in 1997 when I was a plain clothes Detective Constable working in a crime squad in Palmerston North. My squad was called to a rape complaint at a residential address. On our arrival I was assigned officer in charge of the crime scene which was the victims bedroom. I went into the bedroom with about four of my colleagues, including my supervisor. It was quite a small bedroom. As soon as the victim walked in, I felt that horrible anxious feeling building up again. My heart started racing, I felt my chest tightening, and my stomach felt very heavy and I had this massive feeling of uneasiness, it felt like the spotlight was on me, like the whole world was watching everything that I was doing.

As the Officer in charge of the scene it was my job to ask the victim certain questions and reconstruct what happened. I became more and more self conscious because I was preoccupied with these horrible and uncomfortable feelings. My initial urge was to get out of the bedroom before I lost my shit and everyone noticed me losing control. All I could focus on was how to get out of the room. I was so preoccupied and self conscious that I had difficulty asking questions. I spent so much time focusing on these uncomfortable sensations that I began feeling extremely disorientated. I did everything I could to stop the horrible anxious and panicky feelings, but the more I tried to stop these sensations, the more they seem to come on.

I manage to fumble my way through a few questions, but all the while I was looking at the doorway and trying to find a way to get out.

Every time I asked the victim a question, I remember my supervisor had to ask additional questions in order to get the right information from her. Obviously I was in such a tizz trying to get out of the room, preoccupied with trying to get rid of all these sensations, preoccupied with ridiculing myself that this was happening in the first place, and that I was such a failure that I wasn't even able to carryout an adequate scene examination, my poor old supervisor had to step in and rescue me… bloody hell!

This seemed to go on forever but it probably didn't. Somehow I managed to make up some bullshit excuse as to why I needed to go outside and canvas the backyard. Everyone seemed to buy it, and I left the bedroom and rushed outside to the backyard, where I paced up and down the perimeter of the yard trying to calm the fuck down. I spent most of my time ridiculing myself for being weak and useless.

As soon as I got outside I started to feel the panic and anxiety abate and I began to calm down. I took my notebook out and made out I was writing stuff in it, but I wasn't, I was trying to stop myself from freaking out. My Supervisor came out to see how I was getting on. Luckily by this stage I had composed myself enough to go back into the bedroom and complete my crime scene examination.

By that I mean, I didn't feel disorientated anymore, I didn't have that uneasy feeling or that overwhelming urge to escape.

When I went back into the bedroom I was fine and for the rest of the time I was there I didn't experience another panic attack. I was back to my normal self. I finished my scene examination and we all left.

Nothing was ever said about my behaviour. Indeed, as it turns out no one even noticed that I was having difficulty, interesting aye!? More on that later.

I remember sitting back shortly after and wondering once again what the hell just happened, why this was happening, and how to stop it. Of course back then I had no idea what was going on or how to deal with it properly, so I just shrugged my shoulders and boxed on as usual.

Throughout these years I had no idea why this was happening to me and my panic attacks seemed to have a mind of their own. But what I did notice was that the attacks were happening more frequently in social settings. This overwhelming urge to escape was due to the 'fight or flight' or 'panic' response I was experiencing as a panic attack. If I could escape, or get out of the situation, I would. And by doing that, my panic immediately retreated. But what I didn't realise at the time was that I was just reinforcing an anxious pattern of behaviour.

I began to avoid social gatherings where I believed I would experience a panic attack. And when I had to attend any such gatherings, I devised all sorts of coping strategies and techniques that would allow me to escape whenever I was overcome with the uncontrollable urge to 'get the fuck out!'

There were other times, of course, where I just had to grin and bear it, and it was horrible. But interestingly enough, although the experience was horrible, nothing bad actually happened, and the panic attack passed pretty quickly - every single time!

Instead of learning from these lessons, these insights, I began worrying about the next time I would have a panic attack. I had developed a constant feeling of unease in the back of my mind. I was later to learn that this was the start of anticipatory anxiety.

When I had attacks, it was like I was in another world; it didn't seem real, and it was like I was watching a movie. It's hard to describe the desperation, knowing that this was not right, knowing that this was destroying me, not knowing why this was happening, and feeling angry with myself for escaping or for allowing this to happen.

As the years went by, my attacks became more and more prevalent, and I had to devise more and more coping strategies and safety crutches as the ones that I was using had become redundant as the anxiety levels in my brain crept higher and higher. Being a natural leader and mentor, the roles which I was attracted to when I left the police at the beginning of 2000 were always in a leadership or high-profile capacity. These roles required that I engaged with various business sectors, groups, organisations, and communities.

Though I coped well when I was acting in my role; attending professional engagements and working under extreme pressure, it was the social component that I found more and more difficult to deal with. And this inability to cope with social gatherings grew worse and worse. My coping strategies were no longer coping with this aspect of my work.

This is how I developed my social phobia and agoraphobia, which not only affected my business and professional life but also trickled over to my personal and social life. It got increasingly difficult to go out and socialise during the mid-2000s.

Oh and I had become a real prick by this stage too. My behaviour became worse as my anxiety and stress levels began to grow. I became increasingly argumentative, aggressive, cocky, mentally manipulative and controlling, a high functioning, high end Narcissist. This of course wasn't me, wasn't who I really was, this was behaviour, this was who (or what) I had become; My outward behaviour wasn't who I was, but it was who I had become.

At the time of writing this second edition, my behaviour is now aligned to who I really am. Today I am (among other things) loving, compassionate, forgiving and empathetic towards myself and others. I live (most of the time anyway) in gratitude and self love and acceptance. It's a conscious choice that I make every single day. Anyway, back to my story!

I sabotaged so many amazing opportunities because of my phobias. I left jobs because of them. Just when I was ready to go to the next stage, I would do something stupid to destroy the opportunity. I would hate to think what some of my colleagues must have thought of me, all those times when I failed to turn up to social meetings and gatherings, the times when I left early, and the times when I would be excused during a gathering and disappear for long periods, only returning when I had gained control over my panic.

During these periods, I was usually locked in a toilet cubicle feeling absolutely helpless and desperate, trying to control a full on panic attack. During these attacks, I experienced the disturbing sensations, such as derealisation (feeling disconnected from reality), depersonalisation, racing heart, dry throat, and itchy skin. My behaviour changed so much that people perceived me as ignorant, arrogant, or strange.

As a natural leader, I have the ability to communicate and relate to anyone. I can inspire and bring out the best in others. But through this very dark period of my life, this affinity with people was lost (it's back now, thank goodness).

I left a great role with a drug company in 2002 because of my social phobia. Because I didn't know what was going on at the time, I thought the problem was always the job. I sabotaged many great career opportunities during the mid-2000s.

Pretty soon, I refused to go to social gatherings out of fear of having a panic attack; school events, parent teacher meetings, and cafés, where I feared seeing and being confronted by people and having a panic attack. I feared that I would have a panic attack if stopped by people walking down the street, and I did. My tools of coping were no longer working. I felt so desperate, so helpless. I had no idea what was going on.

I sabotaged everything from sporting, business, music, and social opportunities. I lost businesses which ultimately led to my bankruptcy in 2008. I made silly decisions based on poor judgment through fear. This led to the break up with Nikki, the mother of my two beautiful eldest children Finn and Paige-Huia. Nikki endured the worst times of my life, and perhaps this was the last straw for her. I don't blame her. I had sabotaged so many opportunities, lost our fortune and moved my family around so much. She had seen me at my absolute worst.

The height of my panic attacks came while I was working as a team leader at Toyota New Zealand (TNZ), during 2008. I started at TNZ during the month of March, after moving my family back to Palmerston North from Wellington following the collapse of several businesses, mostly in the bio-diesel and alternative fuels sector.

I avoided work meetings, social and business functions. I kept to myself during lunch breaks, spending most of them in the sick bay. I avoided people as much as I could during the day, which was near-on impossible. I spent most of my time locked away in the toilets, waiting for my panic attacks to subside.

So, once again, feeling completely helpless, I resigned from TNZ, after only nine months. My panic attacks had reached the stage where I found it almost physically impossible to go to work, or even leave the house.

That was the last straw for Nikki, and our relationship from that point on went from average to worse, resulting in a split towards the end of 2008. This was the lowest point in my life. I was desperate to find a cure for my panic attacks. If I didn't, I would jeopardise the well-being of my two precious children, and it was this that ultimately gave me the strength and motivation to finally take action and do whatever it would take to heal myself.

I had already gained a huge amount of knowledge and understanding about anxiety conditions. I began researching and studying this area in about 2004. I knew all there was to know about the anatomy of anxiety and the truth behind anxiety conditions. I tried various therapies, programmes, and systems without success but was at a loss as to why I couldn't heal myself.

You see, just like most sufferers, especially the ones who reach out for my help, I knew logically what the problem was, and what I needed to do! I knew I was having panic attacks, and that they were irrational and there was nothing to actually fear. I also knew that I needed to walk into these false alarms and let them do their worst. We all know this logically right? What I didn't know was the how to do what I knew I needed to do.

My breakthrough came when I realised that it didn't matter what I knew intellectually, if I wasn't willing to throw away all coping strategies, techniques, and safety crutches (that make me feel better), if I wasn't willing to stand right in front of my fears, my false alarms, if I wasn't willing to reach out and touch the ghost, resist all urges to run, and let them completely engulf me, I would continue to be trapped in a perpetual cycle of panic. And to be able to do all that, I needed belief and trust, lots of it. I also needed courage, lots more of that. Without belief and trust in myself and a training system, I couldn't possibly muster the required courage to tackle my false fears and alarms head on. It always felt like for every five steps forward I would take, I would end up taking ten steps backwards.

It all boiled down to me being willing to practice and persevere with the right attitude and choosing how I responded, and what I said to myself. My conscious choice of attitude and behaviour determined whether my initial anxious sensations spiralled out of control, or just disolved away to nothing more than an irritation. More on this later.

My healing was very rapid from that point on. I chose to see every anxiety-provoking situation as an opportunity to practice my new attitude. I persevered and became very disciplined with my practice. I just did it; I followed my system, no matter what. I had many, many setbacks before things began to click, but I had belief and trust in what I was doing, and no matter what was happening, I moved forward with courage.

Through my commitment to expose myself to the anxiety provoking situation and practicing and persevering with the right attitude and behaviour, I healed myself of social phobia and agoraphobia, along with the underlying anxiety condition (GAD), using my system outlined in my Building Blocks™.

I will elaborate further on some of my experiences throughout my Building Blocks™.

Today I am at peace; I love and accept myself unconditionally, exactly the way I am. I am grateful for everything in my life, and I have an amazing vision of the future. I feel truly blessed to have suffered the way I have. I found meaning in my suffering, and I now use my knowledge and experience to help others heal themselves. I can instil belief and courage in others because I have been through it all, and if I can do it, so can anyone else. My journey has proven to be a very powerful tool in helping others.

Being at peace in the moment and experiencing joy doesn't mean that I don't step in shit or have really bad days or that things don't go wrong, because just like everyone else, things do go wrong—that's what we call life. Being at peace means living in the present moment, loving, accepting 'what is', embracing the good and the bad that life throws at me, taking positive action on what I can control, letting go of that which I can't control, and not being attached to whatever life throws at me. It's a conscious choice that I make.

My wonderful children, my beautiful wife, and my ability in helping others heal themselves are the greatest gifts I could have ever wished for. I think I am the luckiest man alive.

CHAPTER 2

INTRODUCTION

For fifteen years, I suffered from general anxiety disorder, or GAD as it is affectionately known. My high anxiety and panic attacks developed during my ten-year career in the New Zealand Police. Towards the later part of those years of suffering, my anxiety developed into severe social phobia and agoraphobia.

Now I am healed. How did I do it? Well, that's what this book is all about. And if you suffer from an anxiety disorder, such as GAD, Obsessive Compulsive Disorder (OCD), Post Traumatic Stress Disorder (PTSD), panic attacks, or anxiety-related phobias (social phobia or agoraphobia), then this book is for you too. All that you will ever need to know in order to heal yourself is contained within my Building Blocks™.

For me, for whatever reason, my journey to healing took years and years of study, research, trial and error, and setbacks before I finally cracked the code and worked out what was going on (or what wasn't going on), why it was going on, why other great teachers and programmes didn't work for me, and most importantly, how to heal myself.

During my journey of suffering, I sabotaged business and career opportunities, destroyed relationships, lost businesses and fortunes (going bankrupt in the process), and lost the worst thing that any father could ever possibly lose—the custody of my two children at the time, Finn and Paige Huia.

Having said that, I have gained so much for my experiences; I love my life and myself unconditionally and those around me. I am grateful for my life 'as is' right now; I do not judge others, and I accept them exactly the way they are. I have great empathy and compassion towards others, and I am an amazing father. Before and during my suffering, I was the complete opposite.

'Disorder' is the common term for all of the varying degrees of inappropriate anxiety as I just mentioned. This is a gross misconception, as the above terms are not physical or mental *illnesses* or *disorders*, and do not require any medicinal or psychiatric intervention, treatment, or therapy.

High anxiety is a *behavioural condition*, a *bad habit*, nothing more, and it is also completely harmless. Anxiety is perfectly normal; it's part of our primal survival programming, and we need it to function normally. Anxiety is our friend, alerting us to danger or threat. For whatever reason, your anxiety levels have become stuck on high through learnt behaviour, or Operant Conditioning. You have programmed your subconscious mind to respond anxiously at inappropriate times.

But, it's not a *disorder*; this is the very first truth that you need to embrace and accept if you are to heal yourself completely. *All* of the *disorders* that I mentioned earlier are high anxiety behavioural conditions, only at varying degrees.

So from this moment on, I refer to the various levels of inappropriate anxiety as a 'condition', a behavioural 'condition'.

The answer to building new non-anxious behaviour is not in techniques or strategies to help you cope, deal, or protect you against panic or anxiety-provoking situations, it is in your *attitude*, your interpretation, the meaning you give to the experience that is the answer, the *only* answer.

It is your *attitude* towards your anxious behaviour and corresponding anxious sensations that not only maintains your behaviour but also fuels its perpetuation and survival. All the actions, reactions, and behaviours, worrying and anticipatory thoughts that you currently engage in to protect yourself against your fears are all based on resistance, all based around fear of the fear itself, and as you will find out, it is this fearful, resistant *attitude* that gives life to this horrible but harmless habit.

Your current *attitude* is just sending a message of reinforcement to your subconscious mind that you need more protection.

My Building Blocks™ will help you develop a non-anxious attitude towards panic and anxiety, allowing you to disempower and destroy panic attacks, phobias, and the underlying anxiety condition (GAD, OCD, PTSD) for good.

One of the many teachers that I admire and who was instrumental in my eventual healing is Dr Reid Wilson, author of *Don't Panic*. Here is what he has to say about *attitude*:

> *'Your resistance, your commitment to fight or avoid your discomfort actually causes your continued problem with panic. The single most important way to win over panic attacks is to change your attitude towards the panic.'*

Fighting, resisting, running, protecting, along with a multitude of therapies and interventions have failed you. It's time to change your attitude.

To face your fears, you will need to restore trust and belief in yourself and your ability to handle anxiety-provoking situations. However, before you can do that, you need to have trust and belief in a teacher, programme, or protocol, and the courage to move forward and practice a new attitude towards your fears.

I know exactly what you are going through, because I have been there, and now I am healed. By sharing my story, I hope to make that critical connection with you and help you build trust and belief that the principles contained in this programme work, and restore confidence and belief in yourself that you can return to a normal anxiety-free life.

If I can heal myself, then so can you, no matter how bad you *think* you are. If you are willing to do whatever it takes to get well, if you are willing to do exactly what is outlined in my Building Blocks™, if you are willing to practice and persevere through the inevitable setbacks and challenges that you will face along your journey, then you *will* heal yourself.

How to Use This Book

Warning: I make no apologies for being repetitive throughout my Building Blocks™. Repetition is the mother of all skills, and you will need constant reinforcement as you go about building new non-anxious behaviour.

There are two objectives in the attackpanic programme:

1. To teach you how to stop panic attacks and phobias in their tracks and disempower them completely (See Building Blocks™ 3).
2. To remove the underlying anxiety condition (GAD, OCD, PTSD), and to return you back to a happy, fulfilling, loving, giving, non-anxious person.(See Building Blocks™ 4).

My programme of healing is contained within what I call the Building Blocks™:

Building Blocks™ 1 (BB1). Understanding Anxiety Conditions

BB1 explains what is happening to you and why. All that you need to know and understand about your condition is contained here. You do not need to know anything more in order to heal yourself. Having an understanding around the truth of your condition is critical to you being able to form the required levels of belief and trust in order to move forward into the next BBs and conquer your fears and build new non-anxious habits.

Building Blocks™ 2 (BB2). Your Only Technique—Attitude

BB2 discusses the only technique that is proven to completely heal you from any anxiety condition, and is the only technique that you will ever need—*attitude*. By this I am referring to an *attitude* of non-resistance and unconditional acceptance of your anxious thoughts and sensations, an *attitude* of willingness to facing and experiencing your fearful situations or false alarms and allowing and accepting whatever happens, without trying to fight or control the sensations

- Not giving a shit – as George Carlin would say;
- Giving panic or anxiety permission to hang around.

This *attitude* seems outrageous and counter-intuitive at first; however, it is this paradoxical approach which is the *only* answer. As absurd as this may sound at the start, it is completely opposite to what you are currently doing, and what you are currently doing hasn't worked at ending your suffering, in fact, your resistant *attitude* only serves to perpetuate panic and anxiety. Other teachers and programmes may use different terms or approaches, but stripped down, *all* successful programmes come down to one thing, your *attitude*. Whether you currently suffer from panic attacks or phobias, GAD, PTSD, OCD, or any combination of the above, your *attitude* is the only technique you will ever need.

Building Blocks™ 3 (BB3). Destroy Panic Attacks and Phobias

BB3 will show you how to stop panic attacks in their tracks, disempowering them completely. No coping techniques or strategies, or any other form of intervention is required, just your *attitude* and willingness to practice and persevere with a set of protocols *proven* to not only work, but is the *only* answer to ending your suffering completely.

All ex-sufferers who have healed themselves have done so through this mental *attitude*, whether by accident, or through a programme of healing. This is the only way to completely destroy panic attacks and phobias. This principle isn't new; it's not rocket science, and it isn't my discovery. You will find this paradoxical approach to be the cornerstone of any successful programme.

It is so important that you get this. Whatever else you do to support yourself in terms of techniques, strategies, therapies and treatments will have very little impact on your success in ending your suffering; in fact, they will only make your situation worse and prolong your full recovery. This is the only answer.

Building Blocks™ 4 (BB4). Removing High Anxiety (GAD, OCD, PTSD)

Now it's time to reprogramme your subconscious mind with new non-anxious habitual behaviour. Here I will teach you a set of principles or lifestyle changes for you to implement into your daily life to lower your anxiety and teach your subconscious mind new non-anxious behaviour.

My programme is based around first building a strong foundation of understanding, belief, trust, confidence, and courage in this programme and yourself. Without this foundation, it will be extremely difficult for you to do the work required to heal yourself. Setbacks and challenges are pretty much guaranteed as we go about building your new non-anxious habitual behaviour.

So each BB is designed to provide a foundation for the next BB to build on. *Do not move on to the next BB unless you have accepted the principles contained in the previous BB as truth, as fact.*

So first of all, read this book from cover to cover to get a basic appreciation of all the material contained here. I recommend that you do not take notes or backtrack at this point, just keep reading, even if you come across material that you have difficulty in accepting, just read on with an enthusiastic interest.

Read and absorb every little morsel contained within the Building Blocks™. Review them as many times as it takes until you fully understand and accept the principles as *the* truth.

- You can then go back and review the 'Summary' section of each Building Block™ whenever you need support or reassurance (and you will).

These principles are not only proven to work, they are the only answer to ending your suffering. There is nothing else that you need to know. Seeking more might make you smarter, but it won't make you better. In fact, in my case and my experience, seeking more makes you worse. You invariably just end up more confused and frustrated, and that causes even more anxiety.

At least your situation has gotten so bad, so desperate to the point where you have to do something about it. Rejoice that you have arrived here, as tens of millions of other sufferers will just tolerate their situation as their lot, and plunge forward, not entirely happy, but not bad enough that they have to do something about it, allowing an anxiety condition to restrict their lives.

It's not enough to practice a new system, methodology, routine without manifesting a deep belief in what you are doing and why you are doing it. Destroying fears requires a shift in the subconscious mind, and you cannot impress any change in the subconscious mind without developing absolute belief, trust, and expectancy that what you are doing *will* work.

The subconscious mind will accept anything you believe to be true and will act on it. You know this is the case, as your panic or phobias aren't real and offer no real threat to you; you know this at the conscious level, yet it doesn't make an ounce of difference to your *fear*. You 'believe' it to be true, and so it is for you.

I am not a doctor nor do I hold any psychology degrees. Does that bother you? It shouldn't, the only thing that should bother you is whether or not you're getting better. Let me ask you a question; How have all the doctors and psychologists, therapy and counselling sessions been working for you?

Understand this:

- All the doctors, psychologists, and therapy and counselling sessions didn't help me one bit, nor did they help you. If they did, you wouldn't be reading my book, principally because I wouldn't have had to write it in the first place;
- The teachers that I learnt the most from, and who had the biggest impact on my road to healing, were not doctors, counsellors, therapists (NLP, CBT), psychiatrists, psychotherapists, psychologists or hypnotherapists, they were amazing people who healed themselves and then began teaching others how to self-heal;
- I healed myself through the Building Blocks™ that I developed.

Doctors, psychiatrists, psychologists, and psychotherapists all have their place. However, in my experience, and obviously yours, when it comes to anxiety conditions, the conventional approach to dealing with what amounts to nothing more than a bad habit just isn't working.

You are about to embark on a programme to remove your anxious pattern of behavior. To give yourself the best chance at success, you will need structure and routine to base your practice and perseverance around. Chapter 9: Taking Action will provide you with this initial base.

Medical Examination

Before you begin this programme, you should undergo a full medical examination, first to establish that you do suffer from an anxiety condition, and second to rule out any other illness or disorder, both physical and mental, which maybe causing your anxious symptoms.

If you suffer from an anxiety condition and are otherwise perfectly healthy, then the uncomfortable sensations that you may experience, such as racing heart, blurred vision, headaches, shaking limbs, and pains in the chest, are not symptoms of a medical illness or disorder, such as heart disease or hyperglycaemia. They are normal sensations produced as part of an anxious response and are completely harmless, and therefore can and will be ignored during your programme of healing.

CHAPTER 3

GETTING STARTED

As I have eluded to earlier, GAD, PTSD, OCD, panic attacks or phobias are all part of the same anxiety condition, just at different degrees of severity. You are not mentally ill and you do not have a mental disorder. You have taught yourself through Operant Conditioning, through repetition, to behave anxiously at completely inappropriate times. So essentially we're dealing with a bad habit that requires removal.

The attackpanic program therefore is based around habituation, it will teach you how to reprogram your subconscious mind with new non-anxious behavior.

When you're learning any new skill, behavior or discipline, this process of learning is called Operant Conditioning. You will learn more about this later, but in very simple terms, it is the process of repeating any skill, behavior or discipline until it becomes a habitual pattern of behavior.

This is precisely how you developed your anxiety condition, and this is precisely how you are going to remove your anxiety condition. There is no other way! Avoidance, medication and therapy for example are nothing more than safety crutches and coping strategies;

- They will make you feel better, but they won't make you better;
- Only practicing new non- anxious behaviour WITH the right attitude will make you better. This probably won't make you feel better at the start, but it will make you better.

Now in order to develop any skill, behaviour or discipline into a habit there are 3 things that we need:

- Exposure;
- Intensity;
- Duration.

Exposure
You need to expose yourself to that skill, behavior or discipline that you want to learn to do, that you want to become a habit. You have to do the do, you can't just watch a video, you can't just read a book about it, you can't just go and talk to somebody who will make you feel better!

You must put yourself into the situation, you must practice and persevere with whatever it is that you want to learn, that you want to become good at.

Learning your new non-anxious behavior is no different. You will have to expose yourself to what you perceive to be fearful so you can practice being a non-anxious person. There is no way around this. Your own life experiences will validate this.

Intensity
The more intense your practice is, the faster you can develop your new skill or behavior. The more intense you practice at say playing the guitar for example, the faster you'll improve and the quicker you'll develop your skill and discipline.

The more intensity that you can create around your practice i.e. putting yourself into really scary situations and practicing the correct attitude, the quicker you can develop new non-anxious behavior, and the quicker you can dis-empower panic and anxiety.

Duration
The longer you practice for, the quicker you develop your skill. As an anxiety sufferer the longer you can stay in a situation that is causing you discomfort, again, using the correct attitude, the quicker you develop your new non-anxious behavior and the quicker you dis-empower panic.

Structured programme
- *The more you do the faster you get there;*
- *The more structure you have the more you do.*

The attackpanic programme is a structured programme of habituation, a frame work, a recipe for success. And like all recipes this programme contains ingredients, if you use all the ingredients set out in this book, you will heal yourself very quickly.

So what do you need to succeed?
What do you need to heal yourself from your anxiety condition no matter how severe no matter how long you have been suffering? You need belief. You need belief in me as your coach and trainer, you need to believe in yourself that you can do this, you need to believe in the attackpanic programme.

And just as important as belief you need a vision of what you want to achieve, you need to have the passion, the commitment, the determination and discipline to persevere and practice with whatever it takes in order for you to achieve your vision or goal. For you that's to be a normal non-anxious person.

There is no time like the present – All we have is 'now'
When is the right time to start? Well the truth is no matter who or where you are there is never a right time to start. There is no point in waiting for the weather to improve, until you get some money, until you

get a job, until you leave this person, until this person takes you back, until you finish a course, or until you feel better.

There is never the right time to start, there never will be a right time to start. If you live in this world, and you have warm blood flowing through your veins, chances are there is always going to be some challenge or issue or some excuse that is going to occupy your time and attention and you will forever be holding this off.

The right time to start is now, now is all we have, there is no point in waiting for the right time because it will never ever turn up. There is no point in waiting for tomorrow because tomorrow never comes, now is all you have and now is all you need to start teaching yourself to be a non-anxious person again.

Expectations
Your only expectation should be to practice the correct attitude which is an attitude of non-resistance, an attitude of acceptance for what is right here right now, without any expectation for anything to change (more on that later!) If you expect to heal yourself in a week, and you don't, then you may be disappointed. You may heal yourself in a week but you may not as well, in which case you will be disappointed, then you'll get more frustrated, disillusioned and yes more anxious.

You may even start saying things like the programme doesn't work. The programme works if you work. When you start playing the guitar do you expect to play like your hero in the first week or months? No you don't, you accept that not only does it take time, but your progress depends on how much you are willing to practice, and the quality of your practice.

Do not put any expectations on yourself going through this programme, it will just cause you frustration. Your only expectation should be to practice the right attitude. This is your only job! You must be willing to do whatever it takes, whatever is asked of you if you're wanting to heal yourself. You have to be willing to practice and persevere no matter what. Have your goals and vision for sure, but please don't place any expectations on yourself while you are starting out with building new habits, it will not help you.

So to recap, the attackpanic programme has been developed into a framework which contains all the ingredients that you need in order to heal yourself, but you must be willing to do the work. I can prepare you as much as I can, I can teach you as much as I can but you must be willing to do whatever is asked of you.

CHAPTER 4

THE RIGHT MINDSET

You have no doubt heard this before: *If you keep doing what you have always done, you will keep getting what you have always got.*

The answer to ending your suffering is very simple—do the exact opposite to what you are currently doing. This all seems very scary and counter-intuitive, but it is this non-resistant, paradoxical approach which is the *only* answer.

What would happen if:

- instead of trying to stop, resist, or fight intrusive anxious thoughts, you accepted them unconditionally, let them run their course, allowed them to be present and accepted any outcome?
- instead of anticipating, worrying about an anxious experience or encounter in the future, you fully embraced and accepted whatever happens (knowing and understanding that you are not in any danger or threat)?
- instead of avoiding, running from, or hiding from anxiety-provoking situations, you ran towards them, faced them, actually went looking for them, and accepted any outcome?
- you threw away all the coping strategies, techniques, and safety crutches that you currently use to protect yourself, choosing to experience and accept any outcome?

- you consciously chose to want more, demand more anxious sensations?
- you consciously chose not to fear the fear, to laugh at your fear?
- you learnt how to 'observe' or 'witness' the habitual anxious thoughts arising from the subconscious and consciously chose your reaction, consciously chose a non-anxious attitude?

The answer is, you would get the exact opposite result to what you are currently experiencing; new non-anxious behaviour and the end to high anxiety, panic attacks, and phobias. You see, whilst everything you are currently doing to protect yourself seems like a good idea at the time, it's all based on fear and resistance, and this attitude is rocket fuel for your anxiety condition, feeding the anxiety cycle, and is totally counterproductive to your healing.

You have to reach a point where you are willing to do absolutely whatever it takes to get better. You have to be willing to do what seems counter-intuitive and very scary in order to heal yourself. If you are willing to commit and follow my Building Blocks™, do exactly what is asked of you, then you will heal yourself.

For some of you, once you 'get it', your healing will occur very quickly indeed. For others, it may take a little longer, and this will depend on how quickly you form the necessary belief and trust in my programme and yourself, and how willing you are to stand up to your fears and do the work.

Your 'Why'

The reason or the 'why' you are willing to change, why you are willing to do whatever it takes, is so important as you embark on your own journey of healing, not to mention pretty much everything else you do in your life. It can be the difference between success and failure. You will always find the 'how', to do something as long as you have a compelling enough 'why'. Your own 'why' is the motivation which keeps you going, keeps you putting one foot in front of the other when times get tough and you feel like giving up.

My compelling 'why' I was willing to do 'whatever it takes' to change was my beautiful children. I want to be a father that they are proud of, I want to build a future for them, I want to be there for them, and I want to show them that anything is possible. Whenever things got a little bit tough, I just thought of my children and their welfare and well-being, and that was all the motivation I needed to push through and keep going.

What's your compelling why?

No Compromises

Choose to either do this or don't do this. There is no such thing as 'try'; trying is a noisy way of saying 'No', To 'try' is like taking the scenic route to nowhere, and you will get there very fast. There is no in-between. Any attitude other than 100 per cent commitment will not cut it here when we're dealing with changing habits based on fear. Actually, that goes for *any* new habit that you are trying to develop. Half-hearted attempts will only result in frustration, disappointment, disillusion, and yes, more fear and increased anxiety.

Practice and Perseverance

The biggest stumbling block for you will be your ability to persevere with building your new non-anxious habit. For some reason, when it comes to breaking old mental habits, we forget about perseverance, practice, and setbacks. We are really good at starting a new pattern of behaviour, but if we don't get immediate results and we experience a wee set back or two, we stop practicing and fall back into our old habits. Doubt and procrastination sets in, and the next thing we know we are saying things like 'I tried that and it didn't work.' It wasn't the programme that didn't work, *you* didn't work.

We are creatures of habit, and as such, we can find it difficult to turn our back on old mental habits and persevere with building new ones. When it comes to developing new mental habits, we tend to give up when we don't see immediate results all too easily, even though we don't expect immediate results when learning other skills like playing an instrument or changing a diet.

You must be willing to expose yourself to the anxiety-provoking situation, and you must be willing to practice and persevere with an attitude of non-resistance and acceptance.

Setbacks

No matter what habit you are trying to develop (or break), you will face challenges and setbacks along the way. Building new non-anxious habitual behaviour will be no different; setbacks and challenges are guaranteed. Realize this and accept this as part of your journey.

Here are a few reasons why things may very well get worse for you before they get better:

- We are creature of habits, and habits have a habit of hanging around. By their very nature they are very persistent;
- We tend to do all that we can to make us feel better in the moment. Medication, avoidance, or using other safety crutches and coping strategies like sitting next to an exit in a cafe, being accompanied by a friend for support or not leaving the house for example will make us feel better by relieving the anxious or panicky sensations and intrusive 'what if' thoughts, but this behaviour won't make us better, because we are not dealing with the real issues or the real *'cause*'! These sensations and thoughts are a bi-product, or *'effects'* of underlying high anxiety (the real *'cause'*). Your safety crutches and coping strategies make you feel better by masking the *'effects'*;

- So naturally enough, at the start of your journey of healing, when you throw away all your safety crutches and coping strategies that you use to feel better in the moment, all your horrible sensations and thoughts are going to run riot;
- Just the thought of walking into your false alarm without your safety crutches and coping strategies will trigger more anxiety and panic at the start. And this is perfectly normal. It will appear that things have indeed gone from bad to worse, but in reality nothing has changed, you are just no longer masking the '*effects*';
- Your safety crutches and coping strategies might help you to feel better in the moment, but they will not make you better because they do not address the '*cause*', which is the underlying anxiety condition responsible for the anxious sensations and thoughts;
- You will learn to address and remove the '*cause*' through BB3 & 4. Remove the '*cause*', and the '*effects*' must also disappear.

One Foot in Front of the Other

All things, large or small, have been achieved by taking one step at a time, placing one foot in front of the other. Success is the sum of doing small things day in, day out. Stay in the present moment and do what you need to do today to the best of your abilities. Maintain your vision with unwavering trust; however, don't fall into the trap of looking too far ahead of yourself as you may find yourself becoming discouraged at the enormity of your goal.

When I began writing this book, I had no idea how to write, what to write, and even if I could write. For me, this was an enormous project, and whenever I thought about all the work that needed to be done (that I had no idea how to do), I became overwhelmed with self-doubt and discouragement.

However, I knew what I wanted, I knew why I wanted it, and I had trust that if I just focused on what I needed to do today, without getting too bogged down in the enormity of the project, eventually, the sum of all the little steps taken would equal the achievement of my goal.

Anything is possible when you take things one step at a time. Cultivate a compelling 'why' you are willing to change, maintain your trust in yourself and the Building Blocks™ and just do the work that you need to do today. If you suffer from panic attacks or phobias, then trustfully work through BB3, if you suffer from an underlying anxiety condition, then practice implementing the Golden Rules today.

Let go of any concerns of what tomorrow may or may not bring, for tomorrow never comes. Your only concern should be what you can do now, in this very moment, to the best of your abilities, with whatever resources you have available to you which will move you in the direction of your goals, vision, or desires.

How long will it take for me to heal myself?

Let's take another look at the two objectives of the attackpanic programme:

1. To teach you how to stop panic attacks and phobias in their tracks and disempower them completely (BB3). Healing yourself of panic attacks and phobias, is an instant fix. As you work through the course, you will begin to understand why and how this is possible;
2. To remove the underlying anxiety condition (GAD, OCD, PTSD), and to return you back to a happy, fulfilling, loving, giving, non-anxious person (BB4). This involves reprogramming your sub conscious mind with new non-anxious patterns of behavior. As with all habits, skills or disciplines that you want to learn or get good at, it is going to take time, there are no shortcuts, and there is no substitute for practice and perseverance.

It took persistent action to form your habit, it is going to take persistent action to break your habit. How quickly you heal yourself is going to come down to how committed you are to doing what it takes, and how much you practice and persevere, how much you follow the attackpanic programme.

So, with that being said, in perfect conditions, it is possible for you to be back to normal, back to your true self, doing all the things that you used to be able to do without restrictions, living a full life again without being pushed and pulled around by your anxiety condition within four to eight weeks. That's how habituation works, more on this later.

The less you do, the less you practice and persevere, and the less structure you have around your practice, the longer it is going to take to build your new pattern of behavior. This is no different to learning to drive a car or play the guitar for example. You will learn to play the guitar for example, five times faster if you practiced five times per week, as opposed to only practicing once per week.

PART 2

THE BUILDING BLOCKS™

CHAPTER 5

BUILDING BLOCKS™ 1 (BB1) UNDERSTANDING ANXIETY CONDITIONS

Objectives of BB1
- To explain the truth behind anxiety conditions;
- To arm you with the knowledge, understanding, belief, and trust required in order to face and conquer your fears.

It doesn't matter what you suffer from, whether you suffer from PTSD, OCD, GAD or panic attacks and phobias, the root cause is the same.

It's really important that you put all your current beliefs aside for now and keep an open mind, and be willing to accept a new set of beliefs, beliefs that will move you out of your current situation and towards your future desired state; a new non-anxious person.

The Truth - So What's Really Going On?

Whether you suffer from, GAD, OCD, PTSD, panic attacks, or anxiety-related phobias (social phobia or agoraphobia), the fact is that you are suffering from nothing more than a bad habit, a behavioural condition, a learnt behaviour, which *you* have created.

All of these conditions are all part of what's commonly known as anxiety disorders.

However they are not disorders at all, they are a learned pattern of behavior. This is why I don't use the term 'disorder', I use the term 'condition' as this is more accurate.

The root cause is the same thing: underlying high anxiety firing off inappropriate habitual patterns of anxious behaviour, just at varying degrees of intensity along the anxiety spectrum.

This could be anything from constant intrusive thoughts in the case of a GAD sufferer, or reacting anxiously to loud noises from behind in the case of a PTSD sufferer, or even experiencing panic while standing in a queue at a bank from someone who not only suffers from social phobia, but also GAD and PTSD.

This is a nasty habit in deed, a nasty learned behavior. You feel trapped in a perpetual cycle of high anxiety.

Anxiety conditions are not a mental illness or disorder. You are not going crazy, and you are not mentally ill.

Intrusive and worrying thoughts, horrible and uncomfortable sensations are a bi-product of high anxiety and not a sign of a mental disorder.

There is nothing medically wrong with you.

> *"If you think you are going crazy, you probably aren't"*
> *– Anon*

Medication will not help you remove a learned pattern of behavior, therefore can not make you better, in fact will only makes things worse.

The only thing that can remove a pattern of behavior, is behavior itself.

You have developed this bad habit through Operant Conditioning. Operant conditioning is how we learn any skill or habit. It is the process of repeating a pattern of behaviour over and over until that behaviour becomes a programmed pattern of behaviour, a habit.

All these conditions are very closely related, and as you will see, can overlap each other and therefore you may be effected by more than one, depending on you as an individual and your circumstances.

For example, a soldier or a Police Officer suffering from PTSD, or someone suffering from GAD may trigger an anxious response when exposed to loud noises or sudden movement in a given situation. The sufferer has triggered the same anxious response under the same circumstances, even though they may be suffering from (or at least diagnosed with) different levels of anxiety conditions.

Now, lets take it a step further. When exposed to that trigger, if they do not take action to stop the anxious response, like escaping from the anxiety provoking situation (which is exactly the wrong thing to do!), or using some other coping strategy to make them feel better in that moment, it is highly likely that the anxiety will become more and more intense and uncomfortable, and may even culminate into a panic attack.

If this experience is repeated, and the sufferer experiences more panic attacks, then they run the risk of developing a phobia, which you will learn is a fear of having a panic attack when exposed to a given situation. The sufferer now not only suffers from PTSD or GAD, but also phobias!

What Is Anxiety?

First of all, lets take a quick look at the anxiety scale. If you were to map anxiety on a scale of one to ten, one would be very relaxed and calm, three or four would be your 'normal' baseline non-anxious state, and nine or ten would be the activation of the emergency, 'fight or flight' response. Fluctuations across the anxiety scale on any given day is vital to healthy function.

Anxiety is perfectly healthy and normal, it's part of our in-built survival programming, controlled by our subconscious mind through our autonomic nervous system.

Everyone experiences anxiety, for the most part, when it is appropriate.

Anxiety alerts us to danger, helps us to perform, to react decisively, like when competing in a sport or when protecting or saving someone's life for example. Anxiety is part of the problem solving process, a 'call to action', letting us know there is a problem that needs your attention or action.

On any given day your anxiety levels will rise and fall depending on what you are experiencing throughout your day, eventually settling back down to normal (three or four on the anxiety scale).

So there's no need to be afraid of anxiety, to run from anxiety. Anxiety is designed to protect and look after you. As a sufferer you have trained it to do exactly that, just at the wrong times as you are about to learn.

From this point on, I want you to start looking at anxiety differently to how you have been, I want you to start looking at anxiety as your friend – albeit an over protective and over reactive friend at this point in time – but not for long.

The Emergency Response

All of our automatic vital functions are controlled through our subconscious mind (or unconscious mind, whatever term you wish to use). We trust that our heart will continue to beat and that our bodily functions will perform perfectly without constant conscious effort or guidance; we trust that our subconscious mind will take care of these automatic life-sustaining functions.

It is brilliantly capable of maintaining a healthy equilibrium between expenditure and conservation of energy and is designed to handle extreme activity, responding to an emergency instinctually, in an instant. Shifts between these two poles are perfectly normal and vital to the healthy rhythm of life. Left to it's own devices, the subconscious mind will always seek out a healthy balance.

For example, as part of your built-in survival programming, when the brain detects a real threat or danger it flips the emergency or 'fight or flight' switch. Adrenaline is released into the blood stream, and all hell breaks loose. All your systems react instantaneously to prepare you to run or stay and fight.

All your senses, hearing, smell, sight, and touch become heightened, and you become 'wired', on edge, and agitated. This is a normal response to the adrenaline rush, preparing you for action. Your blood is diverted away from your digestive system, to your brain and lungs, and also out to your skeletal muscles for optimum performance.

You deal with the threatening situation appropriately by running away from it or sticking around and fighting (so to speak). Either way, when the threat is gone and the adrenaline has been used up, the emergency switch is turned off, and your anxiety levels have dropped back down to 'normal'.

The Brain

The cerebrum or cortex is the largest part of the human brain and is associated with higher functions such as thought and action. The cerebral cortex is divided into four different parts called 'lobes'. One of these lobes is called the temporal lobe and is associated with perception and recognition of auditory stimuli, memory, and speech.

The Limbic system, commonly referred as the 'emotional brain' or 'conscious system', is located buried within the cerebrum. Components of the Limbic system include the Thalamus, Hypothalamus, Amygdala, and Hippocampus.

The Amygdala

The Amygdala are a small pair of almond-shaped organs, and can be found in the part of the brain called the Limbic system. Whatever we experience through our life, the full emotional memory of that experience is permanently imprinted within this emotional circuitry.

The primary role of the amygdala is in the processing of memory, emotion, and fear, including the formation and storage of anxiety-related emotions. Furthermore, the amygdala is also responsible for regulating anxiety levels in the body, controlling the release of stress hormones, such as adrenaline, and also triggering the anxious 'fight or flight' response.

Anxiety levels in the body are 'pre-programmed' at a 'normal' benchmark level from birth. This benchmark level is stored in and regulated by the amygdala. Think of the amygdala as a thermostat, with the anxiety needle pre-set to 'normal'.

At this normal level, the anxiety response can only be triggered by real danger. However, through behaviour modification, known as Operant Conditioning (also known as Fear Conditioning), the amygdala can be modified to react differently.

Operant Conditioning

Operant Conditioning is how we learn to do pretty much everything in our lives; whether it's learning a new skill like riding a bike, learning to play a musical instrument, learning to drive, biting your finger nails, or developing a bad habit like an anxiety condition.

We learn new habits and skills by repeated actions and practice or by repeated exposure to an experience until the behaviour or skill becomes second nature. We repeat these patterns in order to become proficient at them so that they become automatic, instinctual, and accepted by the subconscious as perfectly normal behaviour and a habit is formed.

The subconscious mind cannot differentiate with what is real or unreal.

- Operant Conditioning or Fear Conditioning is responsible for the formation of anxiety conditions.

The Learning Process

When we learn or experience something, whether that be learning a new language, skill or habit, whether good or bad, it becomes part of the neural pathways and associations in the brain and is permanently imprinted in the emotional circuitry of the brain.

For example, learning something about a country, its cultures, and history for instance becomes part of your brain's neural pathways. Thinking about that country will activate many other memories of that country as they are all linked together by the neural pathways in the brain. All this information that you learn about this country is tied together into neural associations and stored within the brain, ready to be retrieved. But if you are anything like me, finding it when you need it isn't so easy!

When you learn to do anything, a skill, a habit, anything at all, your brain gradually develops the neural pathways that eventually allow you to perform the thing learnt automatically. The more you practice, the better the quality and effort you put in, the more your brain pathways are 're-wired'. Over time, you find yourself performing the skill or habit without even thinking about it, all the practice has made it automatic.

Initially, the new skill or habit you are learning is difficult and feels unnatural.

But as you practice and persevere, you gradually improve; you become more and more proficient, the skill or habit feels more and more natural. Your brain is 're-wiring' and arranging new neural pathways and associations in order to learn the skill or habit, and as they develop, you become more proficient. The more you practice, the more these neural pathways and associations grow.

It doesn't matter what you learn, it all becomes permanently imprinted within the vast neural associations in the brain, containing over one billion nerve cells.

Without repetition, neural pathways and associations cannot change.

This is the learning process taking place during Operant Conditioning. Everything in your life works like this; whatever you experience, learn, and repeat develops new neural pathways and associations in the brain, and through practice and repetition, over time, you gradually get better and better at it, *whether the thing* learnt *is good or bad, real or unreal*!

As an anxiety sufferer, through Operant Conditioning, the brain has been reprogrammed to habitually and instinctively behave in an anxious manner by re-calibrating the 'normal' benchmark level of anxiety within the amygdala, causing the body to react inappropriately in a way it wouldn't normally. This raises the general level of anxiety, and over a prolonged period, this behaviour can develop into an anxiety condition, reacting inappropriately to certain cues which trigger an anxious response, and in extreme cases, triggering the 'flight or fight' response or panic attacks in situations which shouldn't normally trigger such a response.

Fear Conditioning is the same as Operant Conditioning and is a term given to the development of anxiety conditions. Eminent psychologist, Burrhus Frederic Skinner (1904-1990), who developed the theories behind Operant Conditioning, found that through repetitive behaviour, the subconscious could be manipulated in a way which would alter the involuntary or autonomic reactions stored deep within it, namely the 'fight or fight' response.

Skinner believed that people could imprint their mind with the memory of fear which would overstimulate the amygdala, triggering a fear reaction or the 'fight or flight' response, which, over a prolonged period, could develop into a habit of fear. Put simply, suppose you experience an event or situation which creates an anxious or fearful response, this memory is stored, and you develop a fear of that event happening again; should the event reoccur, you become even more afraid. You remember this fear and feel even more fearful of the fear as you remember the sensations of the fear. Experienced, repeated, learnt, and over time an anxiety condition has been formed deep in the subconscious mind.

John Broadus Watson (1878-1958) was an American psychologist who believed that through Fear Conditioning, he could modify behaviour in infants in order to 'design' them how he wanted. Watson believed that emotions such as fear could be programmed using behavioural modification techniques.

In a highly controversial experiment, Watson successfully conditioned an eleven-month child called Little Albert to become fearful of a rabbit, a dog, and some wool. To do this, Watson simply presented these objects, while simultaneously making a loud noise. This technique was repeated over and over again. Little Albert was subsequently conditioned to respond with fear when presented with the objects alone. Little Albert had conditioned fear, conditioned anxiety.

This is exactly what is happening with anxiety sufferers. The sufferer is exposed to an initial catalyst or trigger—whether it's a financial problem, bereavement, work or business pressures, road rage, or witnessing a traumatic event—provoking an anxious response, giving rise to high anxiety levels within the body. This memory is stored in the amygdala.

If exposure to the situation or environment is ongoing, the memory is experienced over and over, the anxiety thermostat in the amygdala will be reset to a higher than normal level, the anxiety switch becomes stuck in the 'on' position, and the body responds with corresponding anxious behaviour. Through this 'learning process', the body becomes conditioned to behaving in an anxious manner, the subconscious assumes that this behaviour is perfectly normal, and a fear-conditioned habit is formed. The body is conditioned to respond with fear when presented with the initial catalyst or trigger.

It is important to point out here that the problem is not the initial catalyst or the trigger, the problem which needs addressing is the underlying high anxiety which has been programmed in the amygdala. Allow the anxiety levels stored in the amygdala to retreat back to down to normal levels, and the fear response will also disappear.

This will be done using the same method that produced the anxiety condition in the first place, Operant Conditioning. Modifying behaviour, reprogramming the mind with new non-anxious behaviour and reducing the high anxiety levels in the amygdala back down to appropriate 'normal' levels is the only cure for anxiety conditions.

The Nervous System

The nervous system controls every part of your daily life, from breathing and running to learning and memorizing, as well as instinctual reactions.

Your brain is receiving information from your environment through your sensory nerves via the spinal cord. The brain then makes sense of the information and fires off a corresponding response, delivered from the brain out to the rest of the body through the nervous system.

The nervous system is divided into two major divisions: the central nervous system, which is composed of the brain and the spinal cord, and the peripheral nervous system, which is made up of all the nerves that communicate instructions to your limbs and organs.

The peripheral nervous system has two further divisions: the skeletal or somatic nervous system, which provides nerves to limbs and also other areas like eyes and mouth, and the autonomic nervous system which provides nerves to internal organs, including the diaphragm, heart, lungs, and intestines. The autonomic nervous system performs several functions which include regulating heartbeat and digestion.

It was previously believed that the autonomic nervous system was not under our voluntary control; however, over the last few decades, we have discovered that it is possible to consciously influence these processes.

- You, the anxiety sufferer, are proof of this. Through your anxious habitual behaviour, you have created the sensations of a false fear throughout your body, controlling and altering your body's normal processes;
- There is no real danger, but your body is behaving as if there is, altering functions like heart rate, body temperature, digestion, circulation, pupil dilation, blood pressure, and perspiration. You have prepared your body for danger that doesn't exist;
- Through your thoughts, your predominant anxious habitual thoughts, you have influenced the 'autonomic' system.

The autonomic nervous system is further divided into two systems: the sympathetic and parasympathetic nervous systems. The sympathetic system is responsible for spending energy or speeding up the physical response.

If you are confronted with an immediate danger, this system is activated through the release of chemical intermediaries, such as adrenaline into the blood stream to help your body mobilize the energy to either fight or run away from the threat.

This is known as the 'fight or flight' response. When this occurs, certain changes in bodily functions occur to prepare the body to respond: your pupils dilate, your heart rate speeds up, breathing increases, blood pressure rises dramatically, flowing immediately to your limbs, and you are overcome with an immense desire to escape from the immediate environment.

Blood vessels end up causing certain areas of your body to constrict so that blood flow is increased to those areas that are critical to immediate survival, such as heart, lungs, and skeletal muscle stability.

This response has developed through evolution and is critical to ensure that those parts of your body are equipped with the extra resources required to deal with the danger. This 'fight or flight', or panic response is perfectly normal when there is real danger.

The sympathetic nervous system is activated very rapidly, taking only a matter of seconds for the blood to flow from the centre of your body and out to your arms and legs, where it is urgently required to deal with the impending danger. This quick response system is very handy when you are presented with real danger.

However, especially in our modern times, our sympathetic nervous system has become a little too overactive and excited. This is the anxious response in your body; this is anxiety.

You will recall that during an anxious response, blood flow is diverted from the centre of the body; this includes the intestines, which causes digestion to be slowed. The accompanying feeling is commonly known as 'butterflies' and can also manifest itself as nausea and indigestion.

Many of us experience this 'sensation' when public speaking or preparing for an event or competition. This anxious response, under these circumstances, can be very useful in preparing us for the event or competition so that we are ready, mentally and physically to compete. This is perfectly appropriate, perfectly normal.

These 'fight or flight' responses are experienced as sensations throughout your body. In the case of an anxiety condition, when the sufferer activates the anxious response, they interpret these sensations as fearful to varying degrees. When there is no real danger or threat, these sensations are very uncomfortable, scary, and very unpleasant for the sufferer.

Even though the experience leaves the sufferer feeling helpless and scared, these sensations are absolutely harmless and have never and will never harm the sufferer.

If the sympathetic nervous system is the 'anxiety on' switch, then the parasympathetic nervous system (the other branch of the autonomic nervous system) is therefore the 'anxiety off' switch.

The parasympathetic nervous system is responsible for slowing the body down to conserve energy, attending to life-nurturing jobs like digestion. When the parasympathetic system switch is 'on', you feel deeply relaxed and calm.

These two systems are diametrically opposed, they cannot coexist, and they cannot operate simultaneously. You know through your own experiences that you cannot feel anxious and relaxed at the same.

An important aspect to point out here is that because of the way these two systems function, you cannot turn the anxiety switch off simply by consciously trying to control it. All you end up doing is fighting with it, and all that will do is exasperate the anxious response, elevating the sensations to new heights.

The more you resist, the more it persists. The only way to turn the switch off is to activate the parasympathetic nervous system.

As an anxiety sufferer, you know this is true first-hand; when you are experiencing a panic attack, you have no doubt tried to talk yourself out of it rationally at the conscious level to no avail. All that happens is that you get even more wound up, leaving you feeling helpless.

In the case of an anxious response to a real danger, the anxiety switch is turned off when the threat is no longer present; the built-up energy has been expended by confronting and fighting off, or running from the threat.

When the threat is gone and the energy has been used up, the body will return to normal functioning levels, and the anxiety switch will turn off.

That's just how it works.

If you are an anxiety sufferer, you will be experiencing these horrible (yet harmless) sensations of fear, but there is nothing to run from. The only way to turn the anxiety switch off is to turn your conscious thoughts to letting go of the control over the anxious response and pour your intentions on to becoming relaxed. You will have to re-learn to let go and ignore these horrible but harmless sensations and focus on relaxing, and you do that through a non-resistant, fearless attitude.

Your cognitive thoughts (and corresponding behaviour) can activate either the sympathetic or parasympathetic nervous system. Thoughts of worry, fear, being fed up, and negativity are the mental components of anxiety.

The Formation of Anxiety

Whenever I talk about the formation of anxiety, I am specifically referring to the formation of an anxiety condition, which by now you know includes GAD, OCD, PTSD, panic attacks and anxiety related phobias.

Through behavioural modification, the amygdala can be modified to react differently. During high anxiety, the amygdala can be modified to react with higher levels of anxiety, and this can then become fixed causing an *anxiety disorder such as panic disorder, OCD, or phobias. Similarly, those with anxiety conditions can, through a structured programme, modify the inappropriate reactions of the amygdala in order to return it to a more appropriate level, thus eliminating the anxious symptoms associated with the disorder. (*www.Amygdala-anxiety.com*)*

That quote pretty much sums it all up. Let's take a closer look at how anxiety conditions are formed.

Now we all experience anxiety to a certain degree throughout our day, for good and no so good reasons. As you have learned so far this is perfectly normal and vital to healthy function.

- Anxiety is part of our problem solving process, a 'call to action';
- The emergency fight or flight response helps us respond to real danger.

Pressures in our modern life, such as issues and challenges with relationships and personal finances, employment worries and a whole host of other other challenges including the inevitable bereavement of loved ones and pets, traumatic events or some other personal loss can artificially raise our anxiety levels, producing emotions and feelings like frustration, disappointment, worry, and insecurities; they can take us out of the present moment and into the past with regret, resentment, and anger, or into the future with fear, worry, and insecurity.

Our behavior in these states tend to correspond with these emotions.

For example:
- If you are feeling depressed, maybe you can't be bothered getting up and making an effort to say go out and socialize;
- If you are feeling frustrated or fed up, maybe your performance at work suffers;
- If you are feeling irritated or argumentative, maybe you become agitated quickly and decide to pick a fight with your spouse, or unwilling to listen to reason for example.

Now in an anxious state your body can produce sensations that are uncomfortable, yet harmless. And this is a perfectly natural and healthy response to anxiety, which after all, is a call to action.

Depending on the level of anxiety, these sensations can manifest as:

- an underlying irritation, agitation;
- feeling uneasy, unwell, or lethargic;
- interrupted sleep pattern;
- exhaustion;
- headaches;
- numbness;
- sweaty and clammy palms;
- tightness around the chest; and increased heart rate and so on.

Now, for the most part, we are able to maintain a healthy balance between anxious and non-anxious states, rest, and activity.

When we experience anxiety, we generally deal with the situation causing the anxiety appropriately, or if it is an ongoing pressure, like work stress, we are able to balance this demand with activity that promotes relaxation and calm, and we are able to bring our anxiety levels back down to 'normal' healthy levels, like say between three and four.

We all have different ways of doing this: sleeping, physical exercise, mind-and-body relaxation techniques, religious or spiritual practice, spending time in nature, hanging out with mates or your pet, taking a vacation, or engaging in a hobby to name but a few. This is part of the highs and lows of life that we ALL have to deal with.

The problem arises when we get stuck in the anxious state and are unable to come back down to a 'normal', healthy, life-sustaining non-anxious level.

As this anxious state, or lets say behavior is repeated (or practiced) the brain forms new neural pathways and associations. Through repetition, these pathways and associations become deeper and deeper ingrained, and a habit is formed; the subconscious rewires itself, accepting this behaviour as perfectly normal.

Through Operant Conditioning, an anxiety condition (in the form of GAD OCD PTSD) has been formed.

We are all very unique and different, and as such, high anxiety can affect us all in different ways. The anxiety scale (or spectrum) is very wide, ranging from shyness, mild anxiety, all the way up to extreme panic attacks and phobias.

But it doesn't matter where you sit along this scale, or how anxiety affects you; if your behaviour is preventing you from doing things that you would normally be able to do, if you are behaving anxiously, experiencing the sensations of anxiety or fear in situations that are totally inappropriate, then you have an anxiety behavioural condition that requires removal.

High anxiety can cause havoc with your nervous system, sending impulses out to every nerve ending throughout your body: organs, muscles, and skin, creating tension and restricting blood vessels and nerves, causing all those horrible sensations as described earlier. Other nerve-related sensations experienced by sufferers include numbness, pins and needles, cold and hot flushes; all very nasty and horrible experiences, especially when you are unaware of what and why this is happening.

Depending on the severity of your condition, high anxiety may be affecting your life at varying degrees, from just a mild background irritation, to the point where you are beginning to restrict your life; the activities that you once participated in, you now steer away from, the places that you once frequented, you now avoid—all the things that you used to enjoy have now become uncomfortable.

These sensations cannot harm you, they never have and they never will. They are just nerve impulses that *you* are creating through your habitual anxious behaviour. You are in *control* of how you *choose* to react to these sensations.

You can, and will learn to ignore these sensations and move forward with your life, relearning new non-anxious behaviour, resetting the baseline level of anxiety stored in the amygdala back down to normal levels, thereby removing all the associated sensations of anxiety.

Direct behaviour, in this case, non-anxious behaviour, is the only way you can reset the anxiety levels stored in the amygdala. Medication, therapy and counselling *cannot* reset the anxiety levels and cannot remove an habitual behaviour. Only good old-fashioned leg work, actual behaviour, can do this.

As I briefly touched on earlier, the accompanying mental component of anxiety conditions include depressed, fed up, worry, fearful and 'what if' thoughts. I will touch on this later in more detail as I discuss each specific anxiety condition separately.

The Formation of Panic attacks

Your baseline 'normal' anxiety levels have now been reset to a new higher level, at say six to eight. Your new 'normal' threshold produces more anxiety, which further fuels anxious behaviour, reinforcing this bad habit even further. If left unchecked, the cycle will continue and the anxiety condition will get worse. The brain will assume that producing anxious sensations is perfectly normal, and anxiety levels reach a peak.

At this peak, the 'fight or flight' response is activated, triggered by normal everyday situations that do not warrant such a response.

This is an extremely uncomfortable, horrible and fearful experience for the sufferer. Because there is no real threat or danger that warrants such an anxious response, this false activation of the emergency fight or flight response is experienced as a panic attack. Panic attacks are the extreme manifestation of high anxiety, triggering the emergency response at really dumb times!

During panic attacks, you not only focus on your bodily sensations but also become preoccupied with what will happen next. The sensations experienced during panic attacks and phobias are similar to those experienced with an anxiety condition (GAD, OCD, or PTSD), but at a more intense level, and include (but not limited to) the following changes in the body:

- Increased or irregular heartbeats;
- Stomach cramps;
- Tightening and pain around the chest (which may feel like a heart attack);
- Difficulty in breathing;
- Headaches, dizziness;
- Hot and cold sweats;
- Feelings of confusion, depersonalization, derealization;
- Stiff jaw, neck, and shoulders;
- Difficulty swallowing;
- Dryness in the mouth (which may cause nervous coughing);
- Skin rash;
- Clammy or sweaty hands;
- Shaking, tremors;
- Difficulty, concentrating and talking.

These sensations, although extremely uncomfortable and distressing to the sufferer, are completely harmless. They have never harmed you, and they never will. Horrible yes, harmful no.

The urge to escape from whatever triggered your panic response is so overwhelming that you may believe not acting on this urge will result in some catastrophic event, even though, through all your experiences, such an event has never eventuated, and never will.

You follow the urge and escape from the panic-provoking situation. You consciously send the message that the danger has passed, the subconscious picks this up loud and clear and stands all systems down, turning off the emergency switch.

Consciously you are a bit beaten up; you are left feeling a bit shaken and probably preoccupied with what happened. To protect yourself, you constantly monitor your bodily sensations and focus on 'what if' scenarios—this is the start of anticipatory anxiety, which we will be covering at length shortly.

This is the development and manifestation of panic attacks, which may also develop into phobia, which is the fear of having a panic attack when exposed to a certain situation! Here's how that happens.

The Formation of Phobias

During a highly emotional state, in this case an anxious state, whatever you are experiencing in that moment; smells, sites, sounds, actions, activities, situations or anything else in your environment for that matter becomes associated with that emotional state. This becomes etched into your memory.

The next time you are exposed to the panic provoking situation, the emotional state previously experienced in that situation is triggered, in this case a panic attack.

Naturally you focus on the horrible experience and begin to fear that happening again. You may even become pre-occupied with worrying and 'what if' thoughts.

If this experience is repeated several times over, you can become conditioned to panicking. You have trained yourself to panic.

At this point, you fear having a panic attack when exposed to the panic provoking situation. Note that the situation itself offers no real threat or danger, and as such does not warrant such a response!

You modify your behavior and begin taking steps to protect yourself from panicking, like avoiding the situation all together, the ultimate coping strategy!

You have now developed a phobia; the fear of having a panic attack when exposed to a given situation.

I'll go into this in more detail in an upcoming chapter, but it is important to point out here that the sufferer does not actually fear the situation or environment which triggers the panic response. The sufferer fears the sensations themselves, the horrible and uncomfortable sensations of fear. The sufferer doesn't actually fear the queue at the bank, the crowd, the lift, the boss or whatever triggers an attack.

These situations have never harmed you before, and they never will. Logically you are fully aware of this. If you are a sufferer of panic attacks and phobias, you know this and you tell yourself this every time, but to no avail.

Maybe up until now, you were not aware that this is just a bad habit, and up until now, you felt that these sensations were uncontrollable. The fear of experiencing these horrible, scary, uncomfortable sensations is what you *actually* fear.

Draw on your own experiences and you will know the truth in what I am saying. These sensations of fear only exist because you fear them.

Without the fear, you cannot experience fear.

> *When you stop running from fear, fear stops running you*
> (Shaun Grant)

Coping Strategies and Safety Crutches

All these anxious sensations are not only very scary but also extremely horrible and uncomfortable. You are left feeling absolutely helpless as these horrible sensations are triggered seemingly automatically and instinctually.

This begins yet another vicious cycle as you adopt coping strategies and safety crutches in order to control the anxiety-provoking situational or environmental triggers.

Coping strategies and safety crutches are based around conscious fearful and resistant thoughts and behaviour which further exasperate and reinforce to the subconscious mind that the threat is real, and therefore, you need protection by preparing you to fight or run. They will not make you better because they only help you cope (mostly through avoidance), they only address the effects of an anxiety condition; the horrible (yet harmless) sensations of anxiety. They don't address the cause, which is the underlying high anxiety.

Below are a few examples of coping strategies, techniques and safety crutches that sufferers use to keep themselves safe, you may recognize a few!

- Sitting up against the wall in public or crowded places like a café so no one can approach them from behind;
    - As is the case for GAD, PTSD and panic attack sufferers;

- Avoiding leaving the house;
    - In the case of sufferers of agoraphobia and even social phobia;

- Avoiding standing in a queue at a bank for example (yip, it's a thing!);
    - Including sufferers of GAD, PTSD, social phobia;

- Avoiding driving;
  - In the case of sufferers of specific phobias such as driving;

- Avoiding going to social gatherings including shopping and food malls;
  - And if you do go, you have excuses why you might have to leave, or you make sure you are always close to an exit;
  - GAD, PTSD, OCD and social phobia sufferers;

- Taking medication;
  - ALL of the conditions!;

- Obsessive and inappropriate rituals like cleaning or refusing to sit down in a food mall;
  - In the case of sufferers of OCD.

Exercise:
- Think about how your anxiety is affecting you;
- How is it restricting, destroying your life (job, business, relationships, meaningful vision of the future);
- Think about the things that you used to do but now find too uncomfortable and difficult;
- List all the things you are currently using as coping strategies and safety crutches to protect yourself, list them all, they could include the following:
  - Avoidance techniques;
  - Staying home or at some other place of safety;
  - Medication;
  - Planning excuses and exit strategies;
  - Fretting over an upcoming event;
  - Sitting in a certain spot or position so you can escape easily;
  - Checking in, monitoring your sensations and 'what if' thoughts;
  - If you do go anywhere, you take a support person with you.

In the very near future you will learn to notice, become aware of when you are about to use one of your safety crutches, bringing this to your conscious attention, and you will make a conscious decision to say something like 'So what! Fuck it, do your worst, whatever happens, I will be fine!'

You will notice a lot of the coping strategies above involve avoidance! That's because avoidance works, obviously. Avoiding the panic provoking situation will stop you from panicking for sure in the short term, but in the long term it will make you worse as you start to restrict and limit areas of your life around your fears.

Returning To A Healthy Balance

Just as the emergency 'on' response is vital to our survival, so too is the emergency 'off' response. The subconscious will not let you panic forever. Eventually, in order to maintain that healthy balance I referred to earlier, the subconscious will turn the emergency switch off, bringing you back down to normal—*even if you are still in the middle of the panic-provoking situation.*

There are some valuable insights here:

- If you did absolutely nothing, your subconscious mind will eventually turn the emergency switch off;
- The subconscious will always seek a healthy balance, if we consciously get out of the way.

Over the years, I experienced this on many occasions, no doubt you will have too.

Unfortunately though, for many years I was unaware of these insights, along with the understanding of what was happening habitually, and my panic actually worsened.

Here's a typical experience during my suffering:

While running a departmental meeting at TNZ, I noticed the old, familiar uncomfortable sensations building up from out of nowhere, for no reason at all; tightening of the chest, dizziness, trembling, difficulty in concentration, racing heartbeat, dry throat, and clammy palms. The more I focused on them, the more intense they became. I began worrying about them, and they soon worsened. I tried to stop them with coping and breathing strategies that used to work but now didn't.

I tried everything but couldn't stop the sensations. The harder I tried, the more fearful and helpless I felt. This, of course, intensified the sensations through my fear. The subconscious picked all this up and set about protecting me by flipping the emergency 'fight or flight' response.

I had a full on panic attack in front of the entire department, it was horrible (turns out, no one really noticed, interesting, aye?). I had an overwhelming urge to escape, but I couldn't, there was nothing I could do as I was in the middle of reporting. At that point, I just gave in and made a decision to just get on with it; what other choice did I have?

As soon as I made that decision, I felt totally different. The sensations were still present, but the feeling of panic just disappeared completely. I was elated, my super confidence and enthusiasm returned, and the rest of the meeting was a breeze. I totally forgot about the sensations. I can't even remember when, and if, they subsided.

After that I was on a high. I thought I had cured myself. I didn't know how, but I thought I was cured. I was back to my old self. But to my horror, a few days later, I'm sitting among friends minding my own business when I noticed these sensations in the background again. My thought process went something like this:

> *Wait a minute, why is this happening? I thought I could control this? Now what do I do? What did I do? I know, I did this ... Oh no, that didn't work, but it did before. If it doesn't work now, what will? Why did it work before and*

not now? How do I stop these sensations? I can't stop them. Oh for fuck sake, when will this shit stop? How do I stop it? What's happening? What am I going to do? Here it comes. Oh no, I just have to get out, I've got to get out of here...

- So, because I had the ability to escape, I did;
- Sure, once I got the hell out of there the sensations subsided, but this left me feeling in an even worse state than ever before as I began believing that I was incurable, helpless, that no matter what I did, panic would always beat me;
- Running from the situation reinforced to the subconscious mind that the emergency response was required to protect me.

This experience was typical for me over the last four to five years of my suffering. My condition got incredibly destructive before I finally cracked the code, before I finally healed myself.

Here are the insights or 'aha' moments that I didn't understand then but do now:

- If I remained in the panic-provoking situation and gave in to the panic (non-resistance), the subconscious would figure things out and return me back to a healthy state. I didn't realize I was 'inciting' the panic response with my conscious fears;
- The anxious sensations appearing out from nowhere were the result of an underlying anxious habitual pattern of behaviour. It is a record playing automatically in the background;
- Disempowering panic attacks is one thing. However, it won't necessarily prevent the anxious sensations from reappearing again; this can only be done through 'changing the record' by addressing the *'cause'* (underlying high anxiety) and replacing anxious behaviour with new non-anxious behaviour;
- Therefore, anxious sensations were to be expected—until I changed the record playing in the background.

You have programmed your subconscious mind with anxious habitual behaviour, which, in some cases, develops into panic attacks and phobias. You cannot control or stop something surfacing that is happening automatically. You know this as you have been attempting to control your anxiety and panic without success.

Anxiety and panic need fuel to survive, and they get their life-sustaining source through our conscious *reaction* towards the anxious sensations. Our conscious attitude and beliefs we *choose* to hold towards anxiety and panic *is* the fuel that keeps this bad boy alive.

At the moment, you feed your condition consciously with an attitude based around resistance, fear, avoidance, constant monitoring, and worry.

The habitual anxious behaviour is not the problem, your conscious attitude is!

If we consciously get out of the way, the subconscious will do its job perfectly; it will maintain a healthy balance between rest and activity. It knows exactly what to do. If there's a real threat, it will do what it has to. If there's no threat, it will do what it has to.

Here's a quote from one of my favourite trainers and teachers, Dr Reid Wilson:

> *'The unconscious mind is 99 per cent brilliant in its ability to constantly direct the body towards health. For winning over panic attacks, the unconscious needs no fixing and needs no supervision by your mind. It's perfectly fine. It simply needs to be permitted to do its work without intrusion. It's the conscious mind's intrusion that's the problem—that little voice that says 'what if these sensations get worse? Something bad will happen. Watch out.'*

- What if, knowing, understanding, and accepting 100 per cent what I am telling you, and with complete trust and courage you consciously chose an attitude which is non-resistant and fearless (the complete opposite to what you are currently doing which is currently fueling and reinforcing your condition)?;
- What if you allowed the subconscious mind to manage your body's sensations?
- What if you could once again trust that the subconscious mind, which is perfectly healthy and requires no repair, will maintain a healthy balance without any interference from your conscious mind?

The answer is, you would stop feeding the panic cycle, and your panic would die (more on that soon).

Now this will seem counter-intuitive and scary, and may even produce more anxiety at first - In fact I guarantee it will. But think about this very carefully; everything you are currently consciously doing to protect yourself is just fuelling your panic.

Your *choice* of *attitude* is based around the need to keep you on guard to protect yourself; you worry about and anticipate panic, you practice avoidance, and you run from panic.

This very attitude is the fuel panic needs to survive. Why? Because you are sending powerful emotional messages to your subconscious that you are in fact in danger and in need of the emergency response to stay safe.

The subconscious mind will just do what it is told, it cannot reason, it will do whatever you consciously tell it to do, whether it is right or wrong, true or false, good or bad, it cannot make any distinction. You as a sufferer know this truth only too well. You have trained yourself to panic in situations that do not warrant such an extreme response! Your own experience will validate this point.

Case Study 1: Student D

A student of mine who we will name D, suffers from PTSD and panic attacks, so when he goes into public places like cafés, he has to sit with his back up against the wall and in a spot where he can escape in a hurry. He is an ex Police Officer, and does this so he can observe where the loud noise, commotion or any threat is coming from so he can take immediate action to protect himself and those around him.

Sitting in this position is a safety crutch and coping strategy that allows him to keep his anxiety and panic in check, but very restrictive as it limits where he can and will go!

This behaviour is completely inappropriate, as there is absolutely no threat, and the likelihood of any such a threat is so remote that it doesn't warrant any attention.

Logically he knows this already but not taking these measures would trigger inappropriate anxiety and eventual panic. He completely ignores the fact that no one else sitting in the middle of the café is freaking out.

If he was to sit in the middle of the room for example, the stimuli from being in that situation would trigger an anxious response, and he would become agitated and on high alert. All his senses (hearing, vision, even smell) would become heightened and he would become very sensitive to sounds and movement.

Depending on how he consciously deals with these initial sensations, it is very likely that his anxiety levels will continue to spiral out of control until the fight or flight response is activated and an overwhelming urge to escape is acted upon. This emergency response is experienced as panic.

This anxious response is completely irrational. But it is an automatic response to this stimuli. The subconscious mind has been conditioned through experience and repetitive behavior to react this way, to protect him, to flick the panic button.

D cannot stop this automatic response to this situation at this point as it is a learnt behavior, a bad habit. He cannot control the initial anxious response, but what he can do is CHOOSE how he consciously reacts to those initial sensations. More on that later.

D developed his PTSD and panic attacks through his constant exposure to traumatic and high stress experiences over 17 years as a frontline police officer.

Some of you may be thinking that it sounds like he may even suffer from a phobia like social phobia perhaps, a fear of panicking while in a public place. And you could be right, remember, all anxiety conditions are closely related and can overlap.

D was diagnosed with PTSD due to the high anxiety caused by the ongoing traumatic and stressful work experiences, which resulted in always being on high alert, on guard, looking out for threats when in public spaces – a completely irrational response to everyday stimuli.

Now, while in a public place like a café, if D didn't employ his safety crutch as outlined above, it is more than likely that he would panic. So, if he couldn't use his safety crutch he would avoid the situation all together. This approach became extremely destructive and restrictive to his life overtime.

If left unchecked, D would most definitely develop a social phobia of some sort. We'll check in with him and look at more of his story later on.

So you can see how high anxiety can develop into a specific behavioural condition such GAD, OCD and PTSD, depending on the individual and depending on the nature of the catalyst or circumstances for the high anxiety in the first place. And you can also see how these underlying conditions can ALL develop into panic attacks and even phobias.

If you're not crazy, if you do not have a mental illness or disability, and if you are behaving, reacting to normal everyday situations in an inappropriate anxious manner, if you find yourself avoiding situations that you used to like, or if there are things that you used to do but now you find difficult, then you have a behavioural condition, a learned behavior, in this case an anxiety condition, nothing more! It cannot be anything else.

The hows, whys, and when you developed an anxiety condition, the catalyst that triggered your high anxiety in the first place doesn't matter, and doesn't need fixing and in fact can't be fixed. What needs to be fixed is your underlying high anxiety which is a learned pattern of behavior that you created. You taught yourself to be an anxious person through Operant Conditioning, and only you can unteach yourself to be an anxious person through Operant Conditioning, fact!

Think this through very carefully, take what you have learned so far, use your own experiences and you will see that what I am saying is the truth.

Generalised Anxiety Disorder (GAD)

Living with GAD on a daily basis is extremely debilitating and distressing. Anxious behaviour promotes more of the same, you feel stuck in this destructive perpetual cycle.

The sensations that you experience with GAD as previously outlined are generally not as horrible as the sensations experienced during panic attacks, but are still destructive nonetheless. The sensations are just that—sensations, warning you of some threat that doesn't exist. As horrible as they may seem, they cannot and will not harm you. They can, and soon will be ignored.

Some of the persistent and intrusive thoughts you may experience include fed-up, sad, lonely, bizarre or disturbing thoughts, and also feeling depressed, unwell, or even suicidal. GAD sufferers tend to also worry incessantly about money, health, or work. When they look into the future all they see is doom and gloom.

These thoughts are due to chemical changes within the brain in response to the high anxiety. They must not be mistaken for clinical depression. Symptoms or sensations associated with anxiety can mimic depression due to the chemical changes in the brain.

You also tend to become obsessed with monitoring all these horrible sensations and thoughts which only makes your condition worse by causing you to become more distressed, pushing your anxiety levels up higher.

GAD can affect individuals in different ways. The anxiety scale (or spectrum) is very wide, ranging from shyness, mild anxiety, all the way up to extreme panic attacks and phobias.

I've already explained this earlier but it is so important that it is worth repeating here:

- Depending on the severity of your condition, GAD may be affecting your life at varying degrees, from just a mild background irritation, to the point where you are beginning to restrict your life; the activities that you once participated in, you now steer away from, the places that you once frequented, you now avoid—all the things that you used to enjoy have now become uncomfortable.
- These sensations cannot harm you, they never have and they never will. They are just nerve impulses that *you* are creating through your habitual anxious behaviour. You are in *control* of how you *choose* to react to these sensations.
- You can, and will learn to ignore these sensations and move forward with your life, relearning new non-anxious behaviour, resetting the baseline level of anxiety stored in the amygdala

back down to normal levels, thereby removing all the associated sensations of anxiety.

Does Medication help with GAD?

Direct behaviour, in this case, non-anxious behaviour, is the only way you can reset the anxiety levels stored in the amygdala. Medication *cannot* reset the anxiety levels and cannot remove a habitual behaviour. Only good old-fashioned leg work, actual behaviour, can do this.

- There is nothing medically wrong with you.

Mental illnesses such as clinical depression (like Bi Polar for example) are caused by chemical changes in the brain and as such can require medication. Anxiety conditions, on the other hand, are a learnt behaviour and while they can cause chemical changes in the brain responsible for sensations such as mood swings, negative emotions, and thoughts, they are *not caused* by chemical changes in the brain. Medication may provide relief by masking the horrible sensations (the 'effects') by altering the chemical balance in the brain, but it *will not* remove the *cause*; the underlying high anxiety which fuels the anxious behaviour.

If you are on some kind of anti-anxiety medication, the sooner you can get off it the better; all it is doing is masking your sensations. To address the *cause*, you need to build new non-anxious habitual behaviour, and to do that, you have to face your condition 'head on'. You will learn to do this through the Building Blocks™.

This will be a hard pill to swallow (excuse the pun) for some, but medication, when it comes to anxiety conditions, only serve to reinforce the very condition you are trying desperately to get rid of.

The only solution is to relearn non-anxious behaviour through practice and repetition (Operant Conditioning), rewiring the brain with new neural pathways and associations, and replacing the old anxious habitual behaviour.

As mentioned in the earlier section, the anxiety levels stored in and regulated by the amygdala becomes stuck at higher than normal levels; therefore, the body is in a constant state of anxiety, producing all the horrible sensations of anxiety that you experience on a regular basis.

You become over sensitized to external stimuli which wouldn't normally, or shouldn't cause an anxious reaction at all; for example, socialising with friends or family, which used to be fun now become very difficult. You soon find yourself avoiding these situations altogether.

This is a vicious cycle, as the more you behave anxiously, the higher the anxiety levels get pushed up, and the more anxious you become and behave. The more anxious you behave, the more anxious sensations you produce and experience, the higher the anxiety levels rise. When anxiety levels reach extreme levels, panic attacks and phobias may develop.

> *'We are born with only two fears: falling and loud noises.*
> *Any other fear is a learnt behaviour.'*
> (Joseph Murphy)

Shyness, for example, is a mild form of anxiety, at the very low end of the anxiety spectrum. It is a learnt behaviour, a fear probably learnt or passed down through observing and experiencing that behavior in others. It is *not* something you are born with.

Shyness is a mild form of anxiety that can easily be tolerated for an entire lifetime. It doesn't necessarily mean that your life will be drastically restricted and you are able to function quite normally. This level of anxiety is not restricting your life enough to do something about it. In other words, you aren't suffering enough to take action. It's not until the anxious behaviour becomes so destructive that the sufferer must do something about it.

I know this only too well because that is exactly what happened to me. I operated for years, seemingly okay, successful in many areas of my life, but also sabotaging relationships and opportunities along the way. As my high anxiety levels gradually increased, so too did my anxious behaviour. I gradually began retreating from various areas of my life as the sensations and symptoms of anxiety correspondingly increased along with my growing anxiety levels.

It wasn't until my high anxiety escalated into panic attacks, social phobia, and agoraphobia, forcing me to become house bound, destroying career opportunity after career opportunity, putting the welfare of my two beautiful children at risk, that I decided to do something about it once and for all.

I only really did something about my situation because my behaviour had become so destructive, and my situation had become so desperate. To a certain degree, I am very grateful that things got so bad, as I got off my arse and did something about it, and I now no longer suffer from GAD, panic attacks or social phobia.

Maybe you can identify with my story. Maybe you are sabotaging relationships and opportunities because you are allowing high anxiety to dictate your behaviour. Maybe you're not achieving the results that you want or feel you deserve.

Remember that anxiety is a helpful emotion; it alerts us to not only danger but also when there is a problem that requires our attention and action. So you pay attention, identify what the problem is, work out what the solution is, and take action. You pay attention to feedback, make changes, and take further action.

This is *good* anxiety, this is healthy. Anxiety becomes a problem when our habitual behaviour causes us to react inappropriately to situations which shouldn't cause an anxious response, or when we have restricted our lives to the point where we stop doing things that used to be enjoyable but are now a chore.

Obsessive Compulsive Disorder (OCD)

OCD is part of an underlying anxiety condition; it is not a stand-alone condition.

An underlying anxiety condition is responsible for the obsessive and persistent 'what if' or 'catastrophic' thought processes that plague OCD sufferers, which forces them into engaging in certain compulsive mental and/or physical repetitive and unproductive behaviour and rituals.

What's happening?
OCD sufferers believe that if these compulsive rituals are not performed urgently they will experience some form of catastrophe. Performing these rituals provides some relief for them; however, it is usually short lived as the obsessive disturbing thoughts and fears resurface, leaving the sufferer compelled to carry out the rituals again and again.

Some of these rituals can include the following:

- Constantly washing their hands or cleaning their home out of a fear of catching germs;
- Avoiding public places like food malls out of fear of becoming ill;
- A compulsion to keep things in their place;
- A compulsion to count things over and over again;
- A compulsion to check and recheck things out of fear, doubt, and worry;
- Persistent invasive thoughts.

How and why the underlying anxiety condition happened to manifest as an obsessive, uncontrollable urge to carryout a particular ritual is not really that important. As a sufferer, it is so important for you to understand, accept and believe the following to be true, no matter how long you have been suffering, no matter how bad you think you are:

- Providing you have been accurately diagnosed with OCD, and you do not have a mental illness or disorder;
- All you suffer from is an anxiety condition. Your underlying anxiety levels are stuck on high, firing off adrenaline, putting you on high alert and on edge, producing corresponding anxious, worrying and 'what if' thoughts, actions and behavior;
- The anxious response has become a habit. Through repetition you have programmed yourself to be an anxious person, you are stuck in a constant state of anxiety;
- The more anxious you behave, the more you artificially raise anxiety levels which increases your anxious behaviour;
- If you do not find ways to relieve the anxiety, it would eventually rise to extreme levels, at which point you would activate the fight or flight response, experienced as a panic attack;
- For whatever reason, again it's not important, you find that performing some kind of ritual or task provides some form of relief from all your horrible anxious sensations;
- What you weren't aware of, but you will soon begin to understand, is that all you are doing is dealing with the symptoms of high anxiety, the effects, not the cause. All your uncomfortable anxious sensations that you are experiencing are the effects of your OCD, they are not the cause;
- The cause of the anxious sensations is the underlying high anxiety;
- Your rituals are dealing with the effects, not the cause. They appear to give you some form of relief, much like you would if you were to take medication or with some other coping strategy or safety crutch (like good old avoidance!);
- But it's only short lived because you still have an underlying high anxiety condition which is responsible for the uncomfortable sensations;
- Until you address the *cause*, you will always experience these horrible yet harmless sensations, no matter how much you perform your obsessive rituals;

- Your particular ritual provides relief in the moment. But because you still have underlying high anxiety operating in the background, you will soon notice those old familiar ugly sensations again;
- So you go back to your safety crutch or coping strategy which is to perform some ritual and you will receive some short lived relief;
- This is a vicious cycle indeed, a self fulfilling prophecy, which just strengthens your underlying anxiety, intensifying your anxious behavior. It doesn't matter that there is no real danger, your subconscious mind doesn't reason like that, it will just do whatever you consciously tell it. This must be making sense by now?;
- If you don't perform your particular ritual, your anxiety levels will more than likely spiral out of control, activating the emergency fight or flight response to protect you from, well, nothing;
- You become obsessed with performing your ritual in order to provide relief from the sensations;
- This is OCD.

But this is no different to any of the other conditions:

- You have programmed yourself, trained yourself to be an anxious person and to behave inappropriately;
- In your case, you perform rituals to keep yourself safe, to provide temporary relief. This is your safety crutch, your coping strategy, and they are no different to other safety crutches like avoidance, lucky charms, exit strategies, or medication!;
- But you are only performing the rituals because you are trying to get rid of or find relief from the anxious sensations that are popping up seemingly automatically and out from nowhere. You will never find long term relief until you deal with the cause, which is your underlying anxiety condition;

- This is important: Your 'what if' fears are a false alarm, they are bullshit and they are not what you actually fear and you know it! You haven't died yet from eating on a table in a food court for example, in fact you have never become ill from doing so all those times you ate at a foodcourt before you developed this fear, and no one else is falling over ill right in front of your eyes are they!? It is highly likely you ate at many foodcourts with friends and family before you developed this phobia right? What you actually fear, just like any of the other anxiety condition, are the horrible, uncomfortable yet harmless sensations. That's it!;

Whatever your particular fear is, contemplate on what I am telling you and you will see the truth. Look beyond your 'Yes Shaun but I'm different' bias response.

Moving forward
BB2 is going to drill down to what is it that you actually fear. It will teach you the one and only technique that you need to heal yourself; your conscious attitude. This is the really really important stuff.

BB3 will teach you how to completely disempower the panic response, stop panic in it's tracks, without safety crutches and coping strategies. BB3 will give you the trust that you can go into any situation and not fear the fear!

- BB3 will not stop the initial anxious sensations from turning up, it can't because at the moment, it is a habitual pattern of behavior (BB4 will do that!);
- But you will learn that this doesn't matter, it's how you consciously respond, it's the conscious message that you send to the subconscious in the moment that matters;
- No coping strategies, no safety crutches; In your case, no compulsive or obsessive rituals.

BB4 will help you remove the underlying high anxiety (the *cause*). If you adopt and implement the non-anxious behavioural and attitude changes outlined in BB4, make them part of your daily life, make them a habit, overtime you will remove the underlying anxious behavior.

- By doing so you will remove the corresponding obsessive thoughts, and when they are removed, the compulsive and obsessive behaviour and rituals will also disappear.

This is going to take practice, repetition and perseverance on your part though. There is no magic bullet here. You taught yourself to be an anxious person, now you have to teach yourself to be a non-anxious person.

Your subconscious mind is your friend, and will do whatever you tell it to do, including protecting you, preparing you for fight or flight, even in situations that do not warrant such a response. This is good news. You are going to learn how to use the power of your subconscious mind for good, and not evil.

If you are willing to do whatever it takes, if you are willing to practice and persevere, your full recovery is a certainty.

Post-Traumatic Stress Disorder (PTSD)

How does it manifest?
Sufferers of PTSD can experience constant flashbacks, nightmares, inappropriate and intrusive thoughts usually relating to a traumatic event or an initial catalyst. In addition to flashbacks, PTSD sufferers may also experience panic attacks.

The experience of trauma can be devastating to anyone. This could be anything from witnessing or being victim to an horrific event, or experiencing a huge loss, whether it be a bereavement of a loved one or even a pet, or some other loss like a financial loss.

This leaves indelible scars etched into your memory for life. Anyone who has gone through trauma or loss can relate to all the anxiety and pain that such a loss can cause.

Now this of course is part of life and we all have to deal with loss at some stage, unfortunately some more than others. For the most part, through the right support, we are able to move through the grieving and healing process. Counselling and therapy play an important part in moving through the grieving and healing process.

I wish I had of taken the opportunities to go through counselling and therapy all those times I experienced trauma as a young and impressionable police office, I believe it could have made a big difference to me.

Whatever the loss or trauma is that you experienced, it takes time to heal, and with the right support, you learn to accept and move on and live with the loss and get on with your life as a normal non-anxious person (what ever normal is!).

- This is the case for most of us.

You will never forget the event or events, in fact everything is etched into your memory for life. But when you go through the normal grieving and healing process, over time, you look back, and while there will still be pain to a certain degree, your memory no longer triggers all the anxiety that it once used to. Use your own experiences to draw your own conclusions.

For some of us, maybe we don't deal with difficult times in the right way, maybe we don't get or accept the right support, or maybe we operate under extreme conditions for prolonged periods and we don't give ourselves the opportunity to relieve the pressure or stress and come back down to normal stress levels. I know this was the case for me in both scenarios, maybe you can relate to this.

As I have explained earlier, high anxiety produces corresponding anxious behavior, and if this state and behavior is prolonged, you run the risk through repeated behavior of your anxiety levels becoming stuck at higher than normal levels:

- You have programmed, conditioned yourself to behave anxiously;
- This is a learned pattern of behaviour;
- Your sub conscious mind thinks that this behavior is perfectly normal;
- Normal, everyday situations, even sounds and smells can trigger a completely inappropriate anxious response;
- You start avoiding certain situations that trigger this anxious response;
- You use coping strategies and safety crutches to help you manage anxiety provoking situations that you cannot avoid;
- And without your safety crutches or coping strategies, it is highly likely that unless you are able to escape from the situation, your anxiety levels would escalate to the point where the fight or flight response is triggered – and you would experience a full on panic attack;
- If this happens, this highly emotional event is etched into your memory. If this isn't nipped in the butt, a phobia of that situation or thing is formed;
- This is very destructive for you and those around you. You start restricting your life in order to avoid the anxious or panic response;

Case Study 1: Student D

Let's revisit student D. Over his 17 years of policing, D was exposed to many traumatic experiences. He saw his fair share of shit; dead bodies, homicides, rapes, physical and emotional abuse against women and children, violent attacks on innocent victims including himself, and loss, and even killings of colleagues. And through it all he never sought counselling or therapy throughout the course of his career, and never gave himself the chance to work through and resolve the trauma - it wasn't the thing to do back in the day!

Pretty soon D found himself operating in a constant state of high anxiety. His behavior corresponded with his anxiety levels:

- High anxiety put him in a highly sensitized state, all his senses were on high alert;
- He found himself in a constant on edge and agitated state.

Overtime this anxious state became 'normal'. D had programmed himself through Operant Conditioning to be an anxious person:

- He began reacting to everyday normal situation that offered no threat or danger in an inappropriate anxious manner. Certain smells and sounds would trigger flashbacks of past traumatic events;
- This response was now a habit, a learnt behavior, and was happening seemingly automatically;
- This caused D even more distress as he couldn't stop or control the anxious response, and he had no idea what was going on;
- D was later diagnosed with PTSD.

How does it effect daily life?
D found it hard to sleep. Constant intrusive and worrying thoughts, some in the form of flashbacks, some in the form of future insecurities always upset his sleeping pattern. He would lie awake in bed incessantly worrying not only about challenges he was facing at work, but also pretty much everything and everyone.

He didn't realize then that these anxious thoughts were a bi-product of an anxiety condition, fueled by high anxiety levels. If he wasn't stuck in an anxious state:

- He wouldn't have all these inappropriate anxious thoughts;

- He wouldn't keep having these reoccurring flashbacks to the extent that he was having them.

Being on high alert all the time was seriously affecting all areas of his life. He was in such a highly strung, agitated state that he would spin out into a state of panic:

- When he was surprised by sudden loud noises;
- In fact whenever he was surprised for whatever reason;
- When people came into his personal space, this included anyone from friends, loved ones and strangers, depending on how anxious he was at the time;
- When his children would come up and surprise him from behind, he would completely nut off at them and verbally attack them for sneaking up on him - a completely inappropriate response;
- Whenever he went out into a public place, he was always looking around for any threat;
    o If he was in a café for example, he would sit up against the wall and in a position where he could easily see a threat, and also so he could easily escape should the need arise;
    o Of course there was no real threat, and D knew that, but this didn't stop him from triggering the anxious or panic response. This response by now was an habitual pattern of behavior, learned over the course of his policing career;
    o D couldn't figure out why he couldn't stop the anxious sensations when he knew that there was nothing to fear;
    o The turning point for D was when he understood that the problem wasn't the anxiety provoking situation because logically he didn't fear them and he knew that;
    o The problem was how he was consciously reacting to the initial uncomfortable and horrible anxious sensations that were triggered by the situations;
    o What he actually feared were the anxious sensations, not the situation.

What is happening?
- D had taught himself to be an anxious person;
- This was an habitual pattern of behavior;
- Underlying high anxiety was driving the inappropriate flashbacks, intrusive and worrying thoughts about pretty much anything he thought of;
- And this not only affected his sleep, but also his positive vision of the future;
- He had also taught himself to react to normal everyday situations as outlined above with a completely inappropriate anxious response;
- He had trained his subconscious mind to go into survival and protection mode, to flick the panic button when there was absolutely no need;
    o The subconscious mind was only doing what it was told, directed by D's anxious response and conscious thoughts, signaling that he needed protection;
    o It didn't matter that there was no real threat, and that D knew this;
    o It made no difference that this was a false alarm;
    o D's fearful thoughts and actions were fueled by high anxiety;
    o The flashbacks were also driven or fueled by the underlying high anxiety.

So let's quickly recap:
- D's inappropriate flashbacks, intrusive and worrying thoughts are fueled by his underlying anxiety condition;
    o The more he focused on these intrusive thoughts and flashbacks, the more he tries to push them away, the more he gets, and the more intense they became;
    o What you resist, you persist;
    o What you focus on, you tend to get more of;
    o This is a vicious cycle, a self fulfilling prophecy.

- Underlying high anxiety also caused him to react to everyday normal situations in a completely inappropriately anxious manner;
    - Over time, this anxious or panic response became a habitual pattern of behavior;
    - This response was now automatically triggered whenever D was exposed to the anxiety provoking situation;
    - D developed safety crutches and coping strategies to help him control or cope with these situations - if he couldn't avoid them in the first place;
    - Without his safety crutches, D's initial anxious or panic response would spiral out of control and trigger the emergency response or panic attack, experienced as an overwhelming urge to fight or run.

D's conscious reaction to the initial sensations is based on fear, based on resistance, and this attitude actually fuels the anxious response. This attitude seems fair enough as the sensations are very uncomfortable and naturally enough he wants them gone:

- In student D's case, one of the many situations that triggered these sensations was walking into public places such as cafes;
- This is the start of the panic cycle that I explain in detail on page 95.

Now in your case, if you use a coping strategy or safety crutch to handle the anxiety provoking situation (like sitting next to the exit for example), you may successfully foil the onset of a panic attack, but you will be inadvertently strengthening your anxious behavior because your actions are based around fear, resistance, signaling to your sub conscious that you were in fact in danger and therefore needed protection.

I am now introducing you to the idea that it is your conscious choice in the moment on how you react and behave to the initial sensations that decide whether they fizzle out to nothing, or spiral out of control and into a panic attack.

No matter what is happening automatically, no matter what pops up from the subconscious as part of a habitual pattern of behavior, you are controlling what happens next, in this very moment with your conscious choice of how you want to react and behave.

Student D soon realized that when he was surprised by a loud noise, or when startled by his children from behind, even though this might trigger an inappropriate panic response, he had the conscious power in the moment to choose how he wanted to react:

- He understood by this stage that the initial sensations were a learnt response aimed at protecting him from…… well, nothing;
- His subconscious mind had been trained to protect him, but this protection was a false alarm;
- Even though he couldn't stop this anxious response (at this stage) he learnt that he could control what happens next through his conscious choice of how he wanted to react or respond;
- He knew that he had the power to turn off the anxious response through a conscious attitude of non-resistance, fearlessness, disempowering the initial sensations before they spiral into a panic attack.

Moving forward

Here are two awesome quotes from one of my favourite trainers and teachers, Dr Reid Wilson:

> *'Your commitment, your resistance to fight or avoid your discomfort actually causes your continued problem with panic. The single most important way to win over panic attacks is to change your attitude towards the panic.'*

> *'Techniques will not conquer panic, attitude will.'*

BB3 taught D how to completely disempower the panic response, stop panic in it's tracks, without safety crutches and coping strategies. BB3 gave D the trust and the courage to move into any situation and not fear the fear:

- BB3 will not stop the initial anxious sensations, it can't because at the moment, it is a habitual pattern of behavior (BB4 will do that!);
- D learnt that it's the conscious message or instructions that he sent to the subconscious in the moment that matters;
- No coping strategies, no safety crutches.

If you suffer from PTSD, like student D, then BB4 will help you remove the underlying habitual anxious behavior.

If you adopt and implement the behavioural and attitude changes outlined in BB4, make them part of your daily life, make them a habit, you will remove the underlying anxious behavior, and replace it with new non-anxious behavior:

- By doing that you remove the inappropriate flashbacks, intrusive and worrying thoughts;
- And as a non-anxious person you remove the inappropriate anxious response to all those situations that triggered such a response;
- In this normal state, you will worry when there is something to worry about, you will become anxious when there is something to be anxious about, and you will panic when there is something to panic about.

Your subconscious mind is your friend, and will do whatever you tell it to, including protecting you, preparing you for fight or flight, even in situations that do not warrant such a response. This is good news. You are going to learn how to use the power of your subconscious mind for good, not evil.

You are going to learn in the upcoming chapters that you are consciously in control of how you want to react, it is your conscious choice in any moment that determines whether or not your initial anxious sensations and thoughts spiral out of control in any given situation. You will learn how to deal with the intrusive and worrying thoughts and flashbacks.

If you have read my story, you can see how it is very similar to D's. Very similar experiences, but two different diagnoses! It just so happened I was diagnosed with GAD and later social phobia and agoraphobia. But I could have so easily been diagnosed with PTSD as well, I could have easily been given that label.

It ultimately wouldn't have made any difference, because the healing process, the answer is the same, no matter what you have been labelled with.

So I do have some understanding of what you are going through. I've seen my fair share of shit too.

- I can still hear the blood curdling screams from victims crushed and trapped in motor vehicles;
- Or hear the last gasp of breath from a victim dying of stab wounds;
- I can still smell the stench of burnt or decomposing bodies;
- I can still see death, physical violence and sexual abuse;
- I can still see and hear my dad taking his last breath;
- I can still see my mom sitting on the couch with her legs stretched over my daughter Huia's lap, chatting away happily, only to be taking her last breathe a few seconds later right before our eyes.

Certain situations, whether it's something I see, hear, or smell remind me of past experience all too often. If I go into a hospital for example, if I smell things like rubber gloves of all things. But that's just how it is. That's life and we all have to deal with this shit! There is nothing I can do about it, I can't erase the memory, and I never will. I'm not sure if I even want to.

I'm at peace with myself, and I love myself unconditionally, warts and all. I am who I am, where I am, here and now, doing what I am doing because of all my experiences, good and bad, and I wouldn't have it any other way.

But that's all they are now, just memories that come and go, without a second thought. I have made my peace with them, time has healed, and I don't have any attachment to them. I have grieved, and I have healed over time.

Unconditional self love and acceptance, gratitude, forgiveness among other things have a big part to play in the healing process, more on this later.

I no longer have an underlying anxiety condition fueling inappropriate intrusive flashbacks and worrying thoughts. This is how it is for most of us, and so it should and will be for you soon once you have removed your underlying high anxiety condition!

I am working with a large number of soldiers who have also seen their fair share of some pretty ugly shit. I can't even begin to try and understand what they have gone through, and I don't even try to make out that I do. I don't know how anyone can get over some of the stuff that they have seen and experienced.

I have a student in Australia who is a victim of a horrendous gang rape, who is lucky to even be alive following the ordeal. There is no way I'll ever understand what the pain of that memory must be like.

How anyone that has been victim to such horrific experiences can make peace and heal is beyond me. But they do, somehow. Somehow these courageous individuals do manage to make peace and move on. Their lives will never be the same, but they are able to move on!

My job is to remove the underlying anxious habitual condition that is keeping sufferers stuck in a perpetual anxious cycle so that they can get on with their lives as normally as possible, to grieve, make peace, forgive and heal without the distraction of inappropriate anxious behavior.

Case Study 2: Student E

Student E is an ex soldier who has constant and incessant flashbacks from his traumatic experiences while serving throughout the middle east. Interestingly enough, E's traumatic flashbacks were not as a result of what had happened to him or what he saw per se, but as a result of his actions and treatment towards others. Let's just say that E was riddled with guilt and remorse for all the terrible acts that he had carried out on others. We'll leave it at that!

Student E reached out to me online about 5 years ago after having read my book. It had such a profound effect on him that he wanted to interview me on his podcast. Following the podcast E opened up and we discussed his guilt and remorse for his actions, and wanted to know how to deal with his traumatic flashbacks.

Now you can never erase memories or flashbacks. You can't take back what you have done in the past or make it go away. It is what it is, and your actions and memories are here to stay. You can over time however, learn to accept the past and make peace with yourself.

Making Peace With Yourself
I ended up working with E over the following few months, through the healing principles outlined in BB4 (The Golden Rules), helping him to learnt how to make peace with himself and to accept and live with his actions. Over this period the memories and flashbacks never went away, but they began to have less and less of a traumatic impact. Below is a summary of the main things that he did to make peace with himself.

Taking Action Within Your Control
I asked E whether there was anything he could do within his control to make things right, to fix things, to make amends? The short answer was that under the circumstances there was nothing that could be done. Fixing, apologizing or making a reparation for example wasn't an option.

Forgiveness
E then began practicing forgiveness towards himself for his actions. What's done is done, and filling himself with guilt and remorse was of little value. Forgiveness was a choice that he could and had to make. You can imagine that this was pretty difficult at the start, but his only job was to practice forgiveness, not to expect immediate results (which he desperately wanted). And while he was about it, E also practiced forgiving others. Again this wasn't easy at the start, but over time, forgiving himself and others became easier and easier through disciplined practice and repetition.

Unconditional Love & Acceptance
E also began practicing unconditionally loving and accepting himself, warts and all, here and now in the present moment. Of course this wasn't easy, but his only job was to practice without expectation for anything to change and to be ok with not being ok. Whenever E would experience his flashbacks, his only job was to practice forgiveness and unconditional love and acceptance. He chose to focus on this simple yet powerful mantra: 'It is what it is, I can't take it back, what's done is done, but I can use my past to be a better person to myself and others. I am learning to forgive myself and others, and to unconditionally love and accept myself exactly the way I am, here and now.'

E's job was not to stop the flashbacks, his only job was to practice being ok with not being ok, to allow the grief and remorse to flow through, and then to choose to focus on his mantra.

Finding Meaning

E then needed to find a meaning for all his suffering. How could he use his past actions in a positive way or for a higher purpose? What could he possibly learn from his experience?

E pledged to be kinder to himself, to be more loving, compassionate, empathetic and forgiving to not only himself, but others as well. Not only did he change how he treated himself and others, he also began helping others (through his already established online presence) who were suffering from their own traumatic experiences.

I guess to a certain degree we have all done things in the past that we regret and fill ourselves with guilt and remorse, well I know I have anyway. Even to this day I still often have flashbacks of past actions and behaviors that have caused others pain and trauma. But like E, I don't fight these emotions, I allow them to flow through me, and then make a conscious choice to focus on the principles outlined above, every time.

I cover these principles in more detail in BB4, Golden Rules 3 (Finding Meaning).

Panic Attacks

Panic attacks occur as a result of extreme anxiety levels, which send a message to the subconscious mind that you are in real and immediate danger. So for your own preservation, it activates the emergency 'fight or flight' response, creating all the horrible and uncomfortable sensations previously discussed. The response is sudden and creates intense fear within you.

A panic attack is an inappropriate emergency response to perfectly normal everyday situations which do not warrant such a response.

An underlying anxiety condition produces unusual and intrusive thoughts and sensations, popping up from the subconscious. This happens, seemingly automatically and from out of nowhere, catching you by surprise. This is extremely distressing, compounded by the belief that you have no control over the uncomfortable sensations.

The more you focus on the sensations, the more worried and fearful you become, and the more you consciously try to stop the sensations, your memory of previous occasions when you experienced panic attacks surfaces, and you become consciously preoccupied with monitoring your sensations.

This just produces even more anxiety, which feeds and fuels more panic sensations. This causes you to react with even more fear, producing more anxiety and more intense sensations. This vicious cycle convinces the subconscious that you really are in danger and flips the emergency response. Fear breeds fear and a full-on panic attack ensues as the 'fight or flight' switch is turned on.

During a panic attack, you are overcome with an overwhelming urge to escape, to run away. This is an instinctual and normal reaction to the 'fight or flight' response in the body.

Panic attacks can turn up spontaneously, out of the blue, for no reason at all; they do not need an external catalyst to trigger the sensations. All it takes is an unusual sensation or thought, along with memories of previous panic to start the vicious cycle as described above.

Panic attacks can also be triggered by a specific situation or place that causes fear. Panic is a highly charged anxious emotion. Past experiences of panic are etched into your memory. Whatever situation or place you were in at the time of your panic gets associated with the panic. The next time you enter the situation or place, the memory of your inappropriate panic surfaces, triggering the anxious response.

You react consciously to these sensations with fear, starting yet another downward spiral. Your conscious attention on these horrible yet harmless sensations creates more fear, and within a very short space of time, you find yourself in the middle of a full-on panic attack. You have conditioned yourself to habitually respond through Operant Conditioning.

To avoid panic, you adopt certain daily rituals in order to protect yourself. They can include safety crutches or coping strategies such as the following:

- Always ensuring that you have an easy exit, escape route, or excuse to leave a situation;
- Having a support person with you;
- Taking medication to mask the sensations.
- Avoiding drawing attention to yourself, like avoiding eye contact for example;
- Staying alert, on guard, anticipating the next panic attack;
- Monitoring your bodily sensations;
- Carrying a lucky charm with you;
- And the most effective strategy of them all, *avoidance* - avoiding the panic provoking situation altogether.

The *avoidance* technique may work perfectly if you suffer from panic attacks while jumping out of a plane, for example. If you avoid doing that for the rest of your life, you will still manage to live a healthy, prosperous, unrestricted existence without any issues at all. If, on the other hand, you panic every time you leave the house, as is the case for agoraphobia sufferers, *avoiding* leaving the house will lead to a very destructive, highly restrictive life.

Coping strategies and safety crutches do nothing but reinforce to the subconscious mind that the panic response is critical to your preservation, giving this bad habit more strength. Logically you are fully aware that your panic is irrational, but up until now you have been powerless to stop panic attacks because of your conscious attitude towards the sensations.

Your current conscious reaction to panic is based around an attitude of resistance. When you resist anything, it persists. You are trying to resist panic through all your coping and avoidance strategies and safety crutches. Resistance is based on fear. Your conscious fear of the uncomfortable sensations *is* the fuel for panic.

Fear is a strong emotion which occupies your mind in the form of worry and anticipation of the next panic episode and the 'what if' thoughts. This preoccupation of fear, this conscious resistant attitude is not only the fuel for panic but also reinforces the underlying anxiety condition.

You may even get to the point, like me, where these daily rituals of constantly monitoring sensations and thoughts in anticipation of panic actually produced panic attacks, without even exposing yourself to the situation that triggers panic!

If this vicious cycle is not broken, panic attacks can lead to anxiety-related phobias, such as social phobia and agoraphobia. This is exactly what happened to me, and as a result, my life became very restrictive and destructive.

The unusual and horrible anxious sensations can turn up at times when you logically know that there is nothing to fear. Remember that this is happening automatically, habitually. It's like a record playing in the background. So until you change the record—which you will do with my Building Blocks™—these uncomfortable sensations will continue to surface, whether you like it or not, no matter how hard you consciously *try* to stop them.

Earlier I discussed how our subconscious is programmed to maintain a healthy balance, and left to its own devices, it will always seek this balance; it knows precisely what to do and how and when to protect us through its perfect monitoring system. And you may also recall that I earlier discussed that our conscious reaction to the initial anxious sensations produces even more anxiety, which triggers the emergency response. We start doubting our own natural subconscious monitoring system.

Consciously we are 'on guard', watching, monitoring, protecting, avoiding—*resisting*.

I'll say this again, if we can consciously get out of the way, the subconscious mind will be free to find a healthy normal balance. If we consciously stop fueling the panic cycle through our fearful and resistant attitude, there will not be any reason for the subconscious to flip the emergency switch.

You will learn how to do this in BB3 with the Panic Attack Eliminator.

The Panic Cycle

Let's take a closer look at the panic cycle. With practice and perseverance, you will learn how to stop panic in its tracks at any stage during the cycle.

You consciously hold yourself in this pattern with your *attitude*. You will learn how to disempower this uncomfortable yet harmless cycle with BB3:

- The initial anxious sensations or intrusive thoughts (whether triggered by an event, situation, or even appearing for no reason) are registered by the brain;
- Based on memory of past experiences, the conscious mind interprets these stimuli as danger. Unusual sensations and thoughts increase as a result, raising anxiety levels even further;
- The conscious mind increases its focus on the physical sensations, reacting with more fear—raising anxiety levels yet again. *It stops looking for solutions and stops focusing on the facts;*
- Anxiety rises to extreme levels, fueled by the conscious mind interpreting the sensations as a sign of some imminent catastrophic or negative outcome;
- The brain activates the emergency 'fight or flight' response, experienced as a panic attack. *The urge to escape or run from the perceived danger is overwhelming.*

Now you won't be able to stop the initial anxious sensations from surfacing as they are part of an habitual pattern of behavior which we will remove in due course. This is what you have been trying to do up until now without success. The good news is that you don't have to stop anything. All you have to do is choose how you react to these initial sensations.

Your conscious choice on how you react in the moment alone determines whether the initial sensations stick around as nothing more than an irritation, or spiral out of control into a full on panic attack. Whether you react with fear and resistance, or acceptance and non-resistance is your choice, your conscious choice in the moment!

Depending on how you consciously react, you either fuel your anxiety with resistance and fear, instructing the subconscious mind that you are in danger so you need more protection, or with non-resistance, instructing the subconscious that it can stand down, because there is no danger!

At anytime, anytime at all along the panic cycle, you can instruct the subconscious mind to stand down, and it will obey your conscious command!

Whatever you have been diagnosed with, whether it be OCD, PTSD or Agoraphobia, or any of the other conditions, the panic cycle applies to you. Apply what you have learned in the previous chapters regarding your specific condition, combined with your own experiences and you will see the truth.

Anxiety Related Phobias

In very broad and basic terms, a phobia is the fear of experiencing a panic attack when exposed to certain situations or conditions that are completely harmless. The situation or event is not what you fear, it is the fear of a panic attack, triggered by or associated with the situation or event that you actually fear.

- You do not fear the actual situation or event.

This section focuses on the three main anxiety-related phobias: agoraphobia, specific phobia, and social phobia.

- *All these conditions can be completely eliminated through my Building Blocks™.*

Agoraphobia

Agoraphobia is driven by your fear of having a panic attack while away from a place of safety such as your home, not only in open spaces, or in crowded public places such as shopping malls, but also in confined spaces, such as cafés, buses, and standing in a queue at a bank—in fact, just about anywhere where they fear having a panic attack.

Now it's time to repeat myself again. As you are now aware, a panic attack is a perfectly normal and instinctual emergency or 'fight or flight' response, activated by the subconscious mind at totally inappropriate times when no real danger exists.

During this response, there is an overwhelming urge to run or escape to avoid some kind of catastrophe. The fear of not being able exit or escape from a panic-provoking situation drives agoraphobia.

Agoraphobia is one of the most debilitating of all anxiety conditions, as the fear of not being able to escape breeds more fear of the situation. This, along with the associated memory of previous panic, causes you to begin avoiding the situation(s) in order to stay safe. This avoidance behaviour, designed to keep you safe merely strengthens your anxiety condition, which is nothing more than learnt behaviour - *a bad habit.*

Agoraphobia can be experienced in varying degrees, from an underlying lingering and irritating anxiety in anticipation of a panic attack while away from home (place of safety), right up to the extreme end, where the fear of suffering a panic attack becomes so immobilizing that you find it difficult to actually go outside for even just a short while. Eventually, you may even find yourself experiencing a panic attack at home, just by the initial thought of going outside.

The 'place of safety' is different from individual to individual. It is basically anywhere where you consciously believe you will *not* experience a panic attack. It could be your home, it could be your office, anywhere familiar, near a telephone, with friends or family members.

Remember: Just because you have an anxiety condition like GAD, OCD, or PTSD, it doesn't mean that you will also suffer from panic attacks or anxiety-related phobias.

Panic attacks and phobias occur only when your inappropriate anxiety reaches very high levels, activating the emergency response.

Specific Phobia

Specific phobia is an intense or irrational fear of a specific thing that represents no real danger at all. Common specific phobias include a fear of flying, bridges, elevators, closed-in spaces, dogs, spiders, heights, and water, to name but a few. As mentioned earlier, the actual fear is around experiencing the horrible sensations of a panic attack, not the actual specific situation.

- Your acknowledgement of this *fact* is critical to your healing.

To illustrate this, consider for a moment someone who has a phobia of spiders; this condition is very common. Even when presented with a completely harmless species such as a daddy long-legged spider, the sufferer will spin into a panic attack.

No matter how often you tell them that the spider is harmless, it will not make an ounce of difference to them. They already know this; they are already fully aware that the spider is harmless, but it makes no difference.

So what is it that they fear then? They know it is harmless, so how can they possibly have a fear towards it? The answer is they fear the horrible sensations of panic that exposure to the spider triggers. It is the fear of experiencing a panic attack which causes the fear. They fear the fear of a panic attack, the fear of the uncomfortable yet harmless sensations.

For whatever reason, the panic response has been experienced while exposed to a specific situation on one or more occasions. The memory and exposure to this highly emotional response conditions the mind to react with panic whenever you are reintroduced to the panic-provoking situation. Why and how this has happened is not critical to your healing. What is critical is that you accept:

- That you fear the fear of a panic attack. You fear the fear of the sensations themselves;
- Panic attacks occur as a result of an underlying anxiety condition;
- If you learn to stop consciously fearing the sensations and then relearn non-anxious behaviour, the anxiety condition, along with the associated uncomfortable anxious sensations, will disappear;
- *If you didn't fear the sensations, you couldn't experience a panic attack!*

If the object of your specific phobia is easy to avoid, then you may be able to go on with your life without any real disruption or need of treatment. If you have a phobia of snakes, then living in New Zealand will not cause you too many issues. However, if you avoid social gatherings because of a social phobia, then you start sabotaging career or personal relationships and opportunities, and the condition becomes extremely disabling and destructive.

Social Phobia

Along with agoraphobia, social phobia was my territory. These two phobias were my constant companion for many, many years. By themselves, they can cause havoc with a sufferer's life; working in tandem, they can cause real destruction.

I know this better than anyone. I sabotaged and lost relationships, careers, businesses, friendships, and my own fortunes through my own journey of suffering. But here I am today, healed, at peace, full of unconditional self love, acceptance, gratitude, and a deep sense of empathy and compassion towards others. It's hard to believe I once suffered from an anxiety condition at all.

My point is that if I can heal myself, then so can you. I'm teaching you exactly what I, tens of thousands of sufferers around the world who I have helped through this book and my personal cocaching programme over the last ten years, and every other ex-sufferer has done to heal themselves, not *cope*, but *heal* themselves.

Sufferers of social phobia develop an overwhelming self-consciousness in social situations, fueled by a fear of being embarrassed or humiliated in front of others. This all stems from the fear of having a panic attack in front of others and being perceived as someone who is unable to cope with perfectly normal, everyday non-threatening activities or situations.

If left to its own devices, social phobia can play havoc with your self-esteem and confidence, creating even more anxiety and fear of panic and corresponding embarrassment and perceived judgement, which by now as you can appreciate, is a recipe for a vicious cycle of anxious behaviour.

The fear of embarrassment, or of being judged for being visibly unable to cope in front of others, can be so overwhelming that the mere thought or anticipation of entering a panic-provoking situation can cause panic.

The fear can be so chronic that it interferes with a person's interactions, behaviour, and performance in situations such as work, social gatherings, school, and any other routine activity. In its most severe state, social phobia may even cause you to stop going to places like work or school—full stop.

I have first-hand experience of this. My panic attacks and social phobia became so bad that I walked away from an amazing opportunity while working for Te Wānanga O Aotearoa (TWOA) in Palmerston North.

Towards the end of 2005, as the assistant campus director, I was given the opportunity to take over as the campus director.

I was already having a hard enough time, fulfilling my current tasks; just the thought of stepping into the spotlight as the 'big boss' sent me into horrible panic attacks. By this time, I was having difficulty going to work, running meetings, engaging with various stakeholders, and leading my various teams. I began withdrawing myself from any situation that I perceived as threatening, which in my high profile role was almost everything. My only 'place of safety' was home.

I turned down the opportunity, claiming that it would be better for the position to be filled by someone who was strong in Te Reo Maori. Avoiding this promotion made me even more of a prisoner to my anxiety. The buzz around my staff was that I had been overlooked.

Now hearing something like this would affect the best of us, but how do you think it affected someone like me who suffered from an acute anxiety condition?

I remember going home at around that time and breaking down in front of Nikki for the very first time. I had no idea what was going on. I withdrew even more from my previously high profile role as assistant campus director. Somehow, for about the next six months, I managed to always have some 'convenient' excuse as to why I couldn't attend any meetings, or even go to work. Of course this had a flow-on effect with my personal life as I began to withdraw from social interaction. I soon became completely housebound.

This was a disastrous situation to be in. I had two children to care for, and we were a single-income family. If I couldn't go to work, pretty soon people would come and take my furniture! I ended up leaving TWOA in mid-2006. I thought that TWOA was the problem, and if I left, my anxiety would also leave. I was wrong.

This destructive cycle of sabotaging career or work opportunities repeated itself several times before I finally took control and healed myself. The last, and most severe cycle was experienced when I went to work at Toyota New Zealand (TNZ) as team leader for the business planning unit during 2008. My panic attacks were so severe that I would literally spend around three hours each day, locked in a toilet cubical, absolutely petrified of facing my staff and work colleagues, waiting for my panic sensations to die down.

I was responsible for a small team of analysts, and part of my role involved constant interaction with and reporting to the executive management, including the CEO. I lasted nine months there. Actually I'm surprised that I lasted that long. My absence at key reporting meetings didn't go unnoticed. Instead of confiding in my immediate supervisor as to what I was going through, I did what I had always done, I resigned and left with my tail between my legs.

By this time, I was at my wits end. My social phobia had reached absolute rock bottom, and I had put my family at risk yet again. A year earlier, two of my companies had been liquidated; I had lost a fortune and went bankrupt in the process. This was the absolute lowest point in my life. Driven by sheer desperation, motivated by the welfare of my children, I finally decided to once and for all tackle my anxiety front-on. And I did so using the principles contained in these Building Blocks™.

Social phobia may be specific to only one situation, such as speaking in front of others, or in the most severe cases, you may experience panic sensations whenever you are around others.

The most common physical sensations experienced with the panic response is a racing heart, nausea, intense blushing, skin rash, difficulty talking, and trembling hands, all of which can be extremely embarrassing as you will undoubtedly be so self-conscious that you believe that all eyes are on you, watching, noticing you in difficulty and judging you for your inability to cope.

The truth is, no one really notices or cares what you are going through, apart from, of course, those close to you who care and love you, such as your family and friends. But other than those few, everyone else is inherently too preoccupied with themselves and their own problems and issues that they have to deal with to even notice you having difficulty.

I know this only too well. Following my healing, I began sharing my story with friends. Their first reaction was *always* that they had no idea what I was going through as I *always* came across as super-confident and self-assured. I wish I had known that at the time lol.

Our anxiety-fueled perception of ourselves and what we *think* others *see* is so far from the truth of what others *actually* see or perceive about us.

No one is totally squared away, *everyone* has their own issues and challenges that they need to deal with, no matter who they are, and they've got a hard enough job dealing with their own issues to notice you. The truth of the matter is that in most cases, the only one noticing you having difficulty is *you*.

Trust me, my first panic attack in front of others occurred in 1993, and up to about the beginning of 2009, I suffered thousands—and it turns out through talking with a large number of people who knew me throughout those years that bugger all even noticed me stuttering, blushing, trembling, and having difficulty breathing.

What are you currently doing to keep yourself safe?

- Are you preoccupied with embarrassing yourself in front of others?

- Do you have intrusive, worrying thoughts about panicking in front of others?
- When you find yourself in difficulty, do you focus in on your uncomfortable sensations and try your best to turn them off or stop them?
- If that doesn't work, do you then avoid situations that you believe will cause you to panic?
- And following an attack, do you ponder and worry over the experience, chastise and ridicule yourself on your inability to cope like other normal people?
- Do you use coping strategies, techniques, and safety crutches to help you manage?

If you have answered 'Yes' to any of these questions, how has it worked out for you? My guess is that you are still suffering from panic attacks. Why? Because all of your actions and behaviour you currently engage in to protect yourself are based on resistance—fighting against that which you fear.

These conscious actions are fear based, creating more anxiety, strengthening this habitual anxious behaviour. Intuitively, it seems like the right thing to do; to run away from, or avoid that which you fear.

But this attitude is precisely what is keeping you here. The solution to ending social phobia is the same for all the other phobias, panic attacks, and anxiety conditions. It's doing the *exact opposite* to what you are currently doing. We'll get to that real soon.

Social phobia is an interesting one: you fear the fear of experiencing the sensations of panic in front of others, and to make it worse, you also have a fear of being embarrassed, judged, and ridiculed by others who see you having difficulty. And furthermore, deep down at some level you believe that you have to accept others judgement and criticism.

Don't despair, my Building Blocks™ will completely heal you of this highly disabling condition.

Medication

If you suffer from an anxiety condition, and you are currently taking medication to help you *cope*, the sooner you stop taking the medication the better.

Medication will help you *cope* with anxiety, but so will all other safety crutches and coping strategies, like *avoidance* for example. Medication will not heal you. The goal here is to get *better*, not to feel better, not to just to *cope*.

Drugs such as Prozac, Seroxat, and Zispin are common SSRI drugs (selective serotonin re-uptake inhibitors) used to correct serotonin levels in the brain. Serotonin controls moods swings. SSRI drugs are designed to help maintain a healthy chemical balance in the brain.

Clinical depression is a mental disorder, caused by a chemical imbalance in the brain. In this case, drugs are used to successfully correct the chemical imbalance, therefore keeping the disorder under control.

- A chemical imbalance is the cause of clinical depression.
- Depression is the effect of this imbalance.

An anxiety condition, on the other hand, is a learnt behaviour, a bad habit which, as a result artificially raises anxiety levels. Anxiety can *cause* a chemical imbalance in the brain, which produces depression-like symptoms. This chemical imbalance, which produces fearful, fed-up, negative, and depressive thoughts, is the *effect* of anxiety, not the *cause*.

- An underlying anxiety condition is the cause of a chemical imbalance.
- A chemical imbalance is the effect of the underlying anxiety condition.

You have programmed changes in your brain neurology, which also change your brain chemistry. Neural pathways and associations determine which neural chemicals, and at what level, pass through the synapses. Your neural chemistry is determined by your neural pathways and associations, not the other way around.

Medicinal intervention will alter your brain chemistry temporarily, but has no power to change neural pathways and associations. In other words, medication can temporarily hide or mask the symptoms and sensations and the *effects* of an anxiety condition by changing the brain's chemistry, but it will not remove the *cause* or the problem, which is a learnt pattern of behaviour—a bad habit.

Medication cannot and will not remove an underlying bad habit. The only permanent solution is to change your neural pathways and associations through Operant Conditioning. Your brain chemistry will change as your neural pathways and associations change (not the other way around), and this change will be permanent.

In your case, drugs will *never* get rid of a learnt pattern of anxious behaviour, as they target the *effect*, not the *cause*. You will learn that the *only* way to change a behaviour is through behaviour.

Drugs may or may not provide temporary relief from the intrusive and depressive thoughts and sensations (like other coping strategies and safety crutches), but this is *always* only ever short-lived. Under the surface, you still have an anxiety condition running riot; you are still acting and behaving anxiously.

In such circumstances, you will need to increase your medication to compensate for the higher levels of anxiety being experienced.

Furthermore, the side effects and dependency issues associated with medical intervention is a whole new ball game that you will have to deal with, which can make an anxiety condition even worse. If you are taking medication, I don't need to convince you of any of this.

Anxiety is our friend. It is not a disorder. To correct your anxious behaviour, you need to be fully in the present and be aware of all your bodily sensations that your current behaviour is producing. You need to communicate consciously with your subconscious with a non-resistant, accepting attitude in order to teach it new non-anxious habitual behaviour. Drugs and other safety crutches will do nothing for this delicate relationship, apart from causing confusion and distrust, and yes, more anxiety.

If you are a sufferer and you are reading this, you do not need any convincing. Your own experiences will confirm all this.

Johann Hari – Lost Connection

In his book Lost Connections (published 2019), Johann Hari challenges the view that anxiety and depression is caused by chemical imbalances in the brain and that medication is the solution.

Not that you or I need any validation for what we already know to be true through our own real life experiences, but in short, here are the most important points to take away from the very latest research:

1. Overall it has been established that anxiety and depression is NOT caused by a chemical imbalance in the brain;
2. Furthermore, disconnection from the things that are actually important and that provide real peace, joy and fulfillment like meaningful work, meaningful values, other people, the natural world and a hopeful and secure future (among other things) are the real causes of anxiety and depression;
    a. To a significant degree, your depression and anxiety is caused by how you live your life;
    b. BB4, The Golden Rules will help you reconnect with what is important;
3. Medication does jack shit to heal or even help you!

> *You are not a machine that is broken, you are an animal, who's needs have not been met.*
> (Johann Hari)

Hari also has a crack at the medical industry and pharmaceutical companies who sponsor all the research behind their own drugs, and then only publish the results that they want to disclose that support their products.

It's humbling to know that my book attackpanic which I first published nearly ten years ago still holds true today. Truth is truth!

What Are You really Afraid Of?

During high anxiety and panic attacks, what you actually fear are the horrible sensations of fear, not the actual situation that triggered the attack. You fear the horrible sensations of fear manifesting in your body. The fear is not real, and there is no real danger; you are just experiencing sensations, a false alarm produced by anxious habitual behaviour.

- *You are not in any real danger whatsoever.*
- *These sensations are perfectly normal and are completely harmless.*
- *You fear the sensations of fear. You do not fear the situation that triggered the sensations.*

You are not fearful of the crowd of people or waiting in a queue; you have never been harmed by them before, and you never will. There is no killer queue ready to swallow you up whole. You know this consciously, and you know this logically.

- *If you did not fear the sensations of fear, you would not experience fear.*

You are not afraid of heights; no one has ever died of heights, ever. Now, you may be thinking to yourself, 'But Shaun, my fear is of falling and dying, plenty of people die from falling.' I agree. I guarantee that those who do not have a phobia of heights will also fear falling and dying.

Of course you are scared of falling - *Everyone* is scared of falling. Why? Because it will really bloody hurt!

You are not alone here. But when there is no risk of falling (refer to my powerful analogy below of abseiling down the Auckland Sky Tower) and you are still fearful, your fear isn't about falling; it can't be because you know rationally you're not going to fall, no less than you know that you're not going to come to any harm waiting in a queue at the bank.

You are *only* fearful of the seemingly out of control, out of the blue, horrible, and uncomfortable sensations caused by the panic or emergency response. That's it.

Your anxious habitual behaviour tricks the brain into activating the 'fight or flight' response at totally inappropriate times, which causes all the horrible sensations that you fear. And you fear them because up until now, they seem to have a mind of their own, turning up automatically. You cannot control them (luckily you don't have to), and this leaves you feeling helpless and scared.

Whatever the catalyst of your anxiety condition is, whether it is a traumatic event, stressful workplace, relationship, or financial issues, it is irrelevant to your healing.

The problem and the cause of your inappropriate panic response is your underlying anxiety condition:

- *Focusing on the why and how you developed your condition will not help you change this bad habit;*
- *Focusing on the catalyst, memory or triggers, sensations or symptoms, as an anxiety sufferer, only empowers your condition;*

Just Sensations

By now, you are aware that the anxious sensations you experience are designed to put you into a heightened state of awareness, alertness, preparing you for action, to protect you from a danger that doesn't exist.

- As anxiety levels rise, adrenaline is released into the blood stream. This sparks the sympathetic nervous system into action which produces all these sensations designed to raise your awareness and alertness, sensations that you experience as discomfort and fear.

What you may not have consciously considered, however—and this will be a key turning point in your healing—is that this is precisely the same response that occurs when you are engaged in something that you find exciting or exhilarating.

If you are taking a roller-coaster ride for example, or if you are competing or performing in a sport or activity that you love, you are in the present moment, you are fully aware and alert, and you are at your peak ability to perform or experience the moment.

You have activated the same response:
- *Whether you are in a state of panic, or a state of excitement, the same response is taking place in your body;*
- *The difference is the interpretation, the meaning that you are giving to the experience;*
- *The meaning that you give to the experience (joy, fear) is the experience (joy, fear).*

When you are in a state of excitement or you are performing, you don't act surprised or concerned when the sensations appear, you consciously accept them; they are your friend, your helper. You can hang out with them as long as you like, and you are not fearful of them, so it doesn't matter how long they stick around. You don't interpret them as fear or an impending doom or loss of control do you?

- *Your own experience will validate this.*

Now, when you suffer from an anxiety condition, the same sensations turn up unannounced and unwelcomed. Your conscious interpretation is one of discomfort or fear. You become preoccupied and want them to go away because they feel horrible.

- *But they are the same sensations.*

Analogy - Abseiling The Auckland Sky Tower

Here is a very powerful analogy to illustrate this:

Let's take two work colleagues on a team building (both wearing team building T-shirts of course!) exercise on top of the Auckland Sky Tower, preparing to abseil down its face. One happens to love the experience, the opportunity to try something new. She has butterflies and is feeling nervous as she has never tried anything like this before; this is an extreme test for her.

But she is up for it. Even though this is scary, she knows that she is in no real danger, the instructors are experts, all the necessary safety precautions are in place, and all the equipment is in excellent condition.

She is secure in her harness and safety equipment. The likelihood of anything going wrong is very minimal. She is aware of this, but the sheer extremities of the event still make her nervous. Adrenaline is coursing through her body, all her senses are heightened. In this case, the meaning she is giving the experience is one of excitement, challenge, and growth, and therefore that will be the experience.

The interpretation of the event and the sensations is one of excitement rather than fear of some imminent danger. This is the choice that she has made.

Now let's look at her mate right next to her. He has a phobia of heights and suffers from severe panic attacks when exposed to anything above one storey.

He is standing on top of the tower right next to his colleague. He is secured in the same type of harness and safety equipment as his colleague.

He is under the same care of expert instructors and under the same safety precautions. The likelihood of something going wrong is also very minimal, and he knows this just as much as his colleague.

The conditions, event, equipment—everything is exactly the same, except for the experience! The same sensations, caused by the release of adrenaline, are coursing through his body; however, he is conditioned to respond to these sensations with fear.

Fear thoughts increase these bodily sensations and make for a very horrible and scary experience. The conscious meaning he gives to the experience is fear, and therefore fear becomes the experience.

Now, no amount of reassuring and logical talk will stop him from having a panic attack. Logically, rationally, he is aware that he is in no more danger than his colleague, or even the people walking along the street below him, but that is of no significance because he fears the horrible sensations, not the situation. He has interpreted the sensations as fear as opposed to excitement.

The result is a perpetual cycle of uncontrolled fear of doom and feelings of helplessness, which escalates into a panic attack, manifesting into an overwhelming urge to escape.

The same conditions and environment, the same anxious sensations coursing through their bodies, but two very different attitudes, two very different interpretations, two very different meanings, resulting in two very different experiences from the same event.

- The answer to ending panic forever is in your conscious *attitude*. This will be covered at length in BB2.

Anticipatory Anxiety: Frightened About Being Frightened

In my opinion, based on my own experience and that of all sufferers that I have personally worked with over the last ten years, without exception, the biggest problem plaguing sufferers, especially those that suffer from panic attacks, are the *ritualistic* preoccupation and monitoring of their sensations, environment and even thoughts, staying constantly on guard, waiting for some internal sign that an attack is about to unveil itself.

We even go so far as to prepare ourselves with coping strategies and safety crutches should we find ourselves in difficulty. And of course, because you have an anxiety condition, because you are habitually behaving anxiously, you *will* get what you are looking for: more sensations and panic. This is a vicious feedback loop, a self-fulfilling prophecy.

The worrying thoughts about the next attack, projecting yourself forward into a future panic-provoking situation, painstakingly working through all the various negative scenarios *will* trigger corresponding anxious sensations, without even entering the situation.

This convinces your subconscious mind that you are in need of protection. Not surprisingly, when you do enter that (perceived) difficult situation, the subconscious mind, which can't take a joke, remembers all those earlier worrying thoughts and fears and sets about protecting you with a panic response.

This vicious perpetual cycle of behaviour is called anticipatory anxiety, and after having experienced thousands of panic attacks and working with other sufferers, I know this to be true:

- *Anticipatory anxiety is worse than the actual experience of panic.*

This may be hard to believe at first, but think about it; take what you have learnt so far coupled with your own experiences and you will know this to be true.

Anticipatory anxiety is based on fear and resistance. This means that we are trying to fight and guard ourselves against panic. All this resistant behaviour just makes you even more anxious and scared. It is this resistant attitude which is the fuel that panic dines out on.

The funny thing is that when the sensations and panic turn up, we seem to be taken completely by surprise by them, totally unaware that we are the cause of them turning up in the first place, through our anticipatory anxiety.

So how do we deal with anticipatory anxiety? The same way we deal with panic itself, the same way we deal with any anxiety condition—*attitude*. You will overcome anticipatory anxiety through an attitude of acceptance and non-resistance.

Instead of resisting, running, fighting, monitoring, and worrying about the next attack, you will practice accepting your condition 100 per cent, loving and accepting yourself unconditionally, exactly the way you are. If and when an attack happens in the future, you will deal with it there and then.

A non-resistant and accepting attitude also means moving towards that which you fear, your false alarm, expecting panic, provoking panic, wanting to experience panic. This attitude is the exact opposite to what you are currently doing and deprives panic of its life-supporting fuel: *anxiety-producing fear.*

If, with absolute trust and belief in what I'm teaching you, along with as much courage as you can muster, you could learn to *accept* 100 per cent whatever difficult situation you encounter (knowing that you are not in any danger whatsoever), if you could *accept* that you *will* experience another panic attack before you get better (because your current anxious behaviour is a habit), if you went looking for opportunities to provoke your panic response, *then* you will stop acting so surprised when panic turns up.

Expecting and accepting panic takes away the surprise, takes away the need to anticipate and worry about the 'what if' horrible thoughts of doom and gloom which is the very fuel which panic needs to survive.

What's really The Answer?

My Building Blocks™ will teach you how to do two things:

- Destroy panic attacks and phobias, completely and permanently (BB3);
- Remove the underlying anxiety condition by programming new non-anxious behaviour, resetting your baseline anxiety levels (stored in the amygdala) back down to a normal healthy level (BB4).

Whether you suffer from panic attacks or phobias, high anxiety (GAD, OCD, or PTSD) or all of the above, the answer to ending your suffering is the same:

- Your *conscious* attitude.

Attitude is of such importance, I have dedicated an entire Building Block to it. Join me soon over at BB2 as I explain how and why *attitude* is the *only* answer to ending panic and high anxiety.

Truth be known, attitude is probably the answer to everything!

Is Therapy And Counselling The Answer?

WARNING: I am about to go on a meandering rant on why therapy, counselling and medication doesn't, hasn't and will never heal you of your anxiety condition. My opinions are based on fifteen years of personal suffering, nine years of study & research, undergoing years & years of therapy and counselling, undergoing dozens of programmes and courses, trial and error and experiencing successes and failures before finally cracking the code and healing myself, along with nearly ten years experience of helping tens of thousands of sufferers all around the world through this wee book and my personal coaching programme.

The conventional approach to dealing with anxiety conditions, specifically therapy, counselling and medication is fundamentally flawed; always has been and always will be. The main reason is that they only deal with the 'effects' (uncomfortable anxious sensations and the accompanying worrying intrusive fearful thoughts), not the 'cause' (underlying high anxiety).

As long as the 'cause' exists, any attempts to deal with and get rid of the 'effects' will be a fruitless affair.

As a sufferer you will no doubt be able to draw on your own experiences.

Before I dispense any further with my rant, consider this analogy:

One morning you go out to your car and notice that one of the tyres has lost a lot of air due to a slow leak. Upon investigation you discover that the 'cause' is a small pin hole and the 'effect' is a slow leak.

Now you have two options on how you could deal with this predicament:

- The first option is to take the car to a petrol station and re-inflate the tyre. This solves the immediate issue, providing temporary relief so to speak, it's a quick fix, it's cheap (well free actually), fast, convenient and offers little disruption to your plans. However because this option only deals with the 'effects', it is nothing more than a band aid. The next morning you go out to your car only to find that the tyre has deflated again. So you go back to the petrol station, re-inflate the tyre, providing temporary relief yet again. If you continue to deal with the problem in this manner, the pin hole will get bigger over time, it will become more expensive and time consuming to fix and you run the risk of damaging the tyre beyond repair (incurring more costs), not to mention the safety issues of driving on a damaged tyre.

- The second option is to address the 'cause' by replacing the punctured tyre with the spare and then getting the thing fixed! Initially this will require a lot more effort causing an inconvenience as well as incurring upfront repair costs. But once you have dealt with the 'cause' the 'effects' (or symptoms if you like) will also disappear.

And so it is with therapy, counselling and medication. They will make you feel better in the moment, provide you with temporary relief by masking the symptoms, the 'effects', but they do not solve the problem, they do not deal with the 'cause', and therefore won't make you better.

Anxious thoughts and uncomfortable sensation and panic attacks are the 'effects', the bi-product of underlying high anxiety. All your coping strategies and safety crutches that you employ to keep you safe are only addressing the 'effects', and while they may provide some form of relief, making you feel better momentarily, they do not address the 'cause'.

Another pet peeve that really pisses me off is how we are led to believe that anxiety conditions are a mental disorder or illness. Fuck that! I wasn't broken, I didn't have a mental illness or disorder, and neither do you! I programmed myself to be an anxious person, I taught myself to behave anxiously. I was 100% responsible for this conditioned behaviour, and only I, through direct behaviour could remove it.

You buy into this idea that you have a mental illness or disorder at your own expense! This belief leads to a dependency mentality, you are convinced you are broken, and the best you can hope for is to manage and cope with your anxiety. The focus is always on how to make yourself comfortable in the moment through strategies for managing and coping with the uncomfortable sensations and worrying, fearful, intrusive anxious thoughts. Therapy and counselling becomes your safety crutch.

Everything you CHOOSE to believe, whether right or wrong, good or bad, true or false, real of unreal, IS true for you and will become a self fulfilling prophecy through your corresponding attitudes and actions!

Therapy, counselling and medication might make you feel better, might help you to manage and cope, but they will never make you better, never heal you because they do not address the cause, the problem.

- The right support is essential, and you will get this from me, either through this book or by visiting my website (attackpanic.co.nz) or by following or training under some of the awesome trainers and coaches I suggest in Chapter 10 (Further Reading).

Summary of Building Blocks™ 1 (BB1)

Read BB1 in its entirety. If you do not understand any part of it, read it again and again until you 'get it', until you accept this as truth. If you still don't get it, contact me so that I can find out what you are doing which may be causing a block.

This stuff is fact, and you will have to embrace it if you want to build up the courage needed to finally face up to your fears and end your suffering once and for all. Below is a snapshot, a quick reference of the main points for you to review. Once you've fully embraced BB1, you may only need to refer back to the summary below whenever you need support and reassurance:

- You are not ill, and there is nothing medically wrong with you;
- You are not broken and you are not going crazy – 'If you think you are going crazy, you probably aren't';
- You have nothing more than a bad habit; you have taught yourself to behave anxiously through operant conditioning;
- You have an anxiety condition. Anxiety is perfectly normal and healthy, it's just that your anxiety levels, regulated by the amygdala, have become stuck on higher than normal levels, which produce correspondingly anxious sensations on a regular basis, and at times that are totally inappropriate;
- You are not in any danger of coming to any harm whatsoever, nothing has ever happened to you, and nothing ever will. Your own experiences prove this;

- Your anxious sensations are completely harmless;
- You do not actually fear the situation that triggers anxiety or panic, you fear the unwanted and inappropriate sensations;
- The answer to ending panic is your conscious attitude;
- The answer to removing your anxiety condition is in practising new non-anxious behaviour, starting with your conscious attitude;
- If you were to consciously get out of the way, your subconscious mind can be relied upon to seek out a healthy balance;
- Without you consciously adding more fear to the mix, the subconscious can be relied upon to turn off the anxiety response;
- When you notice these sensations, you adopt an attitude of resistance, fighting against them, running from them, avoiding them;
- This attitude will not stop a habitual pattern of behaviour. Because the sensations continue, despite your attitude's best efforts, you react with more fear;
- This of course will cause more anxiety, pushing your anxiety levels up even higher;
- The higher the anxiety, the more intense sensations experienced. The more sensations, the more you fear and the more you resist, and so on and so on. This is a vicious feedback loop;
- Soon your anxiety levels will be pushed up to extreme levels. The subconscious reacts by activating the emergency response in order to protect you from your perceived imminent danger.

CHAPTER 6

BUILDING BLOCKS™ 2 (BB2) YOUR ONLY TECHNIQUE - ATTITUDE

Objectives of BB2
- To explore all the various components that make up the correct attitude in great detail to help you build your understanding, belief, and trust even further;
- To give you the confidence and courage required to face and conquer your fears.

Your *attitude* is how you consciously *choose* to *interpret* or *perceive* the harmless sensations, the *meaning* that you give to them, and how you *react* to them. Your *conscious attitude* and choices you make towards your panic and anxiety is responsible for holding you in this horrible perpetuating cycle.

I don't care how long you have been suffering. I don't care where you sit along the anxiety spectrum. If you comply, practice, and persevere with my Building Blocks™, you will be well again.

I suffered my first panic attack over 29 years ago at the time of writing this second edition. Up until about 13 years ago, I was reduced to being a prisoner in my own home, terrified of facing people, sabotaging businesses, relationships, careers, and opportunities. I tried every form of therapy available; I survived on a diet of safety crutches and coping techniques. You couldn't possibly get any worse than me. Yet when I *finally got it*, my healing was very very quick. In fact, my panic attacks and phobias went away instantly! My underlying anxiety condition took a little bit longer to remove because I had to reprogramme new non-anxious habitual behaviour.

> *Techniques will not conquer panic, attitude will.*
> (Dr Reid Wilson)

Your Current Resistant Attitude

Let's recap on your current attitude towards your anxiety and panic, and what you are doing in order to protect yourself. You may find you are practicing many of these actions or only a few; it makes no difference to the fact that you have an anxiety condition, or to how fast you will heal yourself:

- Staying constantly on guard, monitoring and measuring your anxious sensations.
- Preoccupied with 'what if' or other worrying thoughts about a potential distressing situation (anticipatory anxiety).
- Replaying memories of past situations in which you panicked or had difficulty.
- Using safety crutches, such as cell phones, a support person, or a bottle of medication on hand to help you cope through a situation.
- Restricting your life to avoid anxiety-provoking situations. Refraining from doing things that used to be fun but you now find too difficult to face.
- Using coping strategies to cope with your anxiety or panic. This could be using safety crutches as outlined above, making sure that you have a suitable exit mapped out, therapy or counselling sessions, having a raft of reasons to excuse yourself if the sensations become too overwhelming. The more severe coping strategies

include taking medication, or confining yourself to your home (like I did)—the ultimate avoidance strategy of them all.

Now all this vigilance, anticipation, running, fighting, and guarding against seems perfectly natural and intuitive things to do. I agree, this is the very attitude that I practiced for many years thinking that I was doing the right thing, and that it was the best way to protect myself.

But this attitude is based on resistance, fighting against what you don't want. It is based on fear.

- What you resist persists;
- Your fear is breeding more fear.

Your subconscious anxious behaviour, or if you want to look at it how I did, the record that's playing in the background, is not the problem; it is your conscious FEAR-based *attitude* that's the problem.

Fear creates more anxiety; fear is the fuel for panic.

If you keep doing what you have always done, you will keep getting what you have always got.

If you continue with this current attitude, expect more of the same. Coping strategies, for example, further convinces the subconscious mind that you are using these coping strategies because you are in fear, and therefore you need protection against that fear. The subconscious has no idea what is real and what is not, and it certainly cannot take a joke.

What would happen if you *chose* an attitude completely opposite to the one you are currently holding on to? What if you did the complete opposite to *everything* you are currently doing as described above? What if you *chose* an attitude of *fearlessness* instead of fearfulness? You *must* get a different result.

I know what you are thinking: What? Are you completely nuts? You expect me to walk into panic? Go looking for situations that cause me distress? You expect me to drop all the things I need to keep me safe? You expect me to just stop worrying about my anxiety and to just stop monitoring my horrible sensations? Really?

My answer is simple: *Really*!

This approach seems ludicrous as it appears counter-intuitive to what you should do. This approach is known as a paradoxical intention and involves completely dropping your guard, embracing your fears, walking into them and wanting more, and accepting them and flowing with them.

I bet you're now thinking this: *That's crazy, it's just not that simple. I can't just let go of all my fears and safety nets, it's just not that easy.*

My answer to that is, *have you tried it*?

I can, however, understand your initial concerns; I had them too when I first changed my attitude. It may or may not be easy for you, and this will depend on your level of acceptance and belief in what I am teaching you.

This paradoxical approach may seem scary and may or may not be easy, but how badly do you want to end your suffering? Are you willing to practice and persevere with this new attitude? Are you willing to do whatever it takes to heal yourself?

> *Your commitment, your resistance to fight or avoid your discomfort actually causes your continued problem with panic. The single most important way to win over panic attacks is to change your attitude towards the panic.*
> (Dr Reid Wilson)

You focus in on the horrible sensations; your attention and preoccupation is on these sensations, and you invest all your energy trying to stop them from appearing, worrying about 'what if' these sensations turn up out of the blue. Your corresponding actions and behaviour are focused on avoiding the situation that provokes these sensations.

If you are anything like how I used to be, you probably spend a good deal of your time trying to figure out why these sensations of fear appear out of nowhere, and what you have done to deserve this. You may even feel helpless that you can't consciously turn off these sensations when they arrive.

You are fully aware that the fear towards the sensations is irrational and ridiculous, but you are so frustrated because as much as you try to turn off the anxious response or panic attacks, they just seem to come on even stronger.

You try all your coping strategies, techniques, and safety crutches to control these uncomfortable yet harmless sensations, throwing all your attention and energy into avoiding, running, and resisting. The harder you try, the worse they seem to get and the more frustrated and out of control you feel.

Once something has already happened, you can't turn around and stop it. It's too late; it's like shutting the gate after the horse has bolted. You can't stop a panic attack after it has started. You can't stop the initial anxious sensations (arising as a result of a pattern of habitual behaviour) after they have arrived.

But that doesn't stop you from trying to stop the horrible sensations, does it? Your resistant attitude will never reverse the sensations, will never stop them, but it *will* fuel them and make them worse.

The good news is, you don't have to stop them, ever. You will learn that with a non-resistant, accepting, and fearless attitude, it makes no difference whether the sensations are there or not. You will learn, if you haven't already, that the sensations of panic are the same sensations experienced when you are excited, or when you have had a cup of coffee; the difference is your interpretation, the meaning you *choose* to give them.

You will learn to let them come if or when they come, and let them go when they go, without any fuss or attachment from your conscious mind. You will learn not to fear these harmless sensations.

Non-Resistant Attitude

Do the thing you are afraid to do, and the death of the fear is certain.
(Mark Twain)

So we conquer panic attacks, along with the underlying anxiety condition by adopting an attitude of acceptance and non-resistance. This requires massive amounts of trust and courage at the start as I will be asking you to do exactly the opposite of what you are currently doing. I will be asking you to do the very thing that you are scared of. You will be calling your fear's bluff, walking right into the heart of your fear, your false alarm, your ghost, letting it touch you, letting it do its worst to you.

You will drop all your defences. You will be throwing away all your coping strategies and safety crutches. You will accept and embrace whatever happens to you. You will fear nothing, and you will resist nothing. This applies to all anxiety conditions.

Your job is not to try and stop or control the sensations, to try and turn them off; that will just cause frustration and doubt. Your only job is your attitude—to stop fearing, stop resisting, stop fighting, and begin accepting 'what is' in this very moment:

- This is the only technique that you need to conquer panic and high anxiety. This non-resistant attitude will deny panic of the very fuel that it needs to survive—fear;
- Anxiety will not cause you to lose control or panic. It's your interpretation of fear towards the sensations which causes you to panic;
- *When you do not fear the sensations, you cannot experience fear;*
- *Remember: The sensations you are currently associating with fear are the same sensations experienced when in an excited state—the difference is your interpretation.*

If you can cultivate belief and trust in not only me as your teacher and mentor, but also in yourself again, your road to recovery will be very quick and easy. This is why it is so, so important that you fully understand and accept that what I teach you in my Building Blocks™ is the answer, the only answer. This is why I repeat myself so much, to drum the truth into you so it becomes second nature.

Teachers and trainers like me, who understand exactly where you are and what you are going through, have done all the hard work for you. We teach the same healing principles, just from different approaches. All you have to do is trust in us and yourself, and do the work, and practice and persevere for as long as it takes to build your new non-anxious habitual behaviour.

- Be aware that if you *choose* to practice with a half-hearted approach, such as 'I'll see how it goes,' or 'I'll go until the sensations get too uncomfortable,' then don't expect magic to take place, don't expect too much to change in a hurry. You are still resisting, still sending a message to the subconscious that you are in fear and in need of protection;
- If you approach your work with this mindset, you will be taking two steps forward and five steps back;
- As long as you harbour doubt, your progress will always be hampered;

- For real magic to take place, it's an 'all or nothing' approach—you have to commit to healing yourself.

Throughout all your suffering, have you ever experienced a time during a panic attack when there was nothing you could do to run from the fear-provoking situation, there was nothing you could do to avoid it, and you had no choice but to stand in front of your fear?

As scared and terrified as you may have been, when you finally reached the point where you accepted that there was nothing you could do except grin and bear it, something very odd happened?

Maybe the sensations subsided or even disappeared? Or maybe they didn't disappear, but the feelings of fear disappeared? In a very short space of time, the panic or anxious sensations retreated and went away, and you were left feeling very calm and in control?

It probably didn't occur to you that you just disempowered your panic attack because you let go, stopped resisting, stood right in the heart of what you interpreted as fear and let it do its worst. Okay, you may not have had a choice at the time, but the point is, you *chose* an attitude of non-resistance towards the sensations and situation, and your fear, along with the sensations, disappeared.

You can do this. You have done this; probably many, many times.

Allow me to reiterate:

- Your job is not to try and stop the sensations, your job is to choose your attitude in the moment. That is the only thing you can do, and it's the only thing you need to control for now;
- Without fear of the fear, without the fear of the sensations, you cannot experience fear, irrespective of whether the sensations are present or not. Your interpretation, the meaning you give the sensations or the experience, *is* the experience. Remember my analogy of the two work colleagues on the Auckland Sky Tower?

The difference between fearing and not fearing, the difference between experiencing fear or excitement in any given moment is your *interpretation*, your *attitude*.

By adopting a fearless and non-resistant attitude, you no longer 'fuel the fire' with more anxiety. You effectively get out of the way and allow the subconscious to do its job of maintaining that healthy life-sustaining balance. When you are willing to stand in front of your fears, accept whatever happens, and let it touch you, you are sending a clear message to your subconscious mind that you are not in any danger, and therefore, there is no need for protection.

- Non-resistance is fearlessness; the subconscious picks this up and acts upon the situation accordingly—it doesn't know any better.

Your Best teacher - You

Your experiences will be your best teacher during this time of learning and healing. As you practice, notice what works for you and what doesn't. We are all very different, and while adopting a non-resistant attitude is the only answer to ending your suffering, there are various approaches to take, and this all depends on what works for you as an individual.

For example, while I may have responded well with more aggressive self-talk when facing up to my fears, others may not respond so well, they may benefit from a more subtle approach. As long as the approach is in line with non-resistance and acceptance, it really doesn't matter. Pay attention and notice what works for you. There will be times during your journey when you weren't so overwhelmed by your anxious sensations; these experiences will reveal invaluable insights for you.

When I looked back over my experiences during my road to recovery, I realized that certain things worked for me in the past, but at the time

I didn't realise it. For example, when I acted in complete disregard for my fear (usually because I found myself in a corner, and I had no way out) and assumed a position of indifference or not caring about whatever happens and standing right in the heart of it, the sensations immediately disappeared.

Although this made me feel great, powerful, and excited, I had no idea of what happened or why. I just concluded at the time that I had ended my phobias and panic attacks forever. But then, out of nowhere, I would get another dose of horrible sensations. This was very confusing as I thought that I had cured myself forever on the previous occasion.

After a few cycles of this, I ended up feeling even more frustrated and therefore confused. I didn't realise that I was getting the sensations because of my underlying anxious habitual behaviour. I didn't realise that my underlying high anxiety was producing adrenaline at inappropriate times, which stimulated the sympathetic nervous system into producing all the uncomfortable sensations associated with being anxious.

- Back then, I had no idea that disempowering panic attacks was one thing, but removing an underlying anxiety condition, a learnt pattern of behaviour which triggers the panic cycle, was a separate issue altogether.

Because I didn't know any of this at the time, I just felt even more fearful and out of control. So, sometimes I could stave off attacks, sometimes I couldn't. What I didn't notice, were the times when I stopped panic in its tracks, were the times when I had no choice of escape and so I just had to confront it, and because I had no choice, I just assumed a position of not caring, of non-resistance.

Interestingly, during the times (many times) when I had the option of escaping, the sensations just continued to get worse until I couldn't bear it any longer, and the urge to escape became so overwhelming, I had to act on it or face a certain catastrophe.

All this resistant behaviour just added more fuel to the fire, reinforcing the bad habit and leaving me feeling very frustrated, distressed, confused, and untrusting of my own ability to control normal behaviour.

You see, through my lack of understanding and frustration, I wasn't aware that my error was expecting *not* to have another panic attack just because I managed to disempower the last onslaught of sensations.

Turning Point

The biggest turning point for me was the realization that the sensations appeared from the subconscious because of a learnt pattern of behaviour, a bad habit that I had formed. The subconscious was just playing a record which it thought was perfectly normal and totally independent of what I consciously thought or rationally knew. The subconscious was just doing its job.

I realized that at times when I consciously *chose* to not resist, accept and embrace the sensations, they didn't get any worse; in fact, they seemed to subside instantly, or I just didn't notice them any more.

Most importantly, I realized that this did not necessarily mean that I wouldn't experience fear sensations ever again. However, it did mean that when or if they appeared again, I could choose how I wanted to react. I had the power to consciously choose how I wished to react. I had the power to choose whatever meaning I wanted to give them. That was a very powerful awakening.

The next important thing I realized was that if I had developed a bad habit of anxious behaviour, then this habit would remain until I replaced it with another habit, a more empowering non-anxious one.

I therefore knew that if I *consciously chose to focus* on developing discipline around practicing and persevering with a new attitude of non-resistance, *independent* of what might be coming up from the subconscious, fully believing and trusting in my experiences and learning, then over time the result *must* be a reprogramming of the subconscious mind with new non-anxious behaviour.

And that's exactly what happened.

The Power Of The Subconscious Mind

It is important to spend some time discussing the relationship between the conscious and subconscious mind in the context of your anxiety condition. An understanding of how these two areas of your mind work together, specifically how they work together to hold you in your anxious state will help build trust and belief in not only yourself but also my programme of healing, which in turn will give you the confidence and courage to do what you need to do to heal yourself.

> *Knowledge of the interaction of your conscious and subconscious minds will enable you to transform your whole life.*
> (Joseph Murphy)

The 'conscious' and 'subconscious' mind are the terms generally used to represent the dual role within one's mind, each possessing different distinctive characteristics or spheres of activity.

The 'conscious mind' is the rational or reasoning mind, attempting to make sense of the outside world from information received through all of your senses. It is the part of the mind which makes decisions and choices, based on a set of beliefs, convictions, and habitual or predominant thoughts. These beliefs have been learnt through observation, education, and experience over your lifetime.

The 'subconscious' mind is the seat of all emotions and the storehouse of memory, habits, and programmed (or conditioned) patterns of behaviour. Your subconscious mind cannot reason objectively like the conscious mind; it perceives only by intuition.

The subconscious mind is also referred to as the 'subjective' mind as it is subject to the commands and directions of the conscious mind, and it takes every command seriously; it cannot take a joke and doesn't argue controversially. It is incapable of making comparisons or judgments which are vital to the reasoning process.

Whatever conscious commands, suggestions, decrees, verdicts, or conclusions you give, it will be accepted by the subconscious mind as true, irrespective of whether they are right or wrong, good or bad, and will proceed to bring them into your physical world as conditions and experiences.

> *The subconscious mind reacts entirely by suggestion. In other words, it has no volition of its own. It does not make choices, indulge in arguments, postulate theories, search for answers, wonders at possibilities. It only accepts and acts. Once it is given a suggestion, it immediately sets to work to make that suggestion truth, for it accepts the suggestion completely.*
> (Uell S Anderson)

So how does the conscious mind convey its commands to the subconscious mind? Conscious commands are conveyed through what you predominantly or habitually think about, backed up by beliefs, strong convictions or trust, or whatever else you choose to claim and feel as true. It is immaterial whether the command or suggestion is good or bad, right or wrong, true or false; it will be accepted by the subconscious mind and acted upon according to the nature of the suggestion.

> *The law of your mind is this: You will get a reaction or response from your subconscious mind according to the nature of the thought or idea you hold in your conscious mind.*
> (Joseph Murphy)

Then what happens?

The subconscious mind then proceeds to manifest into your physical world those situations, events, and experiences that align to your commands or suggestions which you hold to be true.

In other words, the subconscious mind is responsible for the creation of all things in your physical world, based on your conscious commands or suggestions.

> *All things that have happened to you are based on thoughts impressed on your subconscious mind through belief.*
> (Joseph Murphy)

How does it do that?

Repeated, predominant, or habitual thinking of your conscious mind, backed by belief and conviction, creates deep impressions or neural pathways and associations in the brain cells, which results in patterns of programmed behaviour (habits). These pathways and associations include ideas, experiences, and knowledge gained over your lifetime and serve to align with and reinforce your conscious beliefs and convictions.

This results in a pattern of learnt behaviour through Operant Conditioning and is developed through repetition and practice. It is precisely how we learn any skill or discipline, from swimming, riding a bike, driving a car, playing an instrument, through to developing an anxiety condition. In the case of an anxiety sufferer, this learnt behaviour is called Fear Conditioning.

Think of your subconscious mind as a record player. Your learnt habitual (programmed) behaviour can be likened to a scratched record, and the grooves in the record are the neural pathways and associations etched into the subconscious mind. The needle of the record player (subconscious mind) runs along the grooves, playing whatever has been recorded, in this case, patterns of behaviour. And because the record is scratched, the needle keeps skipping back to the same spot over and over again, playing the same old tune.

The direction of your life, the opportunities you notice (or don't notice), the things, places, people, and jobs you choose (or don't choose) to pursue, how much money you make (or don't make), and your level of happiness and success are directly related to these habitual programmes playing deep within the recesses of your subconscious mind.

Whatever life situation you find yourself in at this present moment, expect to get more of the same later today, tomorrow, next week, next month, next decade, unless you change the scratched or broken record constantly playing in the background. I will give you the tools to do this in BB4.

> *Your subconscious mind does not engage in proving whether your thoughts are good or bad, true or false, but it responds according to the nature of your thoughts or suggestions. For example, if you consciously assume something as true, even though it may be false, your subconscious mind will accept it as true and proceed to bring about results, which must necessarily follow, because you consciously assumed it to be true.*
> (Joseph Murphy)

Example—Anxiety Conditions

Let's have a look at a typical panic attack or anxiety-related phobia like social phobia or agoraphobia.

They are all symptoms of extreme anxiety, which result in the inappropriate activation of the emergency response. They are nothing more than a bad habit, a learnt pattern of behaviour.

The subconscious mind has been programmed to activate the emergency or panic response when triggered by an event or situation that poses absolutely no danger at all, like talking to a group of people or standing in a queue. It matters not that the response is irrational and inappropriate; the subconscious mind is just doing what it has been programmed to do—remember, it can't take a joke and doesn't reason for itself, it takes its commands from the conscious mind.

This automatic response (albeit a bad habit) is out of our conscious control; it will happen whether we like it or not, as long as the scratched or broken record continues to play deep in the subconscious mind. This initial habitual response from the subconscious mind triggers a response or reaction from the conscious mind.

Your conscious reaction, your interpretation, or the meaning that you give to these initial sensations determines whether they turn into nothing more than a mild irritation that eventually fades, or escalates into a full-blown panic attack.

The intrusive thoughts or uncomfortable sensations appear out of nowhere; you consciously fear them because they make you feel out of control. The fact that you know you shouldn't fear the situation only adds to your frustration, which fuels your fear. The more you resist and try and turn the sensations off, the more anxious and scared you become. These conscious fearful thoughts create more anxiety, releasing more adrenaline—and more horrible and uncomfortable sensations:

- You have just consciously sent a message to your subconscious mind, that you are in danger and in need of protection. So it does its job perfectly and activates the 'fight or flight' response, experienced as a panic attack to protect you from . . . well, nothing;
- At the conscious 'reasoning' level, you know it is ridiculous to fear standing in a queue. However, the problem is not the queue; it is your fearful reaction to the uncomfortable and horrible sensations and the associated 'what if' thoughts of them spiraling out of control and causing you harm or some other negative consequence like being embarrassed or judged;

- The subconscious mind has no idea that there is no real fear, and it cannot draw such conclusions; it is led around by the conscious mind and its fearful commands;
- The result is the activation of the emergency flight or flight response, or panic attack in totally inappropriate situations. The fear was real for you, and it showed up in your physical world;
- *That's the power of the subconscious mind.*

So who's in charge?

The subconscious mind is completely obedient to the commands of the conscious mind, and as stated earlier, commands are the predominant or habitual thoughts or suggestions backed up by strong beliefs or convictions.

To illustrate this relationship further, I will briefly discuss two analogies which helped me to better understand the relationship, as described by Joseph Murphy:

Analogy 1

In the first analogy, the conscious mind can be likened to the captain on the bridge of a ship. The subconscious mind can be likened to the engineers down in the engine room. The captain gives commands to the engineers, who, in turn, control the boilers, instruments, and gauges.

The engineers have no idea where they are going; they just follow orders automatically, good or bad. Even if the ship was heading for rocks, the engineers would still follow the commands of the captain with whom they are completely reliant on; they have no capacity to think for themselves.

In the above example of an anxiety condition, the conscious mind reacted to the initial habitual anxious sensations by conveying commands of irrational and inappropriate fear and danger. The subconscious mind is in complete abeyance and responded with the 'fight or flight' response in an effort to protect you from danger that didn't exist. The subconscious didn't know there was no real danger, it was just following commands from the captain—the conscious mind.

The subconscious mind not only accepts suggestion as truth, but it has the capacity to make literal truth out of such suggestion.
(Uell S. Anderson)

Through your own suffering with high anxiety, panic attacks or phobias, you will have gained first-hand experience of the truth in Uell S Anderson's assertion. The fear of the situation or event that you experience is not real and, in fact, doesn't pose any danger at all, but that doesn't stop the subconscious mind from accepting your conscious commands of fear and then setting about protecting you with the 'fight or flight' response, does it?

Analogy 2

The second wonderful analogy to help you get acquainted with this dual function is to look upon your mind as that of a garden, where the subconscious is like the soil which accepts any seed, good or bad. The soil doesn't discriminate between seeds; it will accept whatever seed is planted in it. Your conscious mind is the gardener and you are planting seeds (thoughts) all day long according to your habitual or predominant thinking.

Negative, destructive thoughts continue to work negatively in your subconscious mind and, in due time, will sprout forth into your outer experience, just as weeds will grow in good soil.

The subconscious mind is creating your world according to your conscious commands or suggestions. This is just how it is and it is working whether you believe it or not, whether you are aware of it or not. It is an immutable law and is working for you, twenty-four hours a day. Whatever you think about you will bring about. You cannot escape this law, and it works irrespective of whether your conscious commands, in the form of your predominant thoughts, are good or evil, right or wrong, rational or irrational.

Where Do Thoughts Come From?

By now you should have a good understanding of the role that the subconscious mind has in creating your life situation. You also now understand that the conscious mind is the captain of the subconscious mind; the subconscious mind will accept whatever conscious commands you give it and will set about creating experiences and situations that align to those commands. Now let's take a look at thoughts themselves.

It is estimated that we have upwards of 60,000 thoughts each day. Each thought has a start and a finish, and they just keep coming, one after the other, in no apparent orderly fashion. Now, this may be hard to get your head around, but we don't actually make or think these thoughts up, they just appear into our consciousness, from where exactly we don't know, but thankfully that's not important. What's important is how we deal with this barrage of thoughts.

Now your conscious mind is the 'observer' of these thoughts.

Imagine that you are sitting in front of a large movie screen as the 60,000 thoughts are streaming across the screen. As you would watch or observe a movie, you watch or observe the thoughts as they flow across the screen.

Your conscious mind observes or notices some thoughts more than others. In fact, out of the 60,000 thoughts that stream across your movie screen, you tend to filter out most of them, and you end up observing the same bundle of thoughts, over and over again.

So what determines what thoughts you consciously observe?

Whatever you have been conditioned (or programmed) to habitually believe to be true about yourself or the physical world you live in, whatever strong convictions you hold about your world dictates what thoughts you tend to focus on and observe. Those thoughts that align to your beliefs and convictions tend to get noticed or observed more and therefore get replayed on the movie screen over and over again.

Those thoughts that don't align tend to get ignored, as if you had popped out for some popcorn and missed a part of the movie. And it is these bundles of thoughts that you consciously pay attention to which you take action on (or in the case of procrastination, no action at all) and therefore shape your physical world.

Every time you observe or notice these bundles of thoughts and then act (or react) on them, you strengthen your beliefs, habits, convictions or conditioning about how you see yourself and the world.

- Our conscious mind observes and picks up these thoughts based on our beliefs;
- Out of the infinity of possible thoughts we could observe, we filter out all those thoughts that don't comply with our beliefs. We end up spending our day, entertaining the same thoughts, day in day out, ignoring or filtering out the rest.

Cause and Effect of Thought

To wrap up our discussion on the subject of thought, it is necessary to talk about the concept of conscious choice-making and 'cause and effect'. You have no doubt heard these phrases before: 'What you sow is what you reap (or you reap what you sow),' 'what you think about you bring about.'

What this means is this:

- Thought = Cause;
- Life situation or circumstances = Effect;
- In other words, your life situation or circumstances are the result of thought.

You are where you are today because of your habitual thoughts. Whatever your life situation or circumstances are right at this moment, they are the direct result of the thoughts you had a moment ago, a day ago, a week ago, or even a month ago. It therefore must follow that your thoughts today will show up in your life situation tomorrow.

Whether you like it or not, whether you want to believe it or not, you are holding yourself in your current situation because of your current habitual thoughts.

What does this mean?

At the end of the day, you are choosing the thoughts that you are observing. Sure they are based on habitual patterns of thinking and particular belief systems, but they are still a conscious choice you are making. You are free to choose whatever thought you wish, no matter what your belief system, no matter what your current life situation or circumstances are.

You have the freedom to choose your thoughts out of the infinity of thoughts that cross your consciousness; you have the freedom to choose how you want to respond to any situation, no matter what that situation is.

Here's the real important part. Most of us choose our thoughts based on what we are observing in our life situation or circumstances. Our outer circumstances direct and dictate our thinking or our choice of thoughts and beliefs.

This is a dangerous and vicious cycle, because if thoughts are the cause, and your life situation is the effect of the thoughts, then choosing your beliefs and thoughts based on your outer world or life situation, *will* produce, you guessed it, more of the same. This is a vicious cycle that must be broken.

If, for example, your current life situation (effects) is one of bad debt and poverty (caused by earlier thoughts and beliefs), and you focus your thoughts around debt and struggle and lack of money, what do you expect the effect in your outside world will be tomorrow? More of the same.

It is so erroneous that most of us allow our thoughts to be dictated by our situation, which is nothing more than the effect of previous thoughts. What a vicious cycle!

- Thoughts *always* precede circumstances (Cause and Effect).

> *We, through intention, can change our brain.*
> (Richard J. Davidson)

Your life situation or circumstances are 'what is', and there is nothing you can do about it. You cannot stop or change a situation that has already occurred, even though you are 100 per cent responsible for it.

The power is in this very moment, the thoughts which you are willing to consciously choose out of the infinity of thoughts and possibilities, irrespective of your current situation. Your current circumstances are the effect of previous thoughts, your current circumstances have absolutely no bearing on what may happen later today, tomorrow, next week, next month, or next year.

It is your conscious choice of thoughts that you allow in this very moment that will be the cause of whatever tomorrow brings.

- An attitude of unconditional acceptance of 'what is' in this very moment is probably the most important ingredient in ending not only panic attacks and phobias (BB3) but also the underlying anxiety condition (BB4);
- Why? Your current anxious condition is 'what is', and nothing will change that. Focusing on the current situation and *choosing* worrying, fearful or resistant thoughts (anticipatory anxiety) will do nothing to change the 'now' and *must* result in more of

the same tomorrow. An attitude of unconditional acceptance of 'what is' in this moment breaks this vicious cycle, slowing down and even stopping the flow of worrying 'what if', resistant and fearful thoughts, giving your mind the opportunity to focus on more empowering and loving thoughts;
- Emotions and feelings behind unconditional acceptance have been proven to reduce anxiety and stress levels.

No matter what your current life situation is, you have the freedom in this very moment to choose your thoughts and beliefs. Whatever thoughts you choose in the present moment will affect tomorrow's circumstances.

- *Do not allow yourself to fall into the trap of basing your choice of thoughts on your current situation. Your current situation is the effect of earlier thought patterns—nothing more;*
- *Choose thoughts and beliefs in this moment, not based on your external circumstances, but on what it is that you desire;*
- *Whatever you consciously choose to think right now, backed by trust and expectancy, your subconscious mind will have no choice in accepting as true, irrespective of your external circumstances and move to bring it to pass. It has no choice in the matter.*

Case Study

As you know, nearly 15 years ago now, I was penniless, jobless, bankrupt, and if it wasn't for my best friend, I would have been homeless. My relationship with Nikki was over, and I had lost custody of my two beautiful children. To add insult to injury, I was suffering from social phobia and agoraphobia.

In a nutshell, my life situation was *crap*!

My life situation today is totally unrecognisable from how it was back then; it's hard to believe that my life was ever like that. How did I make the changes, how did I get here? It was through the very principles I am teaching you in my Building Blocks™, starting with *choosing* thoughts, not based on my current situation but based on what I wanted.

I forced myself to love and accept my life 'as is', I forced myself to be grateful, and I forced myself to focus on my meaningful vision of the future. I took positive action each and every day. I refused to let my life situation determine my thoughts.

You change tomorrow by consciously choosing your thoughts in this present moment.

- *Thoughts are cause; your circumstances are effects;*
- *Change your thoughts; change your life.*

Conscious Choice Maker

Whether we like it or not, everything that is happening in our lives is as a result of the choices that we have made in the past. Unfortunately, most of us make choices unconsciously and therefore do not think that they are choices, but they are.

Even though we are infinite choice makers, we have become bundles of conditioned reflexes, which are being constantly triggered by people and circumstances into predictable outcomes of behaviour.

Whether I insulted you or praised you, you would probably make the unconscious choice to be offended and flattered respectively, *but it's still a choice that you are making.*

Most of us, through conditioning, have repetitious and predictable responses to the stimuli in our environment; our reactions seem to be automatically triggered.

But if you step back for a moment and observe the choices you are making as you make those choices, in just this act of witnessing, you take the whole process from the subconscious realm into the conscious realm, and you will immediately find this to be very empowering.

When you do this, you have access to an infinity of choices.

- No matter what habitual thoughts or emotions arise up from the subconscious, no matter what anyone says or does to you in your external world, you *always* have the *power* to *choose* your response;
- You can't always control what pops up from the subconscious through your current conditioned behaviour, but you can *always* control your conscious *choice* of how you *react*.

You have the power to choose your thoughts in any given moment. You have the power to break away from a subconscious, conditioned response (habitual) to any given situation or any other stimuli by observing the choices you are making, thereby bringing this process up into the conscious level, and therefore giving you the power to *choose* the response which will bring happiness to you and those around you.

You can feel happy and grateful right now. It's your choice. No matter what your life challenges are in this present moment—whether they are of a financial, relationship, or health related nature—no matter how bad you think your situation is, you are not alone!

Everyone, I mean, everyone is dealing with challenges and setbacks of some description. Those that overcome their challenges *choose* to focus their attention on positive action towards what they can control and accept that which is out of their control.

They *choose* to focus on the good in their lives as opposed to the bad.

- Where there is good, there will always be bad if you look hard enough for it. This is the co-existence of opposites that supports life;
- You are making a conscious choice as to where you focus your attention;

- You are making a conscious choice as to how you react to any given situation;
- *You are currently consciously reacting to anxious sensations with resistance, with fear;*
- *You have the power to consciously choose to react to the same sensations with fearlessness, with non-resistance;*
- You can do this right now, in this very moment. You don't need education, training, you don't have to wait for the right time, you have nothing else to learn. You just need the opportunity (and you will get that thanks to your anxious behaviour) to practice, and the trust and courage to *just do it, now*.

Choose to focus on reasons to feel love, acceptance, and gratitude during the day. Anyone, I mean, anyone, no matter what their situation, can find reasons to love.

Bankruptcy is an extremely distressing and destructive experience to go through at the best of times; it's enough to develop an anxiety condition by itself—imagine, if you can, what it must have been like for me who already suffered from panic attacks and social phobia, only to have bankruptcy added to the mix.

Now, given my situation, I could have easily fallen into a deep hole of self-pity, negativity, and depression. However, things were so bad I really had no other option but to change.

I knew, through my studies and research, what others were doing to heal themselves of anxiety conditions, and I had previously experienced success at disempowering panic attacks. But there was always something missing, there was always an ingredient missing from the recipe.

One of those vital ingredients was the realisation that I had the *power* to *choose what I focused* on and *how I reacted* to my life situation and my underlying anxiety condition.

Irrespective of my life situation, I *chose* to focus on unconditional acceptance and gratitude for my life *exactly* 'as it is', and I also *chose* to adopt a non-resistant attitude towards my anxiety and panic: to do exactly the opposite of what I was consciously doing, which was just feeding my condition.

Not only was this attitude the start of the end for my anxiety condition, but it also started a quantum shift in my life situation.

Is there a point to this? Yes, and it's pretty simple: if I can do it, so can you.

Again, no matter what is happening in your life, you have the power to choose where you focus your attention and how you choose to react to your anxiety condition and your life situation.

- *You must muster the courage to rise above your circumstances.*

Whether you have lost your relationship, lost everything you own, you are physically ill, diseased, homeless, or you suffer from anxiety, phobias and panic attacks, you *must* turn away from negativity; don't try to control or fight it, simply *choose* to accept 'what is', focus your attention on gratitude and love (the opposite of fear), and take positive action.

- Don't look too far ahead; take it one step at a time, day by day;
- Accept 'what is', search for reasons to be grateful for your life 'now'. If you turn your attention towards gratitude, you will find things to be grateful for, no matter what your situation;
- Cultivate a meaningful vision of the future.
- Turn your attention away from negativity and your present circumstances and focus on acceptance, gratitude, and your vision;
- Stay in the moment and take action today. Get moving and head towards that which you fear; *choose* to let it touch you and *choose* to accept whatever happens.

Think about this for a while: in any given moment, you are experiencing thoughts and feelings of either love or fear. These two emotions are poles apart, and all the various emotions that we experience are really just varying degrees between these two opposing poles. That's it. Your attention is either on love or fear. Whatever emotion you are focusing on, it is still your *choice*, your conscious *choice*.

Imagination

> *Know this: Whatever you imagine and feel as true, will and must come to pass. Imagination is the most powerful faculty, you are whatever you imagine yourself to be. Imagine the fulfillment of your desire over and over again prior to sleep.*
> (Joseph Murphy)

All conscious thoughts are transformed into pictures by our imagination, whether the thought is right or wrong, true or false. We think in pictures or images. When I say 'elephant', you are creating a picture in your mind of an elephant, based on memory, experience, and beliefs.

- Imagination is your very own superpower, and you *must* learn how to use it for good, not evil.

> *What you form in your imagination is as real as any part of your body. The idea and thought are real and will one day appear in your objective world if you are faithful to your mental image.*
> (Joseph Murphy)

This is happening for you, to you, right now. The problem is that because of your anxious habitual behaviour, you are imagining negative thoughts and fears. *You have the power through conscious choice to stop this right now.*

> *Imagination is more important than knowledge.*
> *Knowledge is limited, imagination encircles the world.*
> (Albert Einstein)

Choose to imagine what you want, as opposed to what you don't want. Know that whatever you predominantly think (imagine) will materialize in your external world. Instead of constantly feeding your imagination with 'what if' scenarios and worrying thought of what you don't want, choose to feed your imagination with thoughts of what you do want.

You can't wait to miraculously get better to feel better. *You must choose to use the power of your imagination to 'feel' better in the now before you can begin to get better.* There is no other way; nothing exists without you first imagining it—*nothing*.

You are currently using your imagination to keep you locked in an anxious state by constantly worrying about the next attack, monitoring your levels of comfort and monitoring your surroundings.

These thoughts carry a huge negative emotional charge and powerful feelings of fear. And these feelings are picked up by the subconscious as truths and as instructions to keep protecting you by keeping you on high alert.

What if, during this programme of healing, you used your powerful imagination to begin imagining the results you wanted? What if you used your imagination and visualisation to experience what it would feel like to be non-anxious as if you were right now? What if you *chose* to consciously focus your attention on what you wanted, as opposed to what you don't want? What if, through practice and perseverance you were able to do that?

You can do that, and you will do that if you are prepared to do whatever it takes and commit to my Building Blocks™. Remember, you are already using your imagination, but for things you don't want. It is only *after* you imagined an anxious or panic-provoking situation that the very anxiety-provoking situation *became your experience.*

We are incredible human beings, capable of manifesting anything in our external world from within ourselves. As someone suffering from an anxiety condition, which may also include panic attacks and phobias, you know this to be true better than anyone else. You have real first-hand knowledge and experience in this truth. Your brilliant mind or imagination is so powerful and creative that you have imagined or conjured up a real fear of that which doesn't even exist.

Visualisation

Visualisation is a product of the imagination. Imagination is a product of the subconscious mind. Visualisation is your ability to build a picture in your mind. Use your superpower (imagination) to visualise a picture of what you desire so vividly that you can feel the joy of receiving that picture. You can smell it, hear it, touch it, taste it, as if you have it right now; it feels real to you now.

Whether you are aware of it or not, you are already visualizing every second of the day through your imagination. As I pointed out earlier, the mind thinks in pictures through your imagination. Therefore, all thoughts are pictures. The problem is that most of these thoughts are about the same thing. And in your case, as an anxiety sufferer, your thoughts will be predominantly anxiety based.

As an anxiety sufferer, you are most likely constantly worrying about the next time you panic, stuck in 'what if' scenarios, staying alert and on guard—this is visualisation. You are picturing all the things you don't want with strong emotions and feelings. You are visualizing fear that doesn't even exist. The *effect* of this visualisation is the experience of real fear in your physical world.

You become what you predominantly think about. *Stop predominantly thinking about negativity and fear.*

This is a choice that you can and must make. GAD causes the sufferer to constantly think negative thoughts and create destructive compulsive rituals. Another by-product of GAD is that you tend to overanalyze everything. This is totally destructive, not only for intimate relationships (trust me, I know this first-hand) but also for all other opportunities that present themselves to you.

Choose your 60,000 thoughts wisely. Use your superpower for good, not evil. Consciously choose to imagine, visualize what you want, not what you don't want. Remember: Whatever you predominantly think about, backed by belief, you bring about.

Through your imagination, visualize the life you want and hold that image (imagine) in your mind, no matter what.

> *When you have fully decided what thing you want to be, form the highest conception of that thing that you are capable of imagining, and make that conception a thought-form. Hold that thought-form as a fact, as the real truth about yourself, and believe it.*
> (Wallace Wattles)

What Does All This Have To Do With My Anxiety Condition?

No matter what your life situation is, no matter how severe your anxious condition is right this very moment, the answer to ending your suffering is your conscious attitude: making a commitment to choose your thoughts, not based on your situation in this moment but based on what you desire.

You cannot afford to fall into the trap of allowing your thoughts to be based around what you are experiencing in this moment, for you will surely secure the same result tomorrow. You *must* rise above your current situation.

As Charles Linden puts it, *'You must transcend your fears.'*

You have the power to choose your conscious thoughts; you have the power to change your beliefs. Your subconscious mind will trustfully obey your conscious commands and bring about new situations and habits.

Even though an anxiety condition is a learnt behaviour, a bad habit, stored deep in the subconscious mind, the answer to ending your suffering sits at the conscious level, your conscious choice of how you react, your attitude towards your situation, and the beliefs that you choose to adopt from this moment on.

This will take a lot of work, and it may or may not be easy, but if you are willing to do whatever it takes and practice and persevere with everything outlined in BB3 and BB4, you will override the panic response, and you will build new non-anxious habitual behaviour.

Meaning/Interpretation

I have mentioned earlier that the sensations that you experience, that you associate with fear, are the same sensations that you experience when you are excited, exhilarated, or engaged in any activity that stimulates you.

What makes the sensations good or bad is your conscious choice of how you interpret them or the meaning that you give to them. A queue is just a queue, a car is just a car, and a crowd of people is just a crowd of people. A loud noise is just a loud noise, it doesn't mean that there is a threat on the other side – and you don't have to jump into action.

It is your interpretation or meaning that you give to them that determines whether the initial sensations escalate into a panic attack.

Remember that you do not even fear the situation or event, you fear the horrible sensations, which are harmless and have never and will never harm you. When you understand and accept that, it will be easy for you to choose a new meaning or interpretation.

Go back and review my Sky Tower analogy. The difference between a wonderful experience and one of sheer terror is a matter of meaning or interpretation of the sensations. You have the same conscious power as me and all the other ex-sufferers who have healed themselves to change the way you react to the initial anxious sensations (which is nothing more than a false alarm), to change the meaning that you give them.

Analogy - Threatening Dog

A dog appears out from a driveway, barking aggressively and launches itself at you. Within a fraction of a second, your body receives this information and interprets the stimuli as danger and activates the emergency response, preparing you to protect yourself by running or fighting.

You react with fear and rightly so, it's a pretty big dog! You then discover that the dog is tied to a chain and is unable to reach you. As soon as you are aware of this, you logically make the conscious choice to no longer fear the situation.

The nervous system takes a wee while to turn off the panic button and turn on the relax button, so the sensations, the heightened sense of awareness are still present for a short while after the event. But that doesn't mean that you continue to interpret the situation as danger and therefore react to the sensations with fear.

You have made a conscious choice that there is no real danger, and so you choose to no longer fear, even when the anxious sensations, the heightened awareness, the 'fight or flight' response is still present in the body moments after the event.

- *You have weighed up the situation, determined that there is no threat, no danger, and have chosen to ignore the sensations, chosen to no longer fear.*

You don't sit there monitoring the fact that the sensations are still there, you don't try to stop or repress the sensations, hope that they will go away. You are indifferent to them, and you ignore them and move on, turning your attention to whatever task you were doing.

Sure enough, after a short while, the adrenaline running through your body disappears, your senses have settled down, and the anxiety levels drop down to 'normal', say 3 to 4, on the anxiety scale. You weren't fixated on your sensations; you didn't try to suppress them, run from them.

You accepted them, let them do their thing and got on with your task at hand, choosing to ignore them and not to fear them even though the sensations were still present long after the threatening or dangerous situation has passed.

And so it is with your initial anxious sensations that at the moment will be popping up automatically due to your anxiety condition. With complete belief and trust in what I am teaching you, you will stand up to your fear, you will make a conscious choice, based on your new level of understanding, to no longer resist or run from or fear these harmless sensations.

You will change your meaning, interpretation from one of fear to one of fearlessness. Without you interpreting the initial anxious sensations as fear, they cannot escalate into panic attacks. The subconscious mind picks up your conscious command of 'no fear' and responds accordingly.

Acceptance

Unconditional acceptance is probably the most important ingredient in your attitude towards your anxious sensations. The more you can accept not only your sensations 100 per cent, but also your whole life, 'as is, where is' 100 per cent, the quicker you will end your suffering.

When you begin to practice this attitude, it may feel very scary and clumsy. This is because this attitude is counter-intuitive to what you think you should be doing to protect yourself. But it is this very attitude which will help you transcend your fear towards the sensations.

Unconditional acceptance of your anxious sensations and associated feelings is an attitude of non-resistance. When you sit back and accept 'what is' 100 per cent, your fear fades away, and you starve anxiety of its vital fuel that it needs to survive. This attitude sends a command to the subconscious mind that there is no danger and that it can stand down.

This makes perfect sense doesn't it? You are currently fighting, running, and resisting the anxious sensations. The answer must be to adopt a completely opposite attitude.

Don't forget that you are practicing a new skill, a new attitude. So don't be surprised if you have setbacks, doubts, uncertainty. That's perfectly normal when you are embarking on learning any new habit. Just keep practicing. BB4 will guide you through implementing acceptance into your life.

An attitude of acceptance is the cornerstone to the attackpanic programme in both disempowering the panic cycle, which you will learn to do in BB3, and removing an underlying anxiety condition, which you will learn to do in BB4.

I will provide a more in depth lesson on acceptance later on in BB4.

Habituation

You must understand that an anxiety condition is nothing more than a bad habit, a learnt pattern of behaviour through Operant Conditioning. It developed just like any other habit, and you can remove it just like any other habit. Understanding the principles around habituation will help you to put things into perspective when things don't seem to be going your way, and give you the trust and courage to keep going if, or when, the going gets tough.

When you embark on a new programme of learning a new skill, discipline, or habit, like starting a new diet, learning to play a musical instrument or riding a bike:

- Do you expect immediate results?
- Do you expect to master the skill or discipline in an instant?

Of course not! Learning something new will take time. Then why do we expect immediate results when it comes to overcoming our anxious condition? It is because of our fear of the intrusive and uncomfortable sensations. We want them gone now, and we don't want to face and push through the fear.

When learning the new habit, our old habits or programming will be fighting for our attention, trying to stay alive. This is because we are creatures of habit, and it is very easy to fall back into the old 'grooves' of the mind.

Most of us are also resistant to change. So we have to push through the initial stages of resistance and practice and persevere with our new skill, ignoring all the initial urges and temptations to fall back to our old habits. Sooner or later, through persistence and perseverance, the new skill or habit will be formed, replacing the old one.

Now, this is hard enough with learning any normal habit, but when it comes to building a new habit based around facing your fear, it can be even harder to push through. You will find yourself at the start resisting change, and you will find it very difficult and scary doing what you have to do to build the desired habit. At the start, your old habit will be fighting very hard for your attention. And because we are dealing with fear, we can be reluctant to do the work required, and we want results *now*.

When learning a new habit, there will invariably be setbacks; you may even go backwards. There may be injuries, moments of doubt, loss of motivation, belief, and confidence, stagnation, challenges, successes, and failures:

- You *accept* and expect your old habits to fight for attention;
- You *accept* that you need to practice, and persevere;
- You *accept* that to maintain your skill level, you have to constantly practice and persevere and that if you don't, you will slip backwards;
- You *accept* that you need constant *exposure* to the skill or discipline that you are trying to learn or master.

This awareness gives you perspective and helps you to maintain your persistence and dedication to practice. Sure you get frustrated and disillusioned from time to time, but you persevere, you practice, and you stick with the programme and eventually, it gets easier and easier. Through Operant Conditioning, you have built new neural pathways and associations in the brain and a new habit is formed.

Here are what I consider to be the most important foundations to building a habit or learning a new skill:

Your Why

I have discussed 'Your Why' previously (The Right Mindset); however, this matter is of such importance that it deserves further discussion. Your success in learning your new habit lies in the 'why' or the reason you are putting yourself through the pain or struggle.

If you have had a near-death experience or suffered a massive stroke or heart attack for example, you realize just how lucky you are to be alive. If your heart attack is due to your lifestyle choices (such as being overweight, smoking, or stressful working conditions), then you will have to make some habitual changes if you want to avoid a premature death.

In light of this 'wake up' call, it is pretty easy to develop a pretty compelling 'why' you should change your lifestyle, and 'why' you are willing to do what you have to do to stay alive.

If you are an anxiety sufferer, you must develop a strong 'why' you are willing to do whatever it is that you need to do to heal yourself. Without it, you will lose motivation as the old anxious behaviour constantly beats at your door. Cultivate a strong 'why' and do not open the door.

At the height of my suffering, I was housebound and jobless, and I had two wonderful children to feed. Because my situation was so bad, it wasn't that hard to develop a compelling 'why' I *had* to do something, and 'why' I was willing to do whatever it took to heal myself.

Maybe you are suffering as bad as I did. If so, embrace the situation, accept it, and use it to fuel your 'why' you are willing to change. Be grateful for this opportunity to heal yourself and get your life back.

Maybe your situation isn't as bad, and maybe your suffering isn't restricting your life to the same degree, but bad enough for you to read my book. If that is the case, use my experiences as a compelling 'why' you are willing to break your anxious habitual cycle *now*, before things get too bad.

Meaningful Vision of the Future

A meaningful vision of the future is one of my Golden Rules for removing underlying high anxiety from your life and is covered in BB4. For the purposes of our discussion on habituation, you must have a clear vision of what you will achieve through learning the new skill or habit. Whether you are learning to drive, ride a bike, or play the guitar, you *must* have a clear vision of what you want to achieve.

Cultivate your vision of an anxiety-free, panic-free future and don't ever let it go.

Belief

This is pretty self-explanatory, but you need to have belief, first in yourself, that you *can* do this, you can break your old anxious habit, and second, you *must* have belief in the programme or system that you are implementing to bring about change. Without belief in yourself or the programme, you will quickly run out of puff and give up at the first sign of struggle or setback.

The purpose of BB1 and BB2 is to build up your understanding and belief in the truth behind anxiety conditions, belief in yourself, and belief in me as your teacher.

Trust

Trust, whether it be in yourself, someone else or something, that if you do this, you will get this result, without question or doubt whatsoever.

The two other elements that make trust so powerful are belief (see above) in yourself and, in this case, my Building Blocks™, and also perseverance (see below).

Trust is the backbone of courage and confidence. If you can cultivate trust in yourself and in my programme, you will easily face your fears and do whatever it takes to build new non-anxious habitual behaviour.

Exposure

Can you learn to ride a bike without actually giving it a go? If you are overweight and want to lose some unwanted pounds, can you achieve it by NOT eating a healthy diet or NOT doing more exercise?

If you want to learn how to play the guitar, can you do it by playing Guitar Hero on any of your devices? Can you learn any skill or habit for that matter, without actually practicing the very skill or habit for which you are trying to learn? Enough said.

There is no way around it; you need to expose yourself to the skill you are trying to learn. Not only that, but the more you expose yourself, the longer you expose yourself, and the more intense your exposure is, the sooner you master the skill or habit.

To overcome panic attacks and phobias, you have no choice other than to expose yourself to that which you 'perceive' as fear; there is no way around it.

You *must* expose yourself to your fears for long enough and frequently enough (using the right tools and attitude of course) to allow your mind and body to work out that there is no danger and that the emergency response can stand down.

Commitment

You must commit 100 per cent to doing the work required of you in BB3 and BB4. A half-hearted attempt or attitude will create frustration and doubt, which will result in more anxiety and more fear, yielding the opposite to what you want to achieve. It's all or nothing; do this or don't. There is no in-between.

You will most probably be uncertain, doubtful, afraid, and not really sure how you will react and handle this work at the start; that's fine, I had the same feelings too. I was scared, but I did it anyway. That's trust, that's courage, and that's 100 per cent commitment. If I can do it, so can you. You have no choice if you want to heal yourself. You simply cannot learn anything new without *exposure* to it.

Everything has already been worked out for you; all you have to do is follow the instructions outlined in BB3 and BB4.

Practice and Perseverance

To become proficient at any skill or habit, you will have to work through all the hard times and setbacks that will inevitably come along, battle with injuries, fatigue, boredom, motivation, and self-doubt. But to be any good, to reach your goal, you must be 100 per cent committed.

Your success will be in direct proportion to your commitment to practice, and also your perseverance.

Repetition is the mother of all skills. The more you practice, the easier the habit becomes.

Persevere with your practice, maintain your vision, belief, and trust in yourself and my Building Blocks™, be 100 per cent committed, and be willing to do whatever is asked of you and whatever it takes. And finally, be scared, but do it anyway—that's courage.

Like I said earlier, make a conscious decision to do this or not to do this. If you decide to do this, then no matter what happens, just do what is outlined in BB3 and/or BB4 (whichever is applicable to you); take one step at a time and don't look back, burn all bridges behind you. Practice and persevere.

Remember—Don't 'try' to do this. 'Trying' is a noisy way of saying no. Any half-hearted attempts to form a new habit will be quickly swallowed up by your old habits. Don't 'give it a go' and see what happens, hoping to get immediate results and then when you don't, you say 'this doesn't work' and give up to your old habits. You may get immediate results, or you may not. That's not important; the important thing is that you stick to the work you have to do.

Setbacks and challenges when forming any skill or habit are guaranteed. You now understand this. So don't be surprised if or when they turn up on your doorstep; embrace them, accept them, and then let them go, and get on with your work.

> *If you start something, see it through, even if the heavens fall;*
> *If you make up your mind to do something, do it. Let nothing,*
> *no one interfere. The I in you has determined, the thing is*
> *settled, the Die is cast, there is no longer any argument.*
> (Charles Haanel (circa 1903))

Deep Breathing

It is very important to understand how breathing works to reduce anxiety and why it won't stop a panic attack. If there is a magic pill for reducing anxiety levels, it would be deep breathing. However, in hot moments, do not expect breathing to stop a panic attack in an instant. There are two reasons for this:

- *A conscious resistant attitude which fuels the panic cycle.* No matter how much deep breathing you do to reduce anxiety levels, if you are reacting to your anxious sensations with fear, you are just stoking the fire of panic and nullifying any positive results that deep breathing may have achieved.
- *The sympathetic nervous system, or panic button if you like, can turn on in an instant.* This is by design: if a car comes screaming around the corner as I am crossing the road, I need the emergency response to kick in immediately so that I can respond to the threat.
- The parasympathetic nervous system, or relax button if you like, takes a wee while to turn on, and this too is by design. It takes a while for your body to go from the emergency 'fight or flight' response back down to normal anxiety levels.
- It takes a while for the adrenaline in the body to get used up and for the associated heightened senses of awareness to drop back down.

So, while deep breathing is very successful at reducing anxiety levels, it won't stop a panic attack immediately; only your conscious non-resistant, fearless attitude will interrupt the anxious or panic cycle and achieve this.

Deep breathing activates the vagus nerve, which is the main route of the parasympathetic nervous system. Activating the vagus nerve through deep breathing turns on the parasympathetic nervous system, bringing the body back down to a relaxed state, slowing the heart rate, lowering blood pressure, relaxing the gut, and bringing the body and mind back down to a state of calm.

The vagus also releases a neural transmitter called acetylcholine, which instructs the body to relax and also reduces inflammation.

Deep breathing can be used during panic for the benefits of what it does (as outlined above), but not with the expectation that it will stop the fear response immediately. If practiced with the right attitude, deep breathing will bring the body back down to a calm state very rapidly.

But don't use it thinking/expecting it to stop a panic attack.

This attitude will only cause frustration and doubt. Use deep breathing, knowing that it *is* working, and it *will* bring the body back down to a calm state very quickly *when* used with the right conscious attitude.

- Only your conscious attitude will interrupt the panic cycle and stop a panic attack;
- Then and only then will deep breathing bring you back down to a calm state very quickly.

Deep Breathing Exercise

Standing or sitting comfortably in a straight and upright posture with your shoulders back, inhale deeply and slowly through your nose, completely filling your lungs.

At the top of your breath, hold for one second. Then exhale slowly out through your mouth for twice as long as it took for you to inhale.

As you exhale, say out loud or in your mind 'relaxing now . . .'; feel the experience of your whole body going into a deep state of relaxation and calm as you say this mantra.

Do at least 3 to 5 reps per session, as many times a day as you wish. You should look to inhale for about 3-5 seconds (exhaling for 5-10 seconds).

I typically use this deep breathing method whenever I think about it, which is lots. I only do about 5 reps, and I can't get enough of it. This simple exercise has a wonderful effect on me throughout my day.

Summary of Building Blocks™ 2

- Everything you are currently doing to protect yourself from anxious sensations and panic—avoiding, running away, staying on guard, constantly monitoring your thoughts, coping strategies and techniques, safety crutches and medication (the list could go on and on)—is not working and is giving you more of what you don't want;
- This attitude is based around fear, based around resistance, and based on focusing on what you don't want. Resistance and fear is the very fuel that anxiety needs to not only survive but thrive;
- To get the opposite result of what you are currently getting, in other words, to finally get what you want, you need to do exactly the opposite of what you are currently doing;
- A non-resistant attitude involves completely giving into your fears, embracing and accepting them, walking straight into them, letting go of having to monitor your thoughts and sensations, discarding coping strategies, techniques, and safety crutches;
- This attitude is based on fearlessness. It is paradoxical in that it is completely the opposite of what you think you should do to protect yourself. It is counter-intuitive to what you think you should do in a 'hot' moment;
- *Without fear of the sensations, you cannot experience fear.* The sensations are just sensations, nothing more;

- *'When you stop running from fear, fear stops running you';*
- A non-resistant attitude deprives, starves anxiety and panic of its vital life-sustaining fuel; *fear*, breaking the vicious cycle that anxiety sufferers find themselves locked into;
- You have the power to consciously choose your thoughts in any given moment, and you have the power to override your predominant habitual thoughts, beliefs, and convictions housed deep in the subconscious mind. You have the power to consciously choose your attitude towards your sensations. You have the power to choose your interpretation or meaning towards your sensations;
- You can do this because the conscious mind is the captain of the subconscious mind, which trust fully acts on the commands of the conscious mind;
- Conscious commands are predominant thoughts, backed up by strong beliefs or convictions;
- An anxiety condition is a bad habit, a learnt behaviour, stored in the subconscious mind. Your conscious fearful and resistant reaction to the initial habitual anxious sensations signals to the subconscious mind that you are in danger and therefore activates the emergency response to protect you;
- A non-resistant attitude sends the message to the subconscious mind to turn off the emergency response;
- We are creatures of habit, and as you embark on learning a new skill or habit, the old habits will be fighting for your attention. There will always be setbacks and challenges along the way. You expect this and push through and persevere with your practice anyway. You can do this based on your belief and trust in yourself and the programme with which you are implementing;
- You need enough exposure to the skill with which you want to learn or master, which will allow you to build new neural pathways and associations in order to form the new habit deep in the subconscious mind;
- Whatever you think about, you bring about. You are a conscious choice maker;

- No matter what is happening in your life, you have the power to *choose* where to focus your attention and how you *choose* to react to your anxiety condition and your life situation.
- *You must muster up the courage to rise above your circumstances*;
- You can't always control what pops up from the subconscious through your current conditioned behaviour, but you can *always* control your conscious *choice* of how you *react*.

CHAPTER 7

BUILDING BLOCKS™ 3 (BB3) DESTROY PANIC ATTACKS AND PHOBIAS

Objective of BB3
- To disempower and eliminate your panic attacks and phobias.

Before we go any further, let's spend the next few minutes reviewing what you have learnt from the previous two Building Blocks™.

You now know *the truth*.

- You are not ill;
- You have a bad habit: you have learnt and conditioned yourself to panic in situations that do not warrant the emergency or 'fight or flight' response;
- Your panic response is a false alarm, a ghost, nothing more. Running from or avoiding your ghost makes things worse;
- You created this condition; you are 100 per cent responsible for your situation;
- You are not in danger of coming to any harm;
- You do not fear the situation or event;
- You fear the uncomfortable and harmless sensations that *you have created* with your amazing imagination;
- Panic attacks are a fear of fear (that doesn't exist);

- No situation, place, or person can cause panic, *only* you. You control panic;
- *You* are fuelling this vicious, anxious cycle with your resistant attitude. You empower panic; you give panic its energy;
- The sensations that you associate with fear are the same sensations that you experience when in a state of excitement, when laughing heavily, or when competing in an event;
- You now know *the answer*;
- Stop running, stop fighting, stop avoiding, stop monitoring your sensations, and stop restricting your life;
- Throw away all coping strategies and techniques, lay *all* safety crutches to rest, and stop feeding and accommodating fear;
- Walk straight into whatever it is that you *think* you fear. Let it touch, and let it do its worst;
- Demand panic to do its worst;
- Look for more opportunities to confront your fears, hunt them down, and call their bluff;
- Accept and be willing to experience whatever happens;
- In other words, stop resisting;
- This non-resistant attitude is paradoxical in that it seems so counter-intuitive to what you should do to protect yourself. Non-resistance is based around acceptance and fearlessness;
- When you no longer fear, you *cannot* experience fear, irrespective of whether or not the sensations are present;
- Trust and courage is all you need to eliminate panic;
- The problem is not the situation that triggers your anxious or panic response, it's not even the uncomfortable sensations, the problem is how you respond in the moment.

Now let's get to work!

The Panic Attack Eliminator

The Panic Attack Eliminator is designed to interrupt and break the panic cycle, wherever you are along this cycle, disempowering and eliminating panic attacks.

You will remember that panic attacks start with an initial uncomfortable sensation or intrusive thought, whether triggered by a situation or just appearing randomly.

You react with fear and resistance, which causes more anxiety, releasing more adrenaline, which means more anxiety, more fear, more resistance, and so on until the cycle culminates in the panic or 'fight or flight' response.

The problem is not the initial sensations that pop up as a result of your underlying habitual anxious behaviour. It is your conscious attitude, your response to the initial sensations, the interpretation, or the meaning that you give to them that determines whether the sensations escalate into the panic or 'fight or flight' response.

Prepare Yourself For Success

Before you give the Panic Attack Eliminator a go, it's so important that you spend some time working through the following questions to prepare yourself, giving you the best opportunity for success.

You must become consciously aware of what you think, what you believe and how you behave during your hot moment. If you can find the courage to let it all hang out, to lean into your false alarm and do the ***opposite*** of how you would normally react, think and behave, you WILL disempower your panic!

So carefully consider and answer the questions below. Write the answers down in your journal. Know this stuff intimately, this is where you need to dig, this is what you will focus on with the Panic Attack Eliminator:

1. Where do your sensations present themselves in your body? You'll know exactly where they are:
   - Are they in your gut?
   - Around your chest?
   - Throat?
   - Heart?
2. Describe your sensations:
   - Tightening of the chest?
   - Flushed face?
   - Dry throat?
   - Difficulty breathing?
   - Racing heart?
   - Disorientation?
3. Your sensations are a false alarm, protecting you against...... well, nothing. What are your sensations telling you to do? What do you feel compelled to do?
   - 'get out of here now?'
   - 'get off the motorway or there will be trouble?'
   - 'clean your hands, again?'
   - 'you must sit here where you can see the exit?'
   - 'this time something really bad is going to happen?'
   - 'today is the day that you are actually going to die?'
   - 'find a way of getting out now before people see you struggling?'
4. What physical or mental rituals do you carryout during your hot moment to try and protect yourself?
   - Scanning the room for the exit points?
   - Taking a bottle of medication with you 'just in case'?
   - Trying to shrink down in your seat to avoid eye contact or draw attention to yourself?
   - Crossing your arms?
   - Pacing up and down?
   - Twitching, scratching?
   - Incessantly cleaning, organising, arranging?

- Altering your body language in an attempt to stop your sensations?
- Choosing to sit in a busy cafe with your back against the wall, choosing to sit in a particular spot for a quick exit?

5. What do you believe will happen if you don't do what your false alarm is urging you to do (question 3)?
   - 'I'm going to catch germs and die?'
   - 'I'm going to die of a heart attack?'
   - 'I'm going to lose control or lose my mind?'
   - 'People are going to see me in trouble and I will be embarrassed?'
   - 'People will judge me and I will have to accept their judgement?'

Now that you have brought your beliefs and behaviour to your conscious awareness, you are ready to jump into the Panic Attack Eliminator.

The Panic Attack Eliminator explained

When the initial sensations or intrusive thoughts that you associate with panic start growing inside of you, follow the protocol below:

1. *Observe*
   - Now, this is all going to sound counter-intuitive, but this is so important that you do exactly as I say, and you can do this with the correct attitude;
   - As best you can, sit there and observe these sensations and thoughts running through your body;
   - If you have answered questions 1 to 4 above, you will be well aware of the initial thoughts and also exactly where your uncomfortable sensations are centred in your body. Go right there now with all your attention and focus;
   - Focusing on your sensations is so important. I want you to STOP focusing on trying to control the situation and pour your

attention onto your sensations. The situation is not the problem, it's not what you fear and it's not where you need to be digging;
- 'Have you lost your fucken mind?' I hear you say. 'I'm shitting myself and you want me to focus on the horrible sensations?';
- Yes I do – I don't want you to try and stop or run from them like you would normally do, I just want you to be consciously aware of them. As best you can, observe the sensations, as opposed to trying to control or remove yourself from the situation;
- You must be willing to allow your sensations to engulf you, to do their worst - to be ok with not being ok. Again, this is completely the opposite to what you have been doing right? This attitude or approach is based on fearlessness, non-resistance!;
- *Your normal way of responding would be to react with fear, with 'what if', 'oh no' thoughts which causes more anxiety and associated horrible sensations. You may even start to feel yourself spiraling out of control, feeding this vicious feedback loop;*
- *It's so important at this point that you interrupt this cycle to give you an opportunity to choose how you want to respond before you get hijacked by your habitual anxious pattern of behaviour;*
- *So in addition to noticing, observing, focusing on the sensations, I want you to say to yourself 'So fucken what!' Use your physiology in a positive, powerful manner. For example, if you are in a social gathering, think to yourself 'So fucken what!' and CHOOSE to standup straight, pull your shoulders back and smile with confidence.*
- Replacing your 'oh no', 'what if' initial thoughts with 'so what' thoughts will help you to interrupt the panic cycle, giving you the opportunity to consciously take back control.

Just do it, no matter what you are feeling! Don't expect anything to change or to feel better (you probably won't at the start!), just do as I say. Your only job is to practice!

- 'Yes but this is really hard Shaun, I'm so scared!' I understand, I've been there done that! But if you want to heal yourself, you

MUST do this. Making yourself **feel** better by employing all your safety crutches like you always have will not **make** you better! At some point you will have to decide once and for all that enough is enough!

2. *Demand more and move towards your fear*
   - Now that you have temporarily broken the cycle and given yourself a wee window of opportunity by observing your sensations and saying 'so fucken what', it's now time to move towards your fear and demand even more of your uncomfortable sensations!;
   - 'What, are you nuts!?' I hear you say. No I'm not nuts, I'm healed, and so will you be if you do exactly as I say!;
   - Remember these sensations are a false alarm, and they are only trying to help, only trying to protect you. So we must send a non-resistant, fearless conscious command to the subconscious, and that is a command of honestly not giving a shit, being willing to let it all hang out;
   - ***So focus right in on where you notice your sensations, your false alarm. Talk to them and say 'Do your absolute worst false alarm!' really DEMAND it, push it!***

This is the critical moment for you, this is going to feel counter-intuitive but you must follow these instructions; whatever your false alarm is compelling you to do (see question 3) and whatever rituals you perform in the heat of battle to keep yourself safe (see question 4), DO NOT DO IT! This is so important. It's time to start taking back the territory by demanding more and moving towards your fear, leaning into your false alarm:

   o Feel the urge to escape to the toilet? Don't fucken go anywhere!;
   o Avoiding eye contact because you don't want the attention? Stand up straight, pull your shoulders back and look straight into their eyes and smile!;

- o Stop cleaning your hands and be willing to let your sensations engulf you;
- o Don't sit next to the exit and surrender to your sensations;
- o If you are searching for some excuse to walk away from a social interaction, stand tall, move forward and engage - no matter what!;
- o Stay in the queue at the bank - no matter what happens!;
- o This is Paradoxical Intention! This attitude and this attitude alone will pop the panic cycle balloon.
- *If you want to use different wording that suits you better, that's fine; just make sure that you are complying with the rules of non-resistance and demanding more. For example, 'Thank you, sensations. I'll let you do your worst,' or 'Please make my heart beat as fast as possible,' or 'Bring it on, I'm not going anywhere,' or 'Yes, give it to me. C'mon, I'm staying right here,' or 'No thank you panic, not today.';*
- NOTE: You must accept the truth that your sensations are nothing more than a false alarm, nothing more. Without this conviction, it is highly unlikely you will approach your practice with the correct fearless attitude, and you will run out of puff at the first sign of discomfort.

You must resist the temptation to carryout your rituals (see question 4):
- o Have the urge to pop a bottle of pills in your handbag? Don't do it!;
- o About to sit at the table right next to the exit? Don't do it!;
- o Overwhelming urge to shrink yourself into your seat to avoid all eye contact and attention? Don't do it!;
- o Overwhelming urge to cross your arms, scratch, twitch, pace up and down? Don't do it!;
- o Have that urge to incessantly clean an already clean pair of hands, or bench top? Don't do it!;
- o JUST DON'T AND BE WILLING TO ACCEPT WHATEVER HAPPENS!;
    - WHATEVER HAPPENS, YOU CAN HANDLE IT!

Important

Magic will happen if you can find the courage to *move towards your fear*. If you take this action, the ultimate in non-resistance and fearlessness when under fire, and honestly be willing to accept *anything* that happens, you will turn panic on its head and take back control in an instant. All you need is trust and courage.

3. *Detach from any outcome*
   - Immediately follow up the above 'demand' with this declaration: *'Whatever happens, I will handle it'*;
   - 'What is' in this present moment *is* all you have. Completely let go of any and all resistance to 'what is'. Remain totally detached from any outcome. Remember, your resistance generates more anxious sensations, which creates more fear, which is the life source of panic;
   - Your only goal is to practice this non-resistant attitude, *not to reduce your sensations*;
   - Don't approach this with your fingers crossed, thinking, 'Okay, I'll do this, but only until things get too hot';
   - If during your practice, your sensations retreat, great. If they don't, that's fine too. Just keep practicing your protocol;
   - A non-resistant, fearless attitude is about being comfortable with whatever happens, it's being ok with not being ok!;
   - If you want to use different wording that suits you better, that's fine; just make sure that you are complying with the rule of detachment. For example, *'It is what it is, and I'm fine with it,'* or *'I'm okay with this, I'll be fine,'* or *'no more running, no more;*
   - If your sensations/thoughts are saying to you 'get me to the doctors now, today I'm really going to die', say to yourself 'I know I'm not going to die today, I never have and never will… this is another false alarm'… and let the sensations flow.
   - You really do need to challenge your beliefs (see question 5), really question what you think will happen to you. Completely give into your belief (you can because it's a false alarm remember!).

You might want to say something like 'If today is the day I die fine, we're all going to die some day!' You haven't died yet because of your false beliefs, and you never will!

*Once again, though, the magic comes paradoxically:
if you are looking for feeling in control, you won't find it.
Your job is simply to do your work: to practice wanting frequent episodes of strong sensations or doubt that last a while.*
(Dr Reid Wilson)

4. *Accept 'what is'*
   - Immediately follow up the above 'declaration' with this commitment: '*I* am learning to *love and accept myself exactly the way I am.*';
   - Open up to and be willing to fully accept and embrace not only your sensations but also *any outcome*;
   - You can't change 'what is' in this present moment. Your only option is to accept 'what is' and completely let go;
   - Don't 'check in' to see if this stuff is working or if your sensations have gone away. Your only job is to practice this protocol. If you find yourself 'checking in', then it means that you are placing conditions on your practice, like 'I'll do this but only if my sensations go away.' If you do that, then you may be disappointed, and your progress will be slow because you are still resisting;
   - You are not trying to remove the sensations - it's too late; they have already arrived. Your aim is to remove your interpretation of fear, resistance, that's it. That's all;
   - Your job is to practice non-resistance, fearlessness, and acceptance. It is irrelevant whether the harmless sensations exist or not;
   - Because you no longer fear, you won't experience fear. Without fear, the sensations are just that, harmless sensations. Without fear, panic attacks cannot occur;

- If you want to use different wording that suits you better, that's fine; just make sure that you are complying with the rule of acceptance. For example, *'I accept my sensations 100 per cent,'* or *'I accept whatever happens,'* or *'it is what it is,'* or *'fuck it, it is what it is,'* or *'no more, no more running,'* or *'what if I could accept my shit exactly the way it is, here, now,'* or *'I love you Shaun, I fucken love you.'*

Whatever you believe is going to happen to you (see question 5 above), now is the time that you call bullshit on it. And the attitude we use to do just that is acceptance and self love! That's right, accept your worst fear, accept the outcome, embrace it, welcome it and learn to love and accept yourself, warts and all, right here, right now exactly the way you are!

Remember your beliefs of what might happen to you if you do not escape from your panic provoking situation is nothing more than a false alarm. You have never come to any harm, and the catastrophic event has never happened, and never will. So to disempower the panic cycle you MUST accept any outcome:

- o Believe you are going to catch germs and die? We are all going to die at some stage, if today is the day you die, accept it and learn to love and accept yourself exactly the way you are – 'fuck it, so what!';
- o Believe you are going to die of a heart attack? We are all going to die at some stage. Millions around the world didn't wake up today, today you did, today you get another shot at the title, another opportunity to be better, but if today is the day you die, accept it and learn to love and accept yourself exactly the way you are - 'fuck it, so what!';
- o Believe that you are going to lose control or lose your mind? You have never lost your mind before, and you never will, your belief is a ghost, a false alarm. But whatever the case, you'll find a way through it and you are learning to love and accept yourself - 'fuck it, so what!';

o   Believe people will judge you and you will be embarrassed? No one's squared away, we are all trying to get by and deal with our own shit. Besides, what others think of you is none of your business, and it doesn't matter what anyone thinks of you; only what you think of you! You are learning to love and accept yourself exactly the way you are - 'fuck it, so what!'

Of course this is a mind game! This attitude is based on non-resistance, and is sending a fearless message to the subconscious that there is no danger and it can standdown. This paradoxical attitude is the only way to turn off the panic response for good (eventually).

Important

You have an underlying high anxiety condition, which is producing the initial sensations that sparks the panic cycle, and until you remove this habit - which you will learn how to do in BB4, these sensations are a sure thing. You can't stop them yet, but that's not your concern anyway. Your only concern is to practice your non-resistant attitude.

- *So stop acting so surprised or feeling like you have just been caught off guard when they show up. Complete acceptance will help you to stop watching over your shoulder, worrying and anticipating the next bout of sensations. Have trust and confidence in yourself that 'when' the sensations turn up, you can handle it.*

5. *Focus on your task at hand*
No matter what is happening, do your absolute best to turn your attention over to the task at hand. If you are talking to a friend, concentrate on engaging in conversation. If you a driving a car, concentrate on driving the car – turn up the radio and sing out loud. If you are talking in front of a group of people, concentrate on engaging with them and articulating your message.

No matter what happens, be courageous, act confidently. If your hands are shaking, ask for more and keep going. If your heart is racing, demand more and let go. If your mouth has dried up and you find it difficult to swallow or speak, have a drink of water and move forward into your task.

Observe, demand more, detach, and accept whatever happens, then get back to your task at hand.

Be aware of your body language, and what you do physically in an attempt to manage, cope with or resist your sensations. As you go about your task at hand, CHOOSE to do the opposite of what your false alarm is telling you to do physically (see question 4):

- If your task at hand is attending a meeting and you feel yourself slumping back in your seat to avoid attention…. DON'T! Sit up straight, shoulders back and smile (even if only to yourself), move forward and engage! Put it out there and contribute to the meeting. As soon as you do this, the experience of fear will disappear.

If done correctly, the experience of fear will fade away, starving panic of the vital fuel it needs to survive and in doing so breaking the panic cycle. Your anxiety level will return come back down to 'normal' and your uncomfortable sensations will slowly disappear.

If the sensations and intrusive thoughts come back into your consciousness, simply go back to step 1 and repeat the cycle. Do this as many times as it takes. No matter what happens, be courageous and 'just do it.'

Unwavering Trust

Trust in this protocol and yourself. Go ahead and practice this new attitude with unwavering trust that if you do this, it will work, maybe today, maybe tomorrow, maybe next week. Whatever the case, it will work.

Your new attitude is based on non-resistance, fearlessness. You are making a conscious decision to get out of the way, to remove fear and resistance from the mix. Without conscious fear, fear cannot exist. The subconscious mind picks up on this and will turn off the panic response.

Have unwavering trust that sooner or later your sensations will retreat. You are not concerned when they will because you no longer fear or resist them, so it really doesn't matter what happens.

Look for More

That's right, I want you to go hunting for opportunities to practice your new attitude. Remember habituation: you need exposure to the skill or thing you want to master in order to master it.

The more you expose yourself to the panic-provoking situation, the more you will be able to practice and the sooner you will banish panic and build new non-anxious habitual behaviour.

You will turn panic on its head. Moving towards it is exactly what it does not expect. Without you running from panic, resisting panic, and fearing panic, it cannot survive.

> *The general rule: The more aggressively you can face your distress and doubt, the more powerfully you will win back your life. If trying to get rid of anxiety and panic tends to keep them around, then what would happen if you did the opposite, if you encouraged them to stay? Keep in mind that this is a mental game. Panic gains territory as long as it gets you to react in a specific way. If you change your reaction, then you start taking back the territory.*
> *(Dr Reid Wilson)*

Do not limit your life by avoiding situations that you think will trigger an attack. This is so important. From this moment on, do not avoid situations because you want to avoid a panic attack. I know this seems scary, but this rule is so important to your healing.

Remember: It is not the situation you fear, you fear the sensations.

Will I have more panic attacks?

Short answer – Yes. I have pointed out in earlier chapters, that disempowering panic attacks is something that through practice you can learn to do right here, right now. However that doesn't mean that you won't experience the panic response again. It is highly likely that certain situations will still 'trigger' the panic response as you will most likely still have an underlying anxiety condition to deal with, and until you remove the underlying anxious behaviour and 'desensitise' yourself from your panic provoking situations, you will continue to trigger the panic response.

But that's ok because what is important is how you respond to the initial anxious triggers and sensations. When you can disempower the panic cycle at will, it doesn't really matter whether or not you trigger the panic response again.

Case Study—My Last Panic Attack

Allow me to share with you one of the last times I experienced a panic attack. As I have stated many times before, I experienced panic attacks as a result of social phobia and agoraphobia for around 15 years. Sometime towards the end of 2008, I was having a typically bad day. At the time, I was working for myself as a management consultant. This was at the height of my anxiety condition.

I was about to go into another meeting, and I was firing off panic attacks just through the very thought of being in the meeting. I tried all the excuses in the world to get out of the meeting, but I couldn't. I had to attend. I had spent so many hours dreading this meeting that by the time I went into it, I was not only terrified but also absolutely exhausted.

As I sat down in front of my clients, I was that spent and that fed up and exhausted that I had no fight left in me. I had nothing left within me to fight my panic. So at that point, I just gave in and said, 'Fuck it, so what, go for it, I'm too exhausted to even care, let alone be afraid. I've got no choice but to be here. There is no way out, so just do your thing. I'm too exhausted. I'm done!'

All of a sudden, the fear, the overwhelming need to escape and run, and all the other usual suspects disappeared in an instant. My senses were still heightened, I could feel the adrenaline flowing through my body, but I felt only slightly nervous. But the fear was gone.

In an instant, everything finally clicked together. I finally understood what it 'feels' like to not resist, to observe the sensations, demand more, detach from the outcome, accept whatever happens, accept 'what is', and get on with the task at hand.

Now I had been previously successful over the years at stopping the odd panic attack, but I didn't know what and how I did it, and because I continued to experience them, I just usually ended up feeling even more confused. But this time was different. This time, I finally got it. I finally understood the process. All the other times I had stopped panic were hit and miss.

I had part of the recipe for success, but there was always something else missing. The missing ingredients for me were as follows:

- The belief that I can win;
- Trust and courage to give in (detach) and let go (accept) of the sensations.

I unwittingly gave into the sensations, flowed with them, and changed my meaning of them. I was that fed up; my attitude was 'What the hell, I'm sick of running. I can't be bothered any more. I'm going to sit right here (because I had no other choice), and I am going to engage with whoever I can, no matter what happens. Do your absolute worst. I'm fed up with running. Do your absolute worst, now.'

The result was surreal. The panic attacks never came. I could feel the same sensations, but I wasn't panicking. I wasn't scared, and all of a sudden, I no longer feared them.

I felt so calm, so at ease, so confident, just like the old me. I didn't use any of the coping strategies or safety crutches that I had relied on throughout the years. Just a decision (albeit out of sheer exhaustion) to let the sensations flow through me.

That social interaction was the most satisfying experience I had had for many years. For the first time in so many years, I was no longer preoccupied with 'what if' thoughts.

I wasn't monitoring my thoughts and feelings, constantly affirming mantras to stave off another attack, thinking about excuses, and planning responses. I felt grounded in the present moment.

Important:
That was the end of panic attacks and the associated phobias for me. Sure, I still had an underlying anxiety condition, but it no longer escalated into panic attacks because I finally had the trust and confidence that I could disempower the panic cycle and to also walk into any situation without fear.

I then committed to making behavioural and lifestyle changes over a period of less than two month that reprogrammed my subconscious mind with new non-anxious behaviour. My anxiety levels, regulated by the amygdala, also retreated back down to a normal baseline level.

These behavioural and attitudinal changes are discussed in BB4. I call them my 'Golden Rules'.

Summary of The Panic Attack Eliminator

1. Observe - Be aware of where your sensations are centred in your body. Focus on them and interrupt the panic cycle by saying 'Fuck it, so what.'
2. Demand more—'Do your absolute worst false alarm.' Do the exact opposite to what your false alarm is telling you to do.
3. Detach from any outcome—'Whatever happens, I will handle it.'
4. Accept 'What is'—'I am learning to love and accept myself exactly the way I am.' Accept your worst fears coming true; they won't, they never have and never will, they are a false alarm.
5. Focus on your task at hand. Use your body language and physiology in a positive way.

The Mantra - Bringing it all together

Now trying to remember and recite the five steps of the Panic Attack Eliminator when you are in the heat of battle will just make you spin out of control even faster. When the 'shit hits the fan' your brain turns into spaghetti, and you immediately focus on running, avoiding, trying to stop or control the sensations, all hell breaks loose and you forget all about the steps. You stop looking at the facts and you lose touch with what you are supposed to be doing and why you are doing it. If you are a sufferer you will know exactly what I am talking about.

So how do we get around this? How do we implement the Panic Attack Eliminator when you are under the pump?

We do this by condensing steps 1 to 4 down into one seamless conscious command, or what I like to refer to as a mantra: 'Fuck it, so what, do your fucking worst false alarm, what ever happens I will handle it. I am learning to love and accept myself exactly the way I am,' or 'Come on, sensations, give me your absolute worst. I want more, whatever happens, I will handle it. I unconditionally love and accept myself exactly the way I am.'

You may want to play around with the wording of your command or mantra, and maybe even consider simplifying it down even further: 'I'll let you do your worst,' or 'I give in,' or 'I accept whatever happens.'

Or, maybe you might even want to take it up a notch and use my 'life hack': *'Yeah fuck you false alarm, I'm staying right her and moving forward!'*

Whatever you decide on, this will be your mantra when you are in a hot moment.

You must be able to recite your mantra in an instant, without thinking too hard, you must practice and practice this mantra until it becomes second nature. Because I can tell you from experience that when the shit hits the fan, there is no way you are going to be able to think through all the steps AND perform them. This will just lead to disappointment, frustration and more anxiety.

You must know intimately the answers to the five questions I asked you earlier in this chapter, and you must be willing to do exactly the opposite to how you would normally think and behave.

So I want you to prepare yourself for your hot moment by first answering the five questions, and then condensing steps one to four into a mantra which is unique for you, which you create that works for you, that triggers the 4 x steps of The Panic Attack Eliminator without you having to remember each one. Your mantra is your trigger that reminds you to let go and let whatever happens happen, to 'be ok with not being ok!', or….. to not give a shit - the ultimate in a non-resistant, fearless attitude!

Examples of mantras that do not comply:

- 'Shit, here we go again… fuck off fuck off.';
- 'Right, if this shit gets too bad, I'm outta here.';
- 'Arrrrrrgggghhhhhhhh. Why is this happening!!??';
- This is it! This time something really bad is going to happen.'

You will recall from my own case study earlier that when I was in the hot moment I said words to the effect of 'fine go for it, I'm too exhausted just do your thing.'

That conscious command, albeit out of resignation and exhaustion was based on a non-resistant and fearless attitude. Therefore it was a mantra that complied with steps 1 to 4. And therefore it turned off the panic button, disempowering the panic cycle.

Wherever you find yourself along the panic cycle, preferably when you first observe the anxious sensations and thoughts, CHOOSE to focus in on wherever your sensations or fears are centred in your body. DO NOT FOCUS ON THE SITUATION OR ENVIRONMENT. Whatever your 'false alarm' is telling you to do…. DON'T DO IT! Whatever you normally do physically in your hot moment to keep you safe, DON'T DO IT! Use your simple and unique mantra to remind you of what you need to do.

YOUR MANTRA MUST COMPLY WITH STEPS 1 to 4!

'Yeah fuck you false alarm, I'm staying right her and moving forward!' This simple mantra is the ultimate 'hack'. It complies with steps 1 to 4 perfectly. It's aggressive nature is based on fearlessness, and sends a clear message to the subconscious that there is no danger, and it can turn off the panic button. If there ever was a secret sauce, a mantra of this nature is it!

Of course you will be a little apprehensive at first, because you are not really certain of how you are going to cope. You may be very clumsy at the start. However, to the best of your abilities, just practice and persevere with unwavering trust. Pretty soon, you will start getting little insights and positive results, and your confidence will grow.

Maybe you will be successful in disempowering your panic the first time you try this. Maybe you won't. Maybe you have to practice 10, 20, 100 times before you are successful. Whatever the case, it doesn't matter in the long run. The only thing that matters is that you practice until you are successful.

Maybe you never have another panic attack again. Maybe you have to experience a few more before you completely eliminate them from your life. Either way, it also doesn't matter in the long run, just go about your practice.

> *'Success isn't final, failure isn't final,*
> *it's the courage to continue that counts'*
> (Winston Churchill)

What determines how quickly you heal yourself is your willingness to let the sensations touch you, engulf you, your willingness to stop resisting and fighting and completely give in to the sensations. Whatever the case, know this:

> *The very second you finally stop resisting, fearing the sensations, is the very moment you disempower panic!*

Practice and persevere with unwavering trust, feel the fear and do it anyway. Pay attention and learn from your successes and setbacks. Be courageous.

Keeping a Journal - Your Feedback Loop

Keep a journal, not only to record the answers to the five questions you answered earlier in this chapter, but also to document your experiences, both good and bad. All experiences are opportunities to gain insights and learn from. If you have a success, it means that you moved forward with the correct attitude and disempowered your panic. If you have a bad experience, it just means that you lost your way and you forgot what you were supposed to do, most likely your brain turned to custard during your hot moment, you couldn't remember steps 1 to 4, and you caved in and did a runner!

Either way both experiences provide vital feedback that you can use to figure out what you are doing and what needs to change. You can then make iterations to your approach and get back out there and give it another crack. You then pay attention to feedback, learn and make further iterations, have another crack and so on.

In your journal I want you to create two columns. In the first column I want you to copy the questions from column one in Figure 1 below. Use the second column to record details of your experiences by answering the questions you copied into column one.

Answer honestly. It's so important that you understand your behaviour, attitude and intentions during your hot moments. The insights that you will gain from this feedback will be instrumental in helping you identify what works, what doesn't work, and what things you could do differently in order for you to be able to move forward and disempower your high anxiety and panic.

Use this feedback to plan and prepare your approach for when you are next exposed to your panic provoking situation. Record both good and bad experiences. It's important to be aware of exactly how you behave in both scenarios.

See Figure 1 below for an example for you to use.

Figure 1: The Journal

Journal	
Column 1.	**Column 2**

1. Question: Describe your experience (good or bad)
   a. What happened (describe the anxiety provoking situation)?
   b. How did you initially respond?
   c. What did you say to yourself (your mantra)?
   d. What actions did you take?
	• I was standing in a queue at the bank. I noticed these horrible sensations turn up and get worse and worse.
	• I tried to stop them but I could feel myself losing control. My chest was tightening, my heart began racing, my stomach was churning.
	• I was looking around and it felt like everyone was staring at me and it felt horrible. I was wishing, wanting these sensations to just stop!
	• I was thinking to myself 'Fuck, not again, what the fuck is happening to me, how the fuck do I stop this shit! Now people are going to see me freaking out – Neat!
	• I felt an uncontrollable urge to get out, so I just left the queue and ran out of the bank with my tale between my legs.
	• As soon as I left the bank the horrible sensations subsided, but I was left feeling very upset with myself. I felt stupid.

2. Question: What was your false alarm (the horrible, uncomfortable but harmless sensations) telling you to do? In other words, what did you feel compelled to do?	To run out of the bank before anyone saw me having difficulty.
3. Did you do what your false alarm told you to do?	Yes, I left the queue and ran out of the bank.
4. Question: Before you gave into the false alarm, how did you behave, or what physical rituals did you carryout in order to try and protect yourself? a. These are your coping strategies or safety crutches	• I monitored my sensations, tried to suppress them and make them stops. • When that didn't work I looked down at the ground so as to avoid eye contact with anyone and then have to heaven forbid engage in a conversation while I was losing my mind. • I turned my back to people, trying to make myself smaller and smaller. • I was preoccupied with what I would say if I had to talk to anyone and what excuse I use to excuse myself.

5.	Were you honestly willing to give in to your sensations and let them do their worst, or did you desperately want them gone? a. Did you follow the Panic Attack Eliminator?	I tried to follow the Panic Attack Eliminator, but when the sensations got too strong I forgot everything and just wanted them gone. I guess I wasn't willing to give into the sensations.
6.	What did you believe was going to happen to you if you didn't do what your false alarm was telling you to do?	Maybe lose control, but mostly I believed that if people saw me having difficulty I would be extremely embarrassed and they would judge me.
7.	Did you give into this belief?	Yes, I couldn't stand being judged or embarrassed so I did what I always do/did.
8.	What could be a better belief to work on?	That I don't give a shit what other's think, after all they have their own problems to worry about. I could work on loving and accepting myself unconditionally.
9.	What could you have done differently?	• Commit to the Panic Attack Eliminator. • Prepare my mantra and stick to it. • Do exactly the opposite to what my false alarm was telling me to do. • Be willing to let the sensations do their worst, lean into them, let them engulf me. • Not give a shit about what others think of me. • Be kind to myself, accept whatever happens, good or bad, practice loving and accepting myself unconditionally.
With these insights, make a promise to yourself that the next time you experience your anxious sensations you will practice and practice the mindset and behaviour that you outlined in point #9 above!	

Breathe

Deep breathing in a hot moment is so, so important in disempowering your panic. During hot moments concentrate on breathing deeply and slowly into your diaphragm. I discuss Deep Breathing in Chapter 6.

No matter what happens or what is happening, maintain a constant rhythm of deep slow breathing. Deep breathing, along with the correct mantra and attitude is a very powerful combination for disempowering the panic cycle.

But remember, deep breathing won't stop the panic cycle unless you have the correct attitude and mantra. All the good work that deep breathing will do will be completely cancelled out by a resistant and fearful conscious attitude.

Student Case Studies

I have already discussed the last time I had a panic attack. Let's review some other real life case studies to illustrate how The Panic Attack Eliminator actually works in real life.

Student C

Sometime in August 2016, while living in Israel, I had a student who had a phobia of elevators. She experienced a massive panic attack while in an elevator over five years earlier, and hadn't stepped foot into another one since.

She was only 17 years old at the time, we won't go into any great detail on how she developed this particular phobia, because that's not important. But suffice to say, she had an underlying anxiety condition from past traumatic experiences associated with bomb shelters (remember, she lives in Israel), ultimately manifesting into a phobia of elevators.

We literally sat down for around 35 minutes and had a chat about what was going on. I explained in very brief terms what you have and are learning right here within these Building Blocks™.

I got her to the point where she believed and accepted a few truths:
- She wasn't mentally ill, she didn't suffer from a mental disorder;
- She suffered from a behavioural condition, she suffered from high anxiety;

- In terms of her particular phobia, she didn't actually fear the elevator itself;
  - Previously she was pre occupied with the fear of being stuck in an elevator;
  - So we put this inappropriate fear into its proper perspective;
    - The risk of that happening was so low that it did not warrant any time and energy focusing on something that was really never going to happen… so she could make the choice to ignore this worry, to not give it any power;
    - After all, it had never happened to her or anyone else she has ever known before;
    - And that I didn't have a phobia of elevators, but rest assured… if I was to get stuck in an elevator, I would probably panic too, and so would most people, she wasn't alone;
    - And just like everyone else, she could choose to worry about it at the time, if it ever happened;
- What she actually feared was the horrible and uncomfortable sensations and thoughts that were triggered by the very idea of going into elevators;
  - They were harmless. Horrible yes, harmful no;
  - They were a false alarm; the subconscious mind was just doing it's job, to protect her against…… well nothing of course.

Setting her up with the right mindset was critical to getting her to the point where she was willing to step up and walk right into the heart of her fear! Once she accepted all this as the truth, I then got her to agree to come with me the very next day to the biggest shopping complex in Tiberias and ride the elevators!

She was obviously freaking out about the very thought of going into an elevator. It had been over five years since the last time she was in one, which was a horrible experience for her. And over the years, the more she avoided them, the more her fear of them grew.

But I explained that her freaking out at the very thought was perfectly normal and to be expected. I then gave her two guarantees:

- I guaranteed that there was nothing I could do to stop the onslaught of the initial anxious sensations and thoughts, they were part of an habitual response at this stage;
    o In fact, they are probably going to be even more intense as she had agreed to throw away her coping strategies and safety crutches (avoidance and medication) and do the very thing that causes her to panic;
    o And she honestly didn't know how she was going to cope!;
    o But she had belief in me as her coach, and that gave her courage… even though she was packing herself;
- But I also guaranteed her that if she did exactly as I said, the initial sensations and thoughts would fizzle out and not escalate into a panic attack.

She said that she didn't know if she could do it. I explained that I understood exactly what she was going through:

- I had been there as well many years ago;
- And that's exactly what all my students that I personal coach say…. before they did what she is about to do.

This was a perfectly normal response; she had been avoiding this for years, and the very thought alone of fronting up to her fear was enough for her to spin into high anxiety! So, even though she knew that she was going to experience high anxiety at the start, and that she didn't know how she was going to cope:

- She felt the fear and did it anyway!

The next thing we did was to prepare her for success by answering the 5 questions as set out on page 169 (Preparing Yourself For Success). I have aready explained at great length why this piece of work is critical.

We then decided on her mantra that she was going to say to herself over and over again (see page 183, The Mantra - Bringing it all together):

> '*So what sensations, do your fucking worst, give me everything you've got. Whatever happens, I can handle it.*'

The next day we drove to the shopping complex and as we approached the elevator I got her to commit to no matter what happens she was not going to turn around and run away, or use any other safety crutch or coping strategy like medication:

Even though she had medication in her bag… more on that later!

No matter what, she was going to stay with me in the elevator, and her only job was to allow herself to freak out, to really push the panic button. I wanted her to make herself panic as much as she could. I really pushed her to want a panic attack, I told her I really wanted her to loose control.

Of course this is a game, this is a trick. This is a paradoxical approach. Genuinely wanting more, being ok with whatever happens is sending a clear message that you really don't 'give a shit' as George Carlin would eloquently put it. You are sending a clear message that you no longer fear.

Now the other important thing was that there were no conditions or proviso's attached, like 'we'll do this but only until it gets too hard, then we'll get the hell out of here!' She was all in or all out. There was no in between. She understood that if she gave a half assed attempt, she would get eaten alive by her fear. Conditions and proviso's are nothing more than safety crutches.

Another important thing I got her to do was maintain deep slow breathing, no matter what was happening.

As we stepped into the elevator I could see she was visibly uncomfortable. She didn't want to be there, in fact she said she wanted to leave. I asked her if she wanted to feel better or get better? Reluctantly she said she wanted to get better. I reminded her again to breath deeply and slowly. I then said that we have no choice, we have to do this, we must do this, she can do this. She is not in any danger, and they are just sensations.

I explained to her that she knew that this was going to happen because the response was nothing more than a habit, but she has the conscious power to decide what happens next. At this point I directed her to focus in on her sensations and start talking to them by reciting her mantra, over and over again. And she did. I told her I wanted her to panic, to panic as much as she could, to push her panic as much as she could. After all, that's what the mantra was asking for!

She actual got a little angry with me and said she was trying!

Then she reached into her bag and pulled out her bottle of medication. I told her that she could take them if she really wanted, but that would defeat everything she had done so far, just getting into the elevator after five years alone was a huge victory, and to give up now would just be a complete waste of time, but I understood if she couldn't resist the temptation to take her medication.

I urged her to put the bottle away and continue with her practice. I reminded her that her job is not to stop the sensations, it was to ask for more, that's all. To her credit, she put the bottle away, and while still a little shaken (well very shaken actually!), she continued focusing in on her sensations and demanding more through her mantra.

And as much as she tried to panic, she couldn't. She obviously wasn't a happy camper as she was coming to terms with these ugly initial uncomfortable sensations, which began way back when we hopped in the car to drive to the shopping mall. But, and this is a very big but, they didn't spiral out of control into a full on panic attack. No matter how much she tried to activate the fight or flight response she couldn't.

The initial uncomfortable sensations stuck around as nothing more than an irritation in the background. She kept reciting her mantra, when I reminded her, and her attention soon moved onto other things.

When she noticed the background irritating sensations and thoughts, she nipped them in the butt with her mantra, and then moved her focus onto the task at hand, which was talking to me.

We went up and down a few times. Got out at a few floors, had a chat about stuff, then got back into the elevator. I'm not going to say that she had the time of her life! But what a huge breakthrough for her. Her very last memory over five years ago of elevators involved freaking out and having a massive panic attack. This day, she not only had the courage to get into an elevator, a busy public one at that with other people cramming in as well, but she also couldn't make herself panic, no matter how much she tried.

If she had of turned around at the start, if she had of taken her medication or used any other safety crutch, she would have certainly avoided panic, but she would have just reinforced her phobia, her anxious behavior. Furthermore, if she had of approached this session with conditions, like 'I'll do this until it gets too hard and then I'm going to pop a pill,' her anxiety would have definitely spiraled out of control until she finally gave in and took her medication, because safety crutches are based on a conscious fear, and conscious fear is fuel for the panic cycle.

But she did it, she fronted up and mentally committed to not use any safety crutches, although she wanted to at the start. The result was that she didn't experience a panic attack. Wow! The only technique she used was a conscious fearless or non-resistant attitude.

She really didn't want to do this, she didn't think that she could do this, but she did it with the correct attitude, albeit with a tinge of stubbornness at the start, and she did what was asked of her. Now this student had to do this several times before she became de sensitized to elevators. Now she routinely uses them.

Truth be known, riding in elevators isn't something she is completely comfortable with, and this has more to do with her underlying anxiety condition that she will have to address one day, as she is still operating day to day in an anxious state.

This happened, this is a true story. In fact this has happened on hundreds of occasion with me when dealing personally with my students, as this is the very process that I take them all through, every time, from start to finish.

It doesn't matter what the student suffers from, the process is identical:

- Give them the understanding of what's really going on;
- Give them the belief and trust that they can do this;
- Give them the right tools to destroy the panic cycle;
    - In this case the Panic Attack Eliminator;
    - Condensed into a simple mantra;
    - Clear instructions of what to do;
- Empower them to do the work, to walk into the heart of their fear without any conditions, caveats, proviso's or safety crutches;
- All my students need is to find the trust and courage to step up to the plate and take a swing, the Panic Attack Eliminator will take care of the rest.

Hand on heart, I have a 100% success rate when my face to face students follow The Panic Attack Eliminator, and we are talking about students from all walks of like, suffering from a wide range of phobias and fears, from:

- Driving phobias;
- Fear of flying;
- Fear of heights;
- Fear of spiders;
- PTSD sufferer with a fear of sleeping bags (that's right, a fear of sleeping bags!);
- Social phobias;
- PTSD sufferer with a fear of running, a running phobia for crying out loud!
- OCD sufferers who stand up to their fears and refuse to carryout compulsive obsessive urges;
- Phobias of water and breathing!;
- And the list goes on.

So you can see now that you can use this very process with your own situation. Follow what I did with my student in this case study.

Now I want to touch on a few more case studies very quickly. First up is an OCD sufferer. One of her obsessive compulsive behaviors was to incessantly call her husband dozens of times a day in order to relieve anxiety and panic.

Normally, if she didn't carryout this compulsive behavior, her anxiety would escalate into a panic attack. So I took her through this exact same process. I explained the same things, I gave her the same set of instructions, threw away her coping strategy, the obsessive behavior, and no matter how hard she tried to panic, she couldn't.

- Ok, the situations were different, one student walked into an elevator, and the other student made a commitment to stop carrying out her obsessive ritual;
- But it didn't matter because its' all the same thing, a fear of the uncomfortable sensations;
- A fear of a fear that doesn't exist.

Student D

Now let's check back in with student D, the PTSD sufferer who we have been following since BB1. D committed to this process, committed to throwing away his safety crutches and made a decision to walk into the heart of his fears and no matter what and accept whatever happened.

So we went into a café and sat in the middle of the room! I took him through the exact same process (including answering the five questions and preparing his mantra). And naturally enough he initially reacted the same fearful way. No surprises there, they all do, it's normal and part of the process. But again, he did exactly what I told him to do, and you guessed it, he couldn't muster up a panic attack either. The situation was different, but the approach, the process was the same.

Another student, a soldier who suffered from PTSD, became so overwhelmed with panic when she ran, that she could no longer sit and therefore pass the required fitness test. This of course would have career ending consequences. I took her through the exact same process and no matter what, I couldn't get her to panic while she was running.

Now when I say I took her through the exact same process, I meant it. We had a chat the night before, I explained a few things, she agreed to go through the process the next day but was convinced that she wouldn't be able to go through with it. And well, the rest is history, because not only did she go through the process without being able to panic, the day after that she went and sat her fitness test by herself and passed[1]

Another student, an ex soldier who suffered from PTSD also had a phobia of driving. When I explained things to him and what we needed to do his first response was that he didn't think that he would be able to it, by that I mean hop in a car and drive.

---

[1] This student was a Captain in the New Zealand Defence Force, and was my very first student that I ever helped back in 2010!

I gave him some home work (the five questions and sorting out his mantra) and we agreed that we would meet up in a week at which point we would go through the process. In his case, he was going to hop in a car and drive while demanding to have a panic attack. He was a reluctant participant, but agreed to do it all the same.

To my surprise I get a phone call two days later from this student and he advised me that he had just driven from Palmerston North through to Napier. This is a three hour drive, and you have to negotiate a very winding and narrow gorge, which is a horrible experience for anybody! I told him that I was very surprised that he mustered up the courage to do something like that based on his earlier reluctance. He told me that he said to himself 'fuck it, I'm just going to do this no matter what!'

So he followed the process. He experienced the usual initial anxious sensations, but he remained committed to The Panic Attack Eliminator, and yes you guessed it, no matter what, he couldn't bring on a panic attack. He did it without me holding his hand, and I thought that was pretty gutsy!

I wanted to share these case studies with you to give you the confidence, the trust, the courage to step up to the plate and take a swing yourself.

I'd love to be there holding your hand for you, but you honestly don't need me there. Follow the instructions outlined in BB3, familiarize yourself with the process. Prepare yourself by answering the 5 questions and condensing down the steps of The Panic Attack Eliminator into your mantra. Then step up to the plate, follow the process exactly, and start swinging!

CHAPTER 8

BUILDING BLOCKS™ 4 (BB4) REMOVING HIGH ANXIETY (GAD, OCD, PTSD)

Objective of BB4
- To remove the underlying habitual anxious behaviour, which fuels GAD, OCD, and PTSD, and replace it with new non-anxious behaviour.
- To reset your baseline anxiety level back down to a 'normal' level.

BB3 showed you how to end panic attacks and phobias by collapsing the panic cycle and, in the process, preventing the initial sensations from escalating into panic.

It's important to remind you that your panic attacks and phobias were the extreme manifestation of high anxiety. Without an underlying anxiety condition, you cannot experience panic attacks or phobias.

In order to remove your underlying anxious condition (GAD, OCD, PTSD), we now need to reprogramme the subconscious mind with new non-anxious behaviour. This will also allow the anxiety levels regulated by the amygdala to be reset back down to a normal baseline level.

Get Off Drugs As Soon As You Can

Drugs do nothing, nothing to address your anxiety condition; all they do is mask all the sensations and symptoms of high anxiety as well as creating other side effects and complications.

While the drugs are masking your symptoms, you will still be carrying out your daily rituals of habitual anxious behaviour, which will be pushing the baseline anxiety levels stored in the amygdala up higher and higher. So pretty soon, you will have to administer a higher dose of drugs in order to continue to mask the symptoms.

Whatever dose you are on, start reducing gradually. Review my discussion under 'Medication' in BB1 (page 105).

The Six Golden Rules

The six Golden Rules outlined below, when implemented into your daily life through disciplined routine and repetition, will enable you to make the behavioural and attitudinal changes that you will have to make in order to become a non-anxious person again.

How badly do you want to heal yourself? Are you willing to do whatever it takes?

Great, because just like learning any new habit at the start, it is not going to be easy, but if you maintain your trust, practice and persevere, you *will succeed*.

Commit to making the Golden Rules a part of your daily life.

Golden Rule 1: Acceptance

Full acceptance of your life 'as it is', including your anxiety condition, reduces anxiety levels, distracts you from worry, and creates a gap in the mind for healing to take place.

To unconditionally accept yourself is to truly love yourself. I use both terms interchangeably throughout the Golden Rules.

From now on, fully and completely love and accept yourself. This is so very important. No matter where you are in your journey, whether or not you are where you think you should be in life, accepting your life as it is now, loving yourself for who you are now is a very empowering feeling.

The only other choice you have is to not accept or love yourself, and the feelings and emotions generated with this attitude can be very disempowering—choose your thoughts very wisely.

Making a choice to love and accept yourself right now will not change at all where you are now, or what your life situation or circumstances are, but it will change the direction of your journey. Not loving yourself has no value apart from promoting further negative and anxious thoughts and is totally disempowering.

A deep and unconditional love and acceptance of yourself promotes positive, empowering thoughts and lays the foundation for a meaningful vision of the future.

Not accepting your life and your anxiety is resisting. And you will just get more of what you are trying to run from; by now you are fully aware of this. You won't win fighting or resisting anxiety or 'what is'. Accept your situation and let go. Love and respect yourself:

- Accept 'what is' now. You don't have any other choice. Your current circumstances cannot be changed; it 'is';
- Do not let your current circumstances (effects) determine your very next thought (cause), for you will surely reap more of what you sow;
- Accept and let go and live by the Golden Rules.

Acceptance also implies unconditional forgiveness. Forgive yourself and forgive others—no matter who they are, no matter what they have done. You are not forgiving for the benefit of those who you forgive; you forgive them, for your benefit.

Non-forgiveness keeps you stuck in the past with resentment, anger, regret and or jealousy. Forgiveness brings you back into the present moment where you can full yourself with love, acceptance, gratitude and a meaningful vision of the future.

This is a conscious choice that you can make. Forgiveness will transform your life.

And finally, acceptance also means that you take full responsibility for your life situation. You are 100% responsible for where you are in your life. There is no one else, or no 'thing' to blame. There is nowhere else you are meant to be, where you are right this moment is 'what is', and there can never be any other way.

You, with your habitual beliefs and thoughts that you ultimately choose to accept and act on, are responsible for your life situation, not your boss, your spouse, your car, your neighbor, it's not the government, the universe, the weather . . . . It's you!

Accept 'what is' now, accept responsibility, and start choosing thoughts and beliefs in this very moment, which will move you in the direction of what it is that you truly want, and deserve. The Six Golden Rules will be your road map.

How to Implement Golden Rule 1

'I am learning to unconditionally love and accept myself exactly the way I am.'

Affirmations, when used correctly (and incorrectly for that matter), are very powerful at programming the subconscious mind with beliefs and corresponding thoughts and behaviours. Affirmations are statements or thoughts that you make, backed up by feelings of belief or non-belief in whatever it is you are affirming.

When you affirm something, pay attention to the feelings or emotions behind that affirmation. There are only two emotions, love or fear. All other emotions are really just varying degrees of either love of fear:

- Affirmations produce that which is being affirmed, not based on the thoughts, but based on the positive or negative emotions or feelings backing up that which you are affirming.

When you say to yourself 'I am learning to love and accept myself exactly the way I am,' what do you feel? If you sincerely mean it, you will immediately notice feelings and emotions of love to some degree. If you sincerely do not mean it, you will produce correspondingly negative and fearful emotions.

What do you feel when you say the above affirmation? If you feel emotions of love, no matter how small, you are on the right track. If you feel negativity, then you have some work to do to develop your understanding and belief in yourself and my Building Blocks™. Either way, you are backing up the affirmation with a belief in either love or fear—and you will surely get a result, one way or the other.

So, to implement Rule 1, first make sure that when you make this affirmation, you mean it with every cell of your body.

Choose to mean it! Start practicing 'meaning' it today. Practice and practice.

Now, I want you to repeat this affirmation as many times as you can throughout your day. Say it hundreds of times if you have to. How badly do you want to get better?

Don't look for any change in your circumstances; just repeat the affirmation as many times as you can. If you find yourself caught up in anxious thoughts, then this is the precise time you should practice your affirmation, with meaning—and accept whatever happens.

Don't expect to feel better at the start, you won't, that's not how it works. Your only job is to practice and practice the Golden Rules. Develop discipline and routine throughout your day and you will get better.

Mirror Work

This is really important stuff. This is where we are going to start digging real deep, and you won't like it at first, but this is going to be critical to your healing, it is critical to the attackpanic programme.

I learnt this practice from Louise Hay back in around 2008. It was one of the hardest things for me to do back then, I felt quite silly in fact! But I practiced and practiced and eventually it became very natural.

All discord, lack, pain, dis-ease, fear, worry, lack of self worth comes down to our inability to love ourselves unconditionally. And there are very few that have this relationship with themselves.

So, I want you to look in the mirror, look straight into your eyes, take a deep breath in, hold, and as you exhale slowly, say:

- 'I love you, I really really love you.' Look straight into your eyes as you say it. Repeat this three times;
- Then say 'I'm sorry I haven't always been there for you, but I'm here now';
- Then say 'I am willing to change, I am changing, I have changed';
- Then say 'I love and approve of myself.' Repeat this 10 times!

This should take you about 1 and a half minutes. I want you to do this mirror work 10 times throughout your day. Two of those times can be as soon as you get up in the morning, and just before you go to bed.

DON'T WAIT UNTIL YOU FEEL GOOD TO DO THIS, 'JUST DO IT'. You will most likely feel stupid at first, everyone does. But practice and persevere, the rewards are worth it.

See Chapter 8 (Taking Action) for further instructions on how to implement Golden Rule 1.

The Correct Use Of Acceptance

Irrespective of what anxiety condition you are suffering from, you will most probably be dealing with uncomfortable sensations and intrusive thoughts on a daily basis. They are a bi product of an underlying anxiety condition, and will go once the underlying condition has been removed, and this will happen through the Golden Rules.

In the meantime, you still have to deal with these sensations and thoughts, and we do that through the correct use of acceptance.

An attitude of acceptance is grounded in non-resistance, fearlessness and willingness to let go and let whatever happens happen.

Your current behavior is based on fear, is based on resistance, it's a conscious choice that you're making to fight against the horrible uncomfortable sensations or the intrusive thoughts that you're experiencing. It seems normal and natural for you to want to fight it, to want them to stop, but this attitude is based on resistance, it's based on fear.

So all you are doing is feeding the anxiety or panic cycle.

An attitude of acceptance is completely the opposite, it's based on letting go, it's based on non-resistance, fearlessness and is the cornerstone to all successful programs available including the attackpanic programme.

But if you feel that you're not making the progress that you should be, it maybe that you're not using an attitude of acceptance in the correct way.

By now you're fully aware that it's your conscious choice of how you react to your initial uncomfortable sensations or intrusive thoughts in the moment that determines whether they fizzle out to nothing, or spiral out of control into high anxiety and even panic. Your conscious choice of fighting and resisting is based on fear, and this very fearful attitude fuels the panic cycle!

The answer is to not try and stop what's already turned up as part of an habitual pattern of behavior. Your only job is to stop fueling the anxious thoughts, making them spiral out of control; you're only job is to consciously choose to practice a non-resistant attitude, and that way you simply do not fuel or perpetuate these sensations and intrusive thoughts. I hope this is making sense to you.

An attitude of acceptance is about letting your sensations and intrusive thoughts come and letting them go without you adding fuel to the fire, without you trying to stop them. It's letting whatever is happening in the moment happen.

And this takes a lot of courage and a lot of trust at the start.

Incorrect use of Acceptance

Conditions/proviso's

So let's look at the incorrect use of this attitude of acceptance. If you practice an attitude of acceptance with a condition or caveat or proviso like, 'okay Shaun I'm going to walk into this situation that causes me discomfort and distress', or 'I'm going to allow the intrusive thoughts to flow through my mind, but only until I can't handle it anymore, then I'm outta here', then all you are doing is resisting, staying on guard, worrying about what is going to happen next, because you desperately want these sensations gone. This attitude is based on fear and you won't be fooling anyone. You know that by now!

Wanting them to stop

If you practice acceptance for the purposes of wanting to stop your uncomfortable sensations or worrying thoughts (which is perfectly understandable, and what you have been doing all along anyway), then that's not the correct use of acceptance either. The fact that you want them to stop means that you're not accepting them, and I'll say it again, this is an attitude based on fear and all you're doing is fueling the anxiety cycle.

The Golden Rules are the foundation of the attackpanic programme, and they start with an attitude of acceptance and an attitude of gratitude for everything in your life in this very moment.

If you find that implementing the Golden Rules is hard, then it maybe that the only reason you're practicing the the rules in the first place, specifically acceptance and gratitude, is because you're desperate for these sensations and thoughts to stop.

And I get that, I understand more than anyone else, I've been there done that. But that desperation for wanting your thoughts and sensations to stop is resistance, it's fear based and is the opposite to acceptance. And all you will get is more setbacks, causing you to become more anxious, frustrated and disillusioned.

Expectation leads to disappointment

You maybe be also struggling maybe because of your expectations. Your expectation is for your habitual sensations and thoughts to stop (naturally enough), but that is not true acceptance. Again this attitude is based on fear.

True acceptance, is to accept whatever is happening right now. To allow your uncomfortable anxious sensations to be there, and this a huge leap of trust because it's completely counter intuitive to what you think you should be doing. It is very scary thinking about this whole idea of sitting right in the heart of your fears and allowing all your intrusive and worrying thoughts to take over your body.

But this attitude of acceptance is key, it's the cornerstone, it's the foundation to not only the attackpanic programme but all other successful programmes as I've mentioned earlier. If you're finding you're getting frustrated with the Golden Rules it's because you're trying too hard. Acceptance is about no expectations, just a willingness to practice your new skill of accepting what is, that's true acceptance.

Of course you want the sensations and horrible thoughts to go, and so you should, and you will, very soon. So of course you should have goals, and a vision of being a non-anxious person again soon. But leave expectations out of it when you are practicing acceptance, it will just get in the way.

And I say practicing (acceptance) because that's exactly what you are doing, practicing; practicing something that you may not have done before, and probably will not be very good at, at the start! It takes time to break old habits and it takes time to build new habits. The Golden Rules will build new non-anxious habitual behavior overtime.

Your anxious sensations and thoughts are a bi-product of an underlying anxiety condition. They are a pattern of habitual behavior, a habit, like a record playing the background. Until you change the record, which is what we will do through BB4, these sensations and thoughts will pop up whether you like it or not. But that's ok. Your only job is to accept whatever 'is', in this very moment. Your job is not to try and stop anything, or to expect anything to stop.

Expectation in this respect is nothing more than a fearful and resistance attitude, and will get in the way of your progress, will get in the way of you practicing acceptance. I hope this makes sense.

Overtime, with practice and perseverance, acceptance and gratitude, along with the other Golden Rules contained in BB4, will remove the underlying anxiety condition responsible for the uncomfortable sensations and intrusive thoughts, and replace it with new non-anxious behavior.

A Quick Recap

The wrong use of acceptance is when you practice this attitude with a caveat, with a proviso; for example when you walk into an anxiety provoking situation and say to yourself 'I'm okay with not being okay, until it gets too bad and then I'm gonna get the hell out of here.'

You're doing the work with a condition and that's the wrong use of acceptance and it will never work, you're not going to fool anybody, especially your subconscious mind.

The other incorrect way of using acceptance is with an expectation, 'I'm going to practice acceptance because I am so desperate for these sensations and intrusive thoughts to stop!'

Conditions and expectations will just get you even more wound up, frustrated and disillusioned, slowing down your progress. You may even begin to believe that you are doomed to this existence, or maybe even that 'this shit doesn't work!' You know, the old 'I tried it, and it doesn't work' scenario. And we don't want that.

Acceptance is accepting everything, warts and all, good and bad! So if you're finding it too hard and nothing is working, you're disillusioned and having setbacks, it could be because of these two incorrect ways of practicing acceptance.

I know, I have been there done that. I have been where you are, I know what you are going through.

Correct use of Acceptance

So what then is the correct use of the attitude of acceptance?

- It's simply practicing being willing to experience and allow whatever is happening to happen without trying to stop it;
- Without trying to resist your initial anxious sensations, without trying to resist or stop your intrusive thoughts;
- It's completely letting go and being okay with not being okay;
- Being okay with whatever's happening in the present moment;
- 'Not giving a shit' - George Carlin.

When your initial sensations and thoughts turn up it's too late to try and stop them, it's like shutting the gate after the horse is bolted:

- You will never be able to stop something that has already happened;
- The second you notice your initial anxious sensations and thoughts, is the very second they have arrived;
- You can't stop them, it's too late, they are already here, that part is now out of your control;
- To try and do so would just cause frustration and disillusion.

The good news is that your job is not to stop something that has already happened, your only job is to control how you consciously react to them, in this very moment:

- That's it, that is your only job;
- It's the only thing you can control;
- Luckily, it's the only thing you need to control;
- And this is where acceptance comes into play;

You have the power to make a conscious choice on how you want to interpret and react to those sensations or intrusive thoughts.

Unconditional acceptance is the cornerstone to your healing (no matter what is happening). This attitude is not about giving up per say, it's letting go of the fear. What we are doing here is exactly the opposite to how you would normally respond to these initial uncomfortable sensations or the intrusive thoughts.

By not reacting to these initial sensations and thoughts you are consciously not adding fear to the mix and it's you're conscious fearful reaction which creates more anxiety:

- Without your conscious fearful reactions towards those initial sensations and thoughts in the moment, they cannot spiral out of control into higher anxiety or even panic;
- What you're effectively doing is consciously moving out of the way, you're not adding any fuel to the mix.

You then make a choice, no matter what is happening to turn your attention onto your task in the moment, or onto something more inspiring, or taking positive action towards a problem or some other project.

The correct use of acceptance will allow you to get on with whatever it is you need to do in the moment, irrespective of what sensations and thoughts have popped up into your consciousness:

You have the conscious power to choose whatever you want to focus on in the moment.

Like all things that you try for the first time, this will take practice as you will have to strengthen your ability to concentrate. But just keep practicing, you will get good at focusing on whatever it is you choose to draw your attention to.

Will acceptance and gratitude for that matter stop your sensations or thoughts?

- The answer is no, it's too late you can't stop something that's already happened;
- But that's not your job, your job is to stop fueling the sensations and intrusive thoughts thereby creating more anxiety;
- You're only job is to make the conscious choice to stop consciously resisting;
- Stop making the situation worse in the moment;

Remember: When you stop running from fear, fear stops running you.

The correct use of an attitude of acceptance won't change your situation right now, it won't get your girlfriend (or boyfriend) back, it won't find you a job or miraculously conjure up some money, or whisk away any other challenge, but it will change your state of mind and attitude:

- And this will change your experience;
- Your experience will change your thoughts;
- And your thoughts will change your actions;
- And your actions shape your physical world.

The Ten Minute Exercise

I want you to do a ten minute exercise, at least once a day to experience what it is like to actually let go, to be okay with not being ok and willing to allow your intrusive thoughts or sensations to exist:

- You probably only need to do this a few times to experience the right feeling, but do the exercise more if you want.

When you truly let go and allow your anxious sensations and thoughts to be there you no longer fear and you're no longer resisting, you take away anxiety's fuel which is fear.

So for a ten minute period I want you to allow yourself to worry, in fact I want you to really make yourself worry as much as you can, really push it. I want you to ask for all the intrusive and worrying thoughts and the uncomfortable anxious sensations to come on as strong as possible.

You've got ten minutes to allow them to come and do whatever they want, really incite your thoughts and sensations to come along and do their worst. I just want you to focus on worrying as much as you can, to just focus on your anxious thoughts.

That's your only job for the next ten minutes; to worry and to feel anxious as much as you can. You are giving yourself permission to feel like absolute crap, with no need try and stop them and gain control, no need to run from them or want them gone.

Find a quiet place where you won't be disturbed and more importantly where you won't be distracted. This is very important for your outcome.

If you can find time to go away and do this exercise now, that would be great, if not, do it as soon as you can following this lesson.

Now, once you have done this exercise, maybe even for the first time, you will have noticed that something very interesting happened:

- At best you would have only been able to focus all your energy and attention on your anxious sensations and thoughts for a couple of minutes at a time before they die down, before other non-anxious thoughts flow into your awareness, into your consciousness.
  There is simply no way you are able to concentrate on worry for more than a few minutes straight, let alone for ten.

- This is because, generally speaking we all pretty much suck at concentration. Concentration is a faculty of the mind that most of us probably haven't developed very well. But we can develop high levels of concentration, it will take a lot of work, but it can be done.

- Sure, after a short while throughout your exercise, your anxious thoughts and sensations may come flooding back, but then they will go again, replaced by other non-anxious thoughts:
  - This is a function of how our mind works, you will recall from Chapter 6 (BB2) that we have around 60,000 thoughts per day, flowing in and flowing out, they all have a start and an ending. They will just keep coming at you, thick and fast, both good and bad thoughts;
  - Everyone, both sufferers and non-sufferers have good and bad thoughts, non-sufferers just don't habitually dwell on them as much as a sufferer would.
- Most importantly, you will have noticed that during the exercise, there were periods when you weren't focused on your anxious thoughts, when you would have had other thoughts that were non-anxious. How long you experienced the non-anxious thoughts during this exercise is not important.
- By giving yourself permission to be an anxious person, you remove the fear, you removed the fixation with your anxious thoughts, you removed your conscious resistance, the need for them to stop (what you resist persists, what you focus on, you get more of):
  - You have removed your conscious fear and resistance, the very thing which fuels anxiety;
  - And the result was that your anxiety dropped, albeit probably only momentarily.
- You have experienced during this exercise what it actually feels like to let go, to be ok with not being ok, to actually accept what is now, to accept whatever happens, to practice acceptance correctly;
- If you can do this for 1, 5, 10 minutes, you have the power to choose do this when and wherever you want.

So you sit there at the start of your ten minute exercise, your approach should be something like:

- 'Here we go, here is my opportunity. I'm allowed to feel all the anxiety and I'm allowed to experience all the worry and intrusive thoughts. All the scary thoughts, the bizarre thoughts of all the crazy things that's going to happen to me, let's have them all, I'm allowed to do this, I'm going to do this for 10 minutes. Do your absolute worse!';

So give this exercise a go and you will experience what it's like when you completely let go, when you step aside consciously and you give yourself permission to be anxious, to be ok with not being ok, and feel the thoughts and sensations dissolve:

- o That is the experience of the correct use of acceptance;
- o This will be a revelation, a turning point and it will be a real aha moment for you;
- o You may only have to do this once to get the experience, you might wish to do this more to build up your trust and confidence.

So putting the 10 minute exercise aside, there are two ways that my students arrive at the point where they experience this aha moment, the feeling where you're practicing acceptance correctly.

The first way is by practicing the Golden Rules, specifically rules 1 and 2, unconditional acceptance and love for yourself and gratitude for your life 'as is'. Practice with trust, courage and belief in yourself and also me as your coach and the program.

Over time through repetition and discipline you will build new non-anxious behaviour.

The second way that you reach that aha moment, that breakthrough is through sheer exhaustion. You're trying (probably incorrectly) the attitude of acceptance, trying so hard, trying to do so much that your anxiety completely overwhelms you. Your anxiety has sky rocketed, your intrusive and worrying thoughts plague you day and night to the point where you have got nothing left, and you are so exhausted and can't fight anymore. And so you give in, you just let go! You stop resisting because you have no fight left, and you really don't give a shit anymore!

Earlier in BB3 I describe as a case study my last panic attack. To summarize, I was going into a meeting and I had been so anxious days before, I was fearing that situation and that meeting so much that I had tried to get out of the meeting unsuccessfully. After days of being so wound up and anxious I was so exhausted that when I walked into the meeting I had no fight left.

So I sat down in front of my clients absolutely spent, and I remember saying something to myself like, 'I've got nothing left, I can't get out I have to stay here I've got no more fight left in me.'

An interesting thing happened, because I was so exhausted I couldn't fight anymore, the very second I stopped fighting the fear and resistance went.

The fuel for anxiety, my conscious fearful reaction in the moment was gone, all I was left with were harmless sensations, but I didn't fear them anymore because I had no energy or fight left to fear.

The sensations stuck around for a while because that's the effect of adrenaline in my body, all my senses were heightened. My point is my fear had gone, so I was no longer experiencing fear. That was an aha moment, that was when I felt what it actually feels like to experience this whole idea of acceptance.

Through sheer exhaustion I just gave up and the second I gave up I experienced no more fear. The point here is, your sheer exhaustion will lead you to absolutely letting go and that's when you'll receive a break through. That's when you will really start to progress.

As I said earlier, we practice acceptance incorrectly by trying too hard because we're so desperate that we want the sensations and the worrying thoughts to stop. But this is a conscious fearful command and it's fueling your anxiety, it's fueling the panic cycle.

If an attitude of acceptance and gratitude is new to you, don't beat yourself up too much if you find yourself struggling at the start. An attitude is a thought process, it's a skill you will have to develop just like any other skill or habit, and you develop it through Operant Conditioning, just like everything else you learn to do, through repetition, perseverance and routine discipline.

Your Mantra

So the best way to practice acceptance is through a mantra or affirmation. Your mantra is a very succinct and short phrase or sentence that you use in a hot moment that reminds you of the correct use of acceptance.

For example if I'm experiencing intrusive worrying thoughts and they're starting to grow in intensity, my mantra might be something like 'Fuck it, so what, it is what it is, whatever happens I will handle it', or 'no more running, whatever happens I'm going to be fine, I'm going to be myself', or 'whatever happens I'm staying right here, no more running'.

In a hot moment you don't want to be trying to think about too many things, that's going to cause you frustration and yes more anxiety.

So your mantra needs to be short and sharp and you need to practice and persevere with it. The simple mantra is all you need in a hot moment to remind you to trigger the proper use of acceptance. Your only job is to practice your mantra, without any expectation for anything to change - That's Acceptance!

Summary

Remember, acceptance and gratitude will not change anything in the 'now', BUT neither will CHOOSING to allow yourself to be constantly stuck in a perpetual negative and anxious state of mind. And both attitudes will result in a correspondingly different state of mind, actions AND results.

You have the power to consciously choose how you want to react to anything in this very moment.

Acceptance and gratitude is all about practicing a non-resistant, non-anxious attitude. The aim of this is to turn off the anxiety or 'panic cycle', by starving anxiety of it's vital fuel it needs to not only make your anxiety worse in the moment, but also to strengthen your anxious habit!

While it is very important to have goals, or as Viktor Frankl would say, 'a meaningful vision of the future', it's also important that we accept what is, 100%, right here, right now, in this moment.

That means accepting who you are, loving yourself exactly the way you are now! That means everything about you...... including your anxious habit. Maybe you will get better, maybe you won't. You should most definitely ALWAYS have that vision, and maybe you will be 'normal' (whatever that means for you) next week, next month, next year! But whatever the case, it is critical that you love yourself exactly the way you are... right here, right now.

The idea is to remove any and all expectation and hope of being well! Expectation and hope used for the wrong reasons can cause frustration, disappointment, dis-illusion, and setbacks, and all this can actually make your habit worse, as this attitude is steeped in fear. Be sure that if you do have an expectation, it is not born out of desperation and fear, for that will surely slow down the process of healing.

So maybe you will be well, maybe you won't, the key is to be ok with not being ok in the now, tomorrow and the future. Of course this is a mental game you are playing with your subconscious! The vision here is to get better. But to win the game you must remove your CONSCIOUS present moment fearful attitude towards your habit! I hope that makes sense.

I am finding that a real stumbling block with some of my students is 'wanting' to be better 'Now'. This wanting is NOT trusting, it's fear and it's resistance, the opposite to acceptance and gratitude!

Your job, day in and day out is to ONLY practice 'being ok with not being ok', no matter what has turned up today! It is not to stop anything or expect anything to change. This is very important. Your only job is to practice acceptance and gratitude.

Take positive action on what you can control 'now', and accept everything else that has popped up today that you cannot control. CHOOSE to be grateful, choose to look for things in your life to be grateful for. CHOOSE to do things that support and nourish you when you can.

Even to this day, when shit happens in my life (as it does for everybody from time to time), and there is nothing I can do about it, I still practice 'not giving a shit!' I will say something like, 'Fuck it it is what it is!' 'I love and accept myself exactly the way I am.' 'Thank you thank you thank you for my abundance.'

Now this of course won't change what is in the moment at all, if the shit has hit the fan, the shit has hit the fan! But it will change how long I allow myself to dwell on something that I cannot control, allowing the emotions and thoughts to come and go very quickly. I am then free to focus on solutions, opportunities, or stuff that inspires me and makes me feel good, and that moves me in the direction of my ideals. Nearly 14 years after I healed myself, this is still my practice, still my routine.

This is a conscious choice that I can make in the moment. This is a conscious choice that you can also make in any given moment. Your only job is to step up to the plate and start swinging, start practicing.

Anxiety sufferers especially spend way too much time resisting their current situation, hoping, wishing desperately for things to be different. This is a resistant and fearful mindset. Fighting against 'what is' is fruitless, it causes fear, worry, resentment, disillusion, depression, envy and enmity, pulling us into the past with regret and anger, pushing us into the future with worry and apathy, ultimately getting in the way of a meaningful vision of the future.

Where we are right now is where we are meant to be, not because I think someone is looking out for us or we are part of some master plan, but because it couldn't possibly be any other way. There is no such thing as 'shoulda', 'coulda', 'if only this', 'if only that'. You are where you are right now because of your past beliefs, attitudes, thoughts and actions, culminating in your current life situations. You are responsible for where you are 100%.

The fastest way to change your current situation and move towards your desired future state (in your case a non-anxious person again) is to change your beliefs, attitude, thoughts and corresponding actions.

And this change starts with accepting your lot, warts and all, right here, right now. Accept your current situation, love your obstacles and challenges, embrace your suffering. Learn to unconditionally love and accept yourself exactly the way you are; your attitude and perspective will slowly change, and so will your motivation and vision of the future. Your daily actions and routine will then correspond to your new attitude.

Golden Rule 2: Gratitude

For me, thoughts of gratitude are the single most powerful habit that I have developed. Admittedly, it didn't come easy, but I used willpower to consciously *choose* to use my imagination to look at my life and see all the things that I ought to be grateful for, thankful for on a daily and consistent basis, until—you guessed it—thinking about 'how grateful I was' became a habit.

Living in a state of constant gratitude makes you feel good, and when you feel good, you are distracted from worrying. Therefore, the more you feel grateful, the more you distract yourself from worry. The more you do that, the more your anxiety retreats. Feeling grateful allows you to use your imagination to solve problems more easily, see opportunities, be more positive and enthusiastic, be kinder to yourself and others, and see a brighter future. Gratitude gives your mind the space to relax.

Your actions are a reflection of your thoughts, and your life moves in the direction of actions. Therefore, the more grateful and accepting you are, the more your life will align and move in the direction of love. Love is the opposite of fear, and fear is what is fuelling your underlying anxiety.

We all have it good, we all have it bad, and it's a fact of life. We will all experience traumatic loss at some point in time. How we deal with the challenges of life, how we let it affect us, how we allow it to either help us survive or thrive is our *choice*, our *conscious choice*.

- If I can do it, so can you.

As I have mentioned before, at the height of my suffering, I was unemployed, penniless, and I had just lost several companies and my fortune, going bankrupt in the process. I was housebound due to my agoraphobia and social phobia. If it wasn't for my best friend, we would have also been homeless, *and* I had two children to feed. I'm not making this shit up, that happened!

In the face of all that, I managed to heal myself in less than two months. How did I do that? I did what I have outlined in BB3 to disempower the panic attacks. I then set about removing my underlying anxiety condition by implementing my 'Golden Rules'. It all started with *consciously choosing* to find things to be grateful for *and* to fully accept and love myself *'as is'*.

I focused on my children, my great health, talents and intelligence, and my family and friends. I still had all my fingers and toes. I was still breathing—I was still alive. I used all my willpower to *choose* to be grateful for *everything* in my life, good and bad. I *chose* to love my obstacles, my challenges, my suffering (through unconditional love and acceptance). Did it come easily at the start? *Hell, no.* My life situation was a fricken train wreck.

Choosing to be grateful at that stage felt about as natural as climbing up a tree backwards. Did I stop being anxious overnight? No. Did I have moments of doubt? Yes. Did I have setbacks? Yes, I had good days and bad days. But I kept going. Irrespective of what was going on in my physical world, I just kept practicing and persevering with being grateful for everything in my life.

How to Implement Rule 2

Every morning, just as you are waking, *choose* to focus on what you are grateful for. Take five minutes as you begin to wake to feel grateful for everything in your life. Say over and over to yourself 'thank you, thank you, thank you for my abundance' and picture everything that you are grateful for. Really feel a deep sense of gratitude.

I simply do not get out of bed until I feel a deep sense of gratitude. I don't wait to feel better, I just choose to focus on gratitude. And no matter how shitty your life might appear at the moment, don't get out of bed until you can feel gratitude.

Here is my mantra I say to myself every single morning, without fail, no matter what is going on in my life:

> *'Today I woke up from my sleep, millions around the world didn't. While I was sleeping, fifteen men in New Zealand died of cardiac arrest. Today I get another shot at the title, today I have another opportunity to be better, to do better, to be kind to myself, to be kind to those around me, thank you thank you thank you for another chance.'*

No matter how crappy I might feel when I wake up; maybe I didn't get enough sleep, maybe my old injuries are coming back to haunt me and are really killing me, maybe I am exhausted from working hard, maybe I have other life worries that we all have from time to time. Whatever the case may be, I just will not get out of bed until I can feel grateful for at least waking up! It's a choice that I make, and so can you!

As you move throughout your day, simply observe how you are feeling. Use whenever you catch yourself worrying and feeling anxious as a cue to *choose* to focus on what you are grateful for. Don't fight the anxious thoughts and feelings, don't try and stop them; notice them, accept them 'as is' *and* then *choose* to turn your attention over to what you are grateful for. If you have to do this hundreds of times a day, then you do it hundreds of times—it will probably be because you are thinking anxious thoughts hundreds of times a day.

Remember: Do not *resist* anxious thoughts and feelings, observe them, accept them, let them flow without judgment or resistance, and, with complete trust, CHOOSE to turn your attention over to thoughts of gratitude like 'Thank you for my children,' 'Thank you for my friends,' 'Thank you for my arms and legs' *and mean it.*

At least once a day, preferably in the morning, spend a minute or two jotting down in a journal all the things you are grateful for in your life. Do it every day. As you do this exercise you *must feel* the gratitude throughout your body.

Practice this more often than not: If, in a thirty-day period, you managed to write about gratitude in your journal for only twenty days, that's fine; you will still be tipping the balance.

Just before you nod off to sleep, while you are in a sleepy state, *choose* to feel grateful for everything in your life. Give thanks for everything. Picture all the things that you are grateful for—really feel the gratitude throughout your body.

And finally, use your powerful imagination to picture everything that you want in your life and give thanks for those things; really feel the gratitude for them—as if you had those things *now*. 'Thank you, thank you, thank you for my healing', 'thank you, thank you, thank you for my new job', 'thank you, thank you, thank you . . . (fill in the blank).'

The last thing you want to be doing when you fall asleep is to *choose* to worry about stuff that has no value at all. You have the power to *choose* where you direct your thoughts. So *choose* to accept and love yourself 'as is' and then turn your attention over to feelings of gratitude!

Get perspective. Seek out role models who are kicking ass in life, who can provide you with inspiration. If you look hard enough, you can always find inspirational people who have managed to overcome way more hardship and adversity (than what you are going through) to get to where they are today.

There is always someone worse off then you who has found a way to thrive. Find them, and use their stories to inspire you to do whatever it takes to heal yourself, starting with gratitude! If they can do it, if they can realize their dreams, then so can you!

Golden Rule 3: Finding Meaning

Dr Viktor Frankl, a psychiatrist who was imprisoned in the Nazi concentration camps during WWII became world famous for his work in *Man's search for meaning*, a book he wrote about his incarceration.

Dr Frankl observed that the difference between those who survived the horrid experience of their imprisonment and those who withered away and died came down to one's ability to develop a meaningful vision of the future, the ability for one to find some kind of meaning in their suffering.

Through his work and observations of others, along with his own suffering, Dr Frankl developed a revolutionary approach to psychotherapy called logotherapy (healing through meaning).

Irrespective of what tragedy or circumstances an individual faced, no matter how bad, no matter how helpless their situation may be, his or her ability to build a meaningful vision of the future, to find a meaning in their suffering, contributed towards whether or not he or she survived the atrocities of the concentration camp.

> *Forces beyond your control can take away everything you possess except for one thing, your freedom to choose how you respond to the situation. You cannot control what happens in your life, but you can always control what you will feel and do about what happens to you. We are never left with nothing as long as we retain the freedom to choose how we will respond.*
> (Dr Viktor E. Frankl)

Regardless of your circumstances, you have the ability to triumph over any tragedy, any predicament by finding a meaning for your suffering and focusing on a higher purpose, a meaningful vision of the future. Anxiety sufferers tend to focus their attention on fed-up and negative thoughts, asking questions like 'Poor me,' 'Why me?' 'If only . . .'

This will not serve you in the slightest. See your own suffering as your opportunity to learn, grow, contribute, and be more empathetic towards others. There is a deeper meaning in your suffering, in your own struggle. Discover that meaning and unlock the special gift that this experience holds for you.

You suffer and endure pain when training for a marathon, for example. You endure mental and physical challenges when you train and diet for months on end, for what only amounts to about five minutes of glory on stage at a body-building competition.

Why? The pain and suffering (means) has a meaning, a purpose, and you are willing to endure it because of your *belief* that it will be worthwhile in the end—the end justifies the means, you have a meaningful vision of the future.

The prisoners in the concentration camps imagined being back in the arms of their loved ones, and that was enough to endure their pain and suffering.

There is no longer any reason to despair; turn despair into meaning and triumph. You have a choice of how you interpret your situation. If the prisoners of the concentration camps can do it, then what's your excuse? Once you discover the meaning in your own suffering, you are able to transcend it.

I found meaning in my suffering. I am a natural leader, mentor, and coach. My purpose or dharma in life is to contribute to the success and well-being of others. I knew from a very young age that one day I would provide my own service that I would not only be an authority on, but a service which would allow me to achieve my dharma. Helping others heal themselves is the greatest gift and service that I could ever have imagined receiving.

There is nothing more satisfying and rewarding than helping others.

Without my experiences, without my own suffering, there is no way I would be where I am today. My effectiveness in helping others heal themselves is directly related to my ability to communicate and build relationships, principally because I have walked the walk—I've been there, done that, and I know what I'm talking about. I have so much more empathy and compassion towards others, thanks to my experiences.

I found meaning in my suffering when I realised it would lead to my life purpose, my dharma, and my dharma gave my future meaning.

You must find meaning in what you are going through today. You must change the way you see your suffering. You don't necessarily have to find a grandiose purpose in your suffering; it could be something as humble as wanting to become a stronger person, with more love and understanding towards yourself and others. Or maybe you want to help others like I do; in which case, your experiences will be invaluable for teaching others how to heal themselves.

> *'Sometimes in life you can't always choose to do what you love, but you can ALWAYS choose to love what you do.'*
> (Shaun Grant)

How to Implement Rule 3

Living with an anxiety condition can rob you of a meaningful vision of the future. High anxiety occupies all your thoughts, preventing you from thinking about a positive future, and when you do look into the future, all you see is more of what you are currently experiencing—suffering. You lose desire and vision.

- Find your purpose, find your dharma, and find a meaningful vision of your future. Have trust in the Building Blocks™ and yourself and reignite your desires, dreams, and goals;
- There is a meaning in your suffering; you have to find it;
- You have to do this work yourself. I cannot do it for you, apart from sharing my story with you to get you started;
- If you cannot do this, or are not willing to do this work, then you are still resisting;

- *If I can do it, if the prisoners in the concentration camps can do it, so can you;*
- Study and learn from the lives and stories of people who have overcome massive adversity and challenges and who have turned their lives around, who transcended their suffering and then went on to achieve success in their own right. These heroes will give you new perspective on your own challenges and inspire and motivate you to move forward and make the necessary changes in your own life to heal yourself, and maybe even one day you can help others as well, if that is something that you are into;
- None of these Golden Rules will happen automatically for you! You have to make a choice, no matter how shit you may feel, no matter how bad you think your life is to practice these rules, no matter what, through thick and thin, with discipline, routine and repetition; with no expectations for anything to change. It's your choice my friend!

Golden Rule 4, Diversion/Distraction

Charles Linden, one of my most respected teachers, who has helped hundreds of thousands of sufferers around the world heal themselves, calls Diversion the 'Holy Grail' in overcoming anxiety conditions, which is why Diversion and Distraction is Golden Rule 4.

Diverting your concentration on to a hobby, passion, or some other higher purpose is a powerful distraction tool. When you combine diversion with acceptance (love), gratitude, and meaning, your healing will be very rapid.

It makes sense that when you are fully engrossed in an activity that you love doing, when your present moment awareness is focused on your hobby, passion, or purpose, you are in a state of pleasure, and you get lost in the moment. This is a 'non-anxious' state, and your attention is diverted away from thinking anxiously.

Diversion gives your anxiety time to retreat as you are no longer preoccupied with it, no longer resisting. Diversion creates 'non-anxious' space in the mind. The longer you divert your mind onto your passion, for example, the longer you will experience a 'non-anxious' state.

If practiced and persisted with, this 'non-anxious' state, in combination with the other Golden Rules of course, will be accepted by the subconscious mind as normal; your brain will have been rewired with new 'non-anxious' behaviour, and the baseline anxiety levels stored and regulated in the amygdala will also be reset back down to 'normal'.

Laughter—The Natural Diversion
Humour helps you rise above the problem, helps you detach from the problem—see it from a distance, gives you a better perspective.
(Dr Viktor E. Frankl)

Laughter has been coined 'the natural diversion' for anxiety. It is a contagious emotion; it is free and has no negative side effects whatsoever. It is impossible to act anxiously when you are in a fit of laughter. Without going into too much detail, here are some of the benefits of laughing:

- Lowers blood pressure;
- Reduces stress hormones;
- Increases muscle flexion;
- Boosts immune function by raising levels of infection-fighting T-cells, disease-fighting proteins called Gamma-interferon, and B-cells which produce disease-destroying antibodies;
- Triggers the release of endorphins, the body's natural painkillers;
- Produces a general sense of well-being;
- Powerful antidote to stress;
- Cardiac exercise;
- Great for relationships;
- Enhances creativity.

*The ability to laugh at a situation or problem gives us
a feeling of superiority and power. Humour and laughter
can foster a positive and hopeful attitude. We are less
likely to succumb to feelings of depression and helplessness
if we are able to laugh at what is troubling us.
Humour gives us a sense of perspective on our problems.
Laughter provides an opportunity for the release of those
uncomfortable emotions which, if held inside, may create
biochemical changes that are harmful to the body.*
(Patty Wooten)

Make laughing your new workout, your new hobby. Make laughter part of your daily routine. Watch your favourite comedy shows, read and listen to whatever makes you laugh, and start a comedy collection and watch your favourite movies two to three times a week.

Get together with friends regularly and laugh, laugh, laugh. Learn to laugh at yourself; consciously *choose* to see the lighter side in everything. Even during tough times, it pays to see the lighter side of life as this puts you in a better state to deal with the situation or problem and helps the healing process.

Remember, laughter is 'the natural diversion'. So don't take yourself too seriously; be the first person to laugh at yourself. Adopt this attitude into your life, and you will destroy anxiety.

Laugh Therapy

If you haven't tried 'laugh therapy', give it a go now. It's very simple to do. Admittedly, the first time I tried it, I was a bit dubious, but I did it, and it was impossible not to laugh.

Try it yourself; the proof will be in the pudding. It's very simple. Here is how it works. To experience a 'deep belly' laugh, just start saying 'hoo hoo hoo, haa haa haa.'

I know this sounds ridiculous, and it is. That's why it works! Pretty soon, you will just start laughing uncontrollably, a 'deep belly' kind of laugh. I don't care how grumpy you might be at the time; you don't need a reason to start laughing, just do this exercise and you won't be able to help yourself.

If you feel silly doing this, then great, you will start laughing at yourself because you look silly and sound silly. Who cares, the important thing is that you are laughing.

Laugh at yourself in the mirror, while you are in the shower, while you're driving. Laugh with others. Find any opportunity to sit down and laugh.

Make laughter on a daily basis your new habit. When a very good friend separated from his wife, he downloaded funny movies and forced himself to watch them on a daily basis; this allowed him to divert his attention away from all the anxious thoughts and allowed him to get through the grieving process and heal rapidly.

This will be very hard to do at the start, especially for anxiety sufferers, but you must persevere, push through and practice. We are born to laugh; it is one of the most natural and easiest things to do. Laughter is the sound of music, it's infectious, and it is healing.

Participate in the idea of love and laughter every day. Throw your newspaper and magazines (unless they are really funny) away, stop reading about how terrible things are in the world. If you have an anxiety condition, reading bad news will only perpetuate your condition. Trust in the fact that if you need to know something really important, somehow, somewhere, someone will let you know.

Read only the stuff that will make you laugh, or that gets you inspired or excited. Read the sports page by all means if you love sport. If you love cars, read the auto section, and if you love property, then read the property section.

But, while you are building new non-anxious habits, stay away from anything in the news or media that is negative. There's no point at this time of adding negativity to your life.

Just practice a new habit, for now, of reading anything that inspires you, that you are passionate about, and, above all, that makes you laugh and feel love. Love and laughter are such easy paths to take when working on convincing your subconscious mind to adopt new non-anxious behaviour.

How to Implement Rule 4

- Find an activity that you are passionate about, that you can get inspired by or fully engrossed in. Let it absorb you. It has to draw all your attention. It must make you feel alive, in this moment;
- It could be a hobby like painting or photography, a life purpose like writing books, an activity of giving to others like volunteer work, anything that will take your mind off worrying and bring you into the present moment with feelings of joy, love, and excitement;
- My children and performing as a musician were powerful diversions for me;
- Turn your attention away from all the negativity in the world. Read only the stuff that inspires or motivates you, and above all, makes you laugh;
- Don't take yourself too seriously; be the first person to laugh at yourself. See the lighter side in everything you experience in your day. Laugh, laugh, laugh;
- Watch funny movies or your favourite comedy shows whenever you can;
- Practice laugh therapy for at least five minutes each day;

Golden Rule 5, Stop Worrying - Eliminating Intrusive Thoughts (Anticipatory Anxiety)

Nothing can disturb you but your own thoughts.
(Joseph Murphy)

Unwanted, anxious thoughts are a by-product of an anxiety condition; all efforts to try and control these intrusive thoughts and make them go will be fruitless. In fact, it will only give them more power, frustrating you further and creating even more intrusive 'what if', 'what's wrong', 'why me', 'I'll never be well again' thoughts.

Remember: Anxious thoughts are the 'effects' of an underlying anxiety condition (the 'cause'). Remove the 'cause', which you are learning to do through the Golden Rules, and the 'effects will also disappear overtime.

Unwanted thoughts can range from just about anything, from worries about health, loved ones, finances, your own abilities, even things that don't make any rational sense. At the height of an anxiety condition, these thoughts can become overpowering and obsessive and never ending. These thoughts maybe based around past experiences or may even border on the bizarre.

High anxiety is the catalyst for intrusive, worrying thoughts, and these worrying thoughts are maintaining your high anxiety levels. The sufferer is locked in an endless cycle of fear and doom.

So how do we deal with this horrible side effect of high anxiety? How do we deal with these intrusive worrying thoughts? We do nothing with them—that's right, nothing. Well, almost nothing. We are no longer going to try to control them or force them out; that is what you have been trying to do all this time to no avail. We are going to do something totally counter-intuitive to what you think you should do.

We are going to give in to them, stop trying to control them, give up all efforts to resist them, and take away their power over you. We are going to detach from them and let them run their course. This will be accomplished through an attitude of unconditional acceptance—Golden Rule 1.

By now, you will be fully aware that the meaning or interpretation you give to your thoughts determines whether they have any power over you. The more you accept everything in your life, your suffering, your journey, your intrusive thoughts, your sensations, the more your anxiety retreats. Your intrusive and worrying thoughts, which are a side effect of anxiety, *must* also retreat accordingly.

The more you stop resisting the ugly thoughts and accept them as part of high anxiety, that they are annoying but harmless, the less attention you give them. The less you focus on them, the less power they have over you.

Unconditional acceptance, not just as a thought, but as a feeling throughout your whole body towards the worrying and intrusive thoughts, renders them powerless.

Unconditionally accept your life as it is now. Where you are right now is exactly where you are meant to be. It can't possibly be any other way. What other choice do you have? There is no such thing as 'should've', 'could've', 'if only', there is only 'what is'.

It doesn't mean that you adopt a view of 'this is as good as it gets.' Your future is based on your thoughts, actions, and decisions that you make in the present moment. You can be, do, and have anything you want. But whatever it is that you want in the future will be determined by what and how you are thinking now.

> *You cannot harbor negativity ten hours a day and*
> *expect to bring about beautiful conditions.*
> (Charles Haanel)

So accept your life 'as is'. This attitude is not about giving up and inaction; quite the opposite, in fact. It's about accepting that things will happen that we don't necessarily want to happen, that some things are out of our control, but that we always have the conscious choice on how we react—acceptance puts you in a more positive state, opening the door for a more positive outlook and corresponding thoughts; our thoughts and actions right this very moment, determines our circumstances tomorrow.

How to Implement Rule 5

Implement Golden Rules 1 to 4. Acceptance, Gratitude, Meaning, and Diversion *will* remove your underlying anxiety. Remove the underlying anxiety, and you will remove the inappropriate worrying and intrusive thoughts.

RULE 5 Mantra

Below is a mantra I want you to start using whenever you are overcome with your anxious, intrusive or anticipatory worrying thoughts:

> *'Fuck it, so what. It is what it is right now, and whatever happens I will handle it, always have, always will. I am learning to love and accept myself exactly the way I am.'*

Then say *'Thank you thank you thank you for my abundance'* or *'What if I could learn to be grateful for my life right now?'* (in the morning you can replace this gratitude mantra with the mantra outlined in rule 2).

Choose to say this over and over again with absolute acceptance for what is. You will have to practice and practice this, it certainly will not come naturally at first. Choose to get up and move, doing something to distract you (rule 4), all the while reciting your mantra.

Your only job is to practice and practice this approach, and it applies no matter what you are doing when you are overcome with these intrusive thoughts, day and night; when you are doing the dishes, when you are in your car, when you wake up during the middle of the night, or first thing in the morning when you awake (used in conjunction with rule 2 mantra).

The Problem Solving Process – Interrupting the anxious feedback loop

We need to be able to slow down the onslaught of anxious and worrying thoughts before they spiral out of control.

If we can take a step back and separate ourselves from these initial anxious thoughts by noticing or observing them, even for just a fraction of a second, we can interrupt the cycle and give us an opportunity to consciously choose how we want to react or respond without being pushed and pulled from pillar to post with our anxious habitual behaviour and conditioned responses.

When we are overcome with worry or we are in a hot moment, we can forget to take a moment and consider our options of how we could respond. The Problem Solving Process allows us to do this.

There is nothing wrong with having anxious, worrying or fearful thoughts, they are perfectly normal and healthy, they are a call to action, a warning sign that there is a problem that you need to face and address.

We need to figure out whether there is good reason for why we are feeling anxious, or whether it is all 'white noise', a bi-product of underlying high anxiety. If it is real, then you do everything within your control to fix the problem. If the problem is in fact 'white noise', then you have the present moment power to choose your attitude, choose how you want to respond.

Work through the process outlined in Figure 2 below to drill down to the problem and root cause of your experience and then you can consciously choose how you wish to respond.

The Problem Solving Process below is pretty self explanatory to work through, however if you want more information on how to apply it, visit attackpanic.co.nz for tutorial videos on how to apply The Problem Solving Process.

Figure 2: The Problem Solving Process

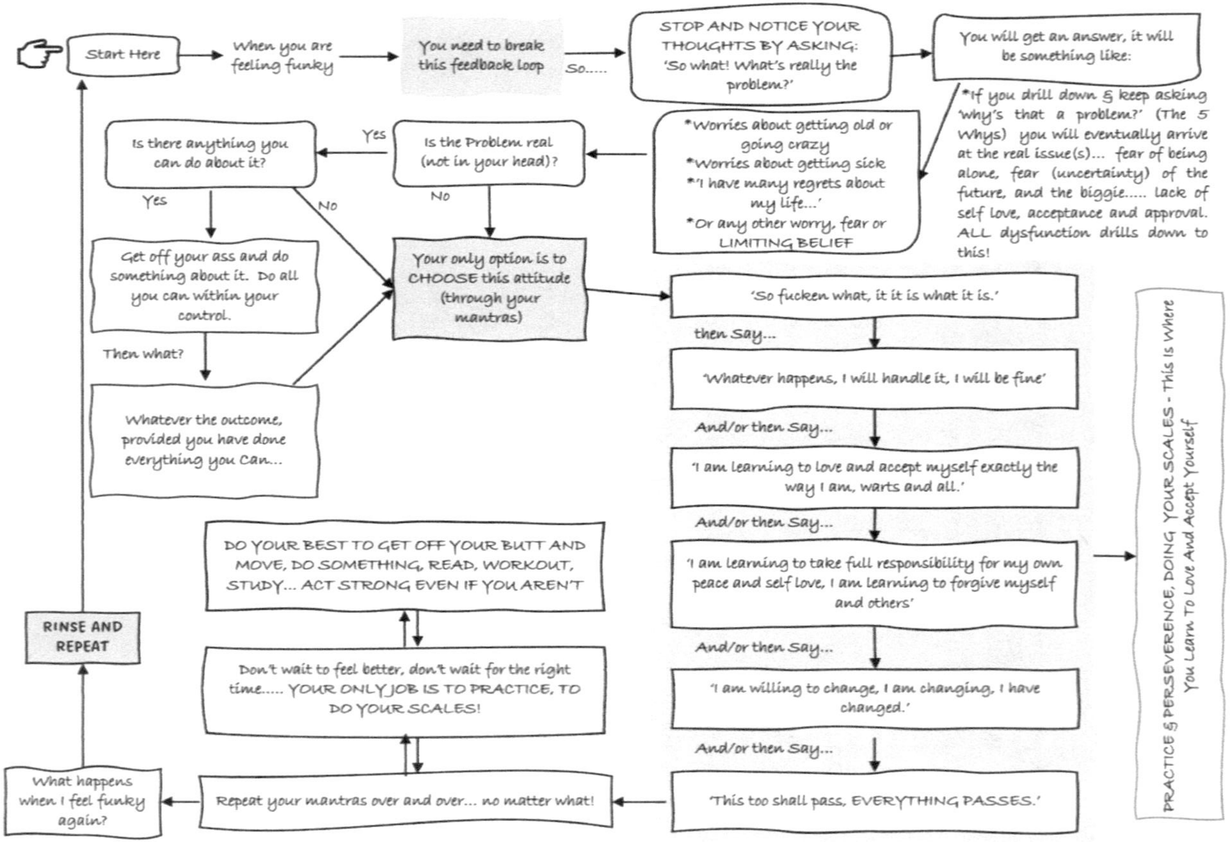

As I have mentioned in Chapter 6 (The Power of the Subconscious Mind), we are bundles of conditioned responses, reacting and responding to situations automatically based on our underlying beliefs and bias. The Problem Solving Process will allow you to break this feedback loop, bring your awareness to the actual problem or limiting belief, empowering you to consciously choose how you want to respond.

There is one other point I want to raise in Rule 5:
- Stop going to counselling or therapy. If conventional therapy and counselling worked, we would all be healed, and I wouldn't have wasted fifteen years of my life (although I'm not complaining now), and I wouldn't be writing this book. Why don't they work? Well, a few of the issues I have experienced are as follows:
  o They tend to drag up the past, the initial catalyst or trigger of your anxiety. Again all you are doing is fuelling your anxiety at the subconscious level, giving it more power. I'm not interested in the trigger; I'm interested in lowering your baseline level of anxiety. The only way you can do that is developing new non-anxious behaviour at the subconscious level. Remember, you fear the sensations, not the situation;
  o Therapy sessions make you feel really good when you are in session, but the minute you leave that safe environment, you invariably forget what you were supposed to do, and you need to go back to get pumped up again, and again;
  o They focus on addressing the sensations, the effects, not the cause (an underlying anxiety condition);
  o If the therapist or counsellor hasn't 'walked the walk', it will be difficult for them to 'talk the talk'. You believe me because I have been where you are. In fact, I have probably been to a much more destructive place than most of you. I healed myself completely. So 'I know that I know.' I truly understand where you are coming from and what you are going through. This develops a real connection with you, and you are more inclined to *believe* me;

- o Discussions at the rational and conscious level will never work. Resetting your baseline anxiety level in the amygdala can only be achieved through a change in behaviour at the subconscious level.

I discuss this further on page 115 (Is Therapy And Counselling The Answer?).

Golden Rule 6, Relax

When you are in a deeply relaxed state, you stop worrying; you are in the present moment, and you are calm; stress disappears and anxiety retreats. You can think and see with clarity of mind; you can see things (good and bad) in a more positive light.

This 'non-anxious' state is precisely what the mind and body needs in order to reduce anxiety levels and reprogramme the subconscious mind with new non-anxious behaviour.

The more you experience this state, the quicker you can remove the underlying anxiety condition and all the associated symptoms and sensations.

We *all* know intuitively that if we are stressed out, or overworked, we need to take time out to just chill out, 'recharge the batteries', so to speak. It is common knowledge that if you are stressed out and you don't take time out, sooner or later something has to give.

For an anxiety sufferer, deep relaxation is critical to your speedy recovery. For non-sufferers, deep relaxation is critical to reducing stress and reducing anxiety levels—preventing an anxiety condition.

We are all different, and what works for one may not work for the other; this has more to do with your level of trust and belief in a certain practice rather than the efficacy of the practice itself. You will need to find a way to allow your body and mind to completely relax, to lose yourself in the present moment, to slow the thinking down to give your mind and body the opportunity or 'space' to calm down.

The following are the relaxation techniques that I use and recommend:

Meditation

Meditation has many benefits, but specifically to you, meditation slows the mind and places you in a deep state of relaxation, just the thing that you need to allow your anxiety levels to retreat.

In my experience, not all meditation techniques are created equal, and there are many techniques available. I practice 'Transcendental Meditation' and find that it works just fine for me. I love it for its simplicity and profound effect it has on me.

Shop around and try various techniques; you'll find the one that's right for you.

Guided Visualisation Exercises

Visualisation exercises are very very powerful. When done properly, these exercises have the ability of placing your conscious mind in a deeply relaxed state. Once the conscious mind is out of the way, the subconscious mind is susceptible to any suggestions that you give it.

Whatever you visualise (or suggest) in this state, the subconscious mind has no choice but to accept. This is the fast track to getting whatever it is that you want.

You can download my free visualisation exercise audio files specifically developed for anxiety sufferers from my website (attackpanic.co.nz).

Self-Hypnosis/Hypnotherapy

See Visualisation Exercises above; they are one and the same.

Deep Breathing

See my discussion on deep breathing in BB2.

Nature

At least once a day, or whenever you possibly can, get outside and reconnect with nature. Go for a bushwalk, spend time in a garden, or take a stroll along the beach. Spend at least 10-15 minutes each day in nature.

On a clear night, spend at least ten minutes gazing up in wonder at our magnificent universe. Feel the connection, the serenity, and the gratitude for our wonderful universe.

While spending time in nature, practice your deep breathing exercise. *Choose* to focus your attention on acceptance and gratitude. This includes accepting any intrusive or worrying thoughts; just let them do their thing without attachment.

There are, of course, many other relaxation techniques out there such as yoga, tai chi, EFT or meridian tapping, and passive relaxation (reading, listening to music—not watching TV).

Experiment with what works for you. Take your time. Don't be in too much of a rush; you have the rest of your life ahead of you. Just maintain trust that you will find the right technique for you.

How to Implement Rule 6

I still practice deep breathing every day through a structured routine, or whenever the thought comes into my mind. It's easy to do anywhere, and I experience a wonderfully relaxed state. I also continue to meditate once a day, and I use visualisation exercises for everything that I want to manifest into my life.

Go to my web site and download the free visualisation exercise audio files, specifically developed for anxiety sufferers. Using headphones, listen to the exercise at least once a day, preferably in the morning.

Find a quiet comfortable place, where you will not be disturbed for about 12 minutes and listen to the exercise. Do this for at least one month.

Find a meditation technique that works for you, and meditate at least once a day.

Perform the deep breathing exercise from BB2 as many times as you like throughout your day.

Spend time in nature every day.

What's important is that you practice the above exercises more often than not. If you forget to do the meditations and visualisations for a day or two, don't beat yourself up. Just make sure you do them consistently.

If you can't manage to meditate and do the visualisation exercises on the same day, that's fine, but make sure that you do at least one of them each day.

If you can implement this rule into your daily life on a consistent basis, you will experience a dramatic reduction in your anxiety levels and speed up your recovery.

Practice and persevere. Be kind to yourself when things don't seem to be working. Have trust and keep going.

Summary of The Golden Rules (BB4)

Rule 1: Acceptance
Rule 2: Gratitude
Rule 3: Finding Meaning

Rule 4: Diversion/Distraction
Rule 5: Stop Worrying—Eliminating Intrusive Thoughts (Anticipatory Anxiety)
Rule 6: Relax

Don't be fooled by the apparent simplicity and obvious nature of the above rules. Of course, the solution is simple, it's just hard to implement at the start because we are all creatures of habit, and generally, we are resistant to change. Our old habits are going to be fighting for survival, and they will be hard to break.

1 x Golden Rule Per Day

For the next four weeks, as part of your daily structure and routine, read 1 x Golden Rule each day. Start with Golden Rule 1 on Monday, Golden Rule 2 on Tuesday and so on. Sunday can be a day off.

How to start

The most important thing here is to get started with Golden Rules 1 & 2. Just focus on practicing and persevering with these two rules first. The best way is to develop discipline around a daily routine. I provide more support and advice on how to do this in the next chapter (Taking Action).

After a while, your attitude towards the future will change, you will start seeing a brighter future. This is Golden Rule 3 (Finding Meaning). It will happen automatically when you implement Golden Rules 1 & 2 and make them part of your daily attitude and life.

Golden Rules 1 & 2 will allow worrying thoughts to come and go without attachment, allowing you to focus your attention on other stuff, preventing you from getting stuck on dwelling on your negative thoughts. This will help you implement Golden Rule 4 (Diversion/Distraction).

The Daily Planner is also a powerful tool that you can implement to further divert your attention onto things and activities that you need to do during the day, especially things that you plan to do that inspire or nurture you. The planner is a very powerful diversion tool, and when used in conjunction with your new attitude of acceptance and gratitude, your anticipatory anxiety or intrusive thoughts (Golden Rule 5) will also be eliminated. I discuss the Daily Planner in more detail on page 251.

Golden Rule 6 (Relaxation) is just something that everyone should be implementing throughout their day, whether they have an anxiety condition or not. It's just good for you.

CHAPTER 9

TAKING ACTION

When it comes to integrating the Golden Rules into your daily life, there is no such thing as 'one shoe or size fits all.' We are all different; what works for me may not work for you. You will need to find out when and what works best for you. No one else can do it for you.

Having said that, there are a few things you *will* need to do and understand in order to be successful at making the Golden Rules a part of your life. Here are some very important tools that you should use to provide structure, discipline and routine around your practice.

How to Get Started

- Fully understand the principles of habituation, in particular Practice, Perseverance, Exposure, and Setbacks.
- Fully understand the power of your subconscious mind.
- For the next four weeks, read 1 x Golden Rule each day (Sunday is a free day).

BB3: Dealing with Panic Attacks and Phobias

Review The Panic Attack Eliminator (BB3) over and over again until you absolutely know exactly what you have to do and why.

Make sure that you have your mantra sorted. This is so, so important. That mantra must comply with steps 2-4 of the Panic Attack Eliminator. In short, your mantra must be based on an attitude of not giving a shit, and being ok with not being ok, giving yourself permission to panic:

- Being prepared to accept whatever happens – because whatever happens, nothing will happen!

You can use one of my mantras or you can create your own. Why is this important? In a hot moment, you haven't got a hope in hell of remembering steps 2-4, and trying to recall them at this time will just cause you more frustration and anxiety, adding fuel to the panic cycle. A simple mantra for you to recall, which will remind you of the correct attitude, or which will trigger the right attitude is all you need.

You must also know the answers to the five questions (page 169) so you are aware of your false beliefs that you need to challenge and turn your back on.

I then want you to plan how you are going to take care of yourself when you go and confront your hot moment. By that I mean practice your mantra until it is ingrained into your mind. So, when the shit hits the fan, you don't start searching for what to do, you will know what to do. You just start repeating your mantra, with the correct attitude! This certainly doesn't mean that you plan how you are going to escape when things get too hot, or what strategies you are going to use in order to cope.

Then step up to the plate and start swinging, start practicing your new attitude. The outcome is not important. What is important is that you take a swing, that you are willing to experience whatever outcome:

- If it is a bad outcome, ask yourself what you are doing wrong? I guarantee that the problem will be a resistant and fearful attitude. Learn from your experience, and step back up to the plate and have another swing;

- Keep practicing. You may have successes and failures, learn from them and keep moving forward;
- Remember: Disempowering panic attacks is one thing. It doesn't mean that you have stopped the habitual sensations and thoughts from turning up as part of an underlying pattern of behavior (BB4 will help you to remove this underlying pattern of behaviour). The important thing here is that you now know that you can turn off the panic button;
- Whether the experience is good or bad, take time out to contemplate on what happened. Use the Journal (see page 186) to organize your thoughts. Analyse what you did, and what you 'could have' done differently. Applying the lessons learned, promise to get back out there, step up to the plate and have another swing.

Also Remember: Your only job is to practice the correct attitude in the moment and that is giving yourself permission to panic. Of course, this is a mental game, but this is the only way to remove the conscious resistance and fear towards your sensations, and it is your conscious reaction to the initial sensations that determine whether or not they spiral out of control.

BB4: Removing the underlying anxiety condition (GAD, PTSD, OCD) – Implementing the Golden Rules

I want you to say to yourself - 'I am learning to love and accept myself exactly the way I am.' Do this without expectation of anything changing. Just practice saying it. Write it out on post it notes to remind you to say it at the start. Whenever you are reminded, just say it, in your mind or out loud, as many times as you can until that idea leaves your mind and you start focusing on something else. Just say it when you are reminded to, whether you are prompted by post it notes or the thought just pops up. This practice is not conditional to whether you are feeling good or bad…. it is just a habit of thought that you are developing.

Every morning and every evening do your mirror work (page 205). Now you may find this piece of work hard at the start, you may even feel a bit silly! That's ok, JUST DO IT!

The other thing I want you to practice saying is 'thank you thank you thank you!' When you practice this, use your conscious choice making ability to think of all the things you are grateful for. No matter how good or bad you think you have it, there are always heaps of things that you ought to be grateful for right here, right now!

Again, practice whenever you are reminded to do this throughout your day, write 'thank you thank you thank you' out on post it notes and stick them all around the place at the start to remind you to practice!

Now, before you get out of bed in the morning, and before you go to sleep in the evening, I want you to be thinking about how grateful you are…. so lay there just as you are waking and just as you are nodding off and say, 'thank you thank you thank you', and think about all the things that you are grateful for! Your only job is to practice, not look for or expect any change aye? Just practice. After a while, with practice, you will be able to focus your concentration on long periods of acceptance and gratitude

Below is my gratitude mantra that I say to myself every morning before I get out of bed, and also what I write in my journal each and every day (well most days anyway):

> *'Today I woke up from my sleep, millions around the world didn't. While I was sleeping, fifteen men in New Zealand died of cardiac arrest. Today I get another shot at the title, today I have another opportunity to be better, to do better, to be kind to myself, to be kind to those around me, thank you thank you thank you for another chance.'*

When you notice good periods throughout your day, bask in that moment, for it will pass. Remind yourself to contemplate on gratitude for this moment, and all the things you are grateful for. You have the conscious choice making ability to do this. This period will fade away, and that is ok, but it will return, and when it does, practice gratitude again!

When you notice bad periods during your day, this is the time to PRACTICE your MANTRA grounded in ACCEPTANCE for what it is right this very moment.... without any expectation for anything to change; your only job is to just practice your mantra! No more running, no more safety crutches or coping strategies, just a conscious choice to not give a shit, to being ok with not being ok. Don't look for any change, be willing to be here, now, with whatever is going on. But you now know that this bad period will also move on and fade away!

Here is the mantra that I want you to repeat to yourself when you are experiencing your intrusive, worrying and anticipatory thoughts:

> *'Fuck it, so what. It is what it is right now, and whatever happens I will handle it, always have, always will. I am learning to love and accept myself exactly the way I am.'*

Move forward and as best you can focus on your task at hand.... BETTER STILL, CHOOSE TO DO SOMETHING THAT MAKES YOU FEEL GOOD, OR THAT SERVES OTHERS!!! With the correct use of acceptance, the bad periods will fade faster than if you tried to stop the sensations or run from them. They will come back of course, just like good periods, cool, this is your opportunity to practice again, and again, and again.

Do your breathing exercise as many times as you are reminded to do throughout your day. Just five reps at a time.... or more if you can! This is good shit. Again, don't expect or look for any change, just do it because it feels good at the time.

Whenever you are reminded, by whatever means (this includes when you find yourself feeling anxious) practice your acceptance and gratitude mantra and breathing. You don't have to wait for the right time to begin practicing your mantras and breathing. There is never a right time, there is only now! Don't wait to feel better, don't wait until you get another job, or any other reason that you can make up.

Good periods and bad periods will flow in and out like the tide. Practice your gratitude mantra when things are going well, practice your acceptance and gratitude mantra when things aren't going well.

The Daily Planner

The Daily Planner is a very important tool in developing discipline around practicing and persevering with your new, non-anxious routine, day in, day out. This is the 'how to' bit that you have been missing. Discipline, routine and practice is how you learn to do anything, and relearning to be a non-anxious person again is no exception.

So use the Daily Planner to block out periods where you will practice and implement all of the Golden Rules:

- When are you going to meditate or do the visualisation exercises?;
- When are you going to spend time in nature?;
- Even enter your morning and evening affirmations of acceptance and gratitude that you must do when you wake;
- Even plan your laugh therapy sessions;
- When are you going to work, eat, hang out with family or friends, or complete your chores?;
- When are you going to set time aside during the day for your hobby, passion or higher purpose?;
- When are you going to do your concentration exercise?;
- When are you going to do your deep breathing exercise?;
- When are you going to read your 1 X Golden Rule for the day?

Fill your planner in with everything you intend to do in your day—and do it. Fill your whole day with activity around your Golden Rules:

- Filling up your day with activities is an excellent way of diverting or distracting your mind away from paying too much attention to worrying and intrusive thoughts;
- When you are busy and focused on an activity, you are in the present moment and your attention is diverted away from worry.

Always plan ahead by filling out your daily planner the night before. I urge you to not plan your day on the same day. You will most likely get distracted and end up not doing your planning until half way through the morning; in which case you have just missed half your day. This will probably make you frustrated, and more anxious:

- Plan your day, get moving and take action, no matter how big or small. Focus on what needs to be done today. Do your best to complete all the tasks that you have entered into your planner. Move what you don't complete over to the next day or delete it if the task no longer applies.

Whatever the task is, big or small, place your full attention on it, get in the moment and complete the task to the best of your abilities. Don't worry about the next task, focus your attention on what you are doing in that moment - this is a powerful diversion tool:

- However, other things will surely crop up, and sometimes you won't be able to stick to the plan. Accept whatever happens and move on. Just do your best, and remember, as long as you follow your planner, more often than not, you will win.

Be kind to yourself, don't beat yourself up if you struggle with this at the start. If you haven't done this before, you probably will struggle at the start. Just keep practicing, and with perseverance, this will become a powerful habit.

My Daily Planner

Figure 3 below is an example of how I plan my day. Feel free to use this as a template to get you started. This is pretty much my routine that I have been practicing every single day (well, by that I mean more often than not) for nearly 14 years now.

Figure 3: My Daily Planner

		DAILY PLANNER
Date:	Name:	Daily Rituals
		MR - Morning Rituals: (see Explanation Notes) -
		1. Deep Breathing
5am		2. Gratitude Mantra
	MR	3. Self Love and acceptance Mantra
6am		4. Mirror Work
	Walk, run, exercise	5. Visualisation Exercise (audio file)
7am		AR - Afternoon Rituals: (see Explanation Notes) -
		1. Deep Breathing
8am		2. Gratitude Mantra
		3. Self Love and acceptance mantra
9am	5 min Exposure exercise (see email explanation notes)	4. Mirror work
		5. Meaningful Vision of the future Visualisation
10am		ER - Evening Rituals Prior to Bed (see Explanation Notes) -
		1. Mirror Work
11am		2. Breathing Exercises
		3. Gratitude Mantra
12pm	AR	4. Self Love and acceptance mantra
	5 min Exposure exercise (see email explanation notes)	5. Meaningful Vision of the future Visualisation
1pm		6. Visualisation Exercise (audio file)
2pm		
		Taking Action Towards Vision of The Future -
3pm	5 min Exposure exercise (see email explanation notes)	1. From your meaningful vision of the future, chunk your vision down into bite sized tasks into a list
4pm		2. Prioritise your list of tasks into an action plan
		3. Enter your prioritised tasks into this planner and 'get it done.' No matter what is happening, however you are feeling, take action!!
5pm	Acknowledgement (see email explanation notes)	
		Distraction -
6pm		1. Find stuff you love to do, or figure out what you can do for someone else.
	5 min Exposure exercise (see email explanation notes)	
7pm		2. Block out times during the day when you are going to take massive action!
8pm		Set Your Watch To Chime Every Hour -
		1. Every hour, on the hour, start practicing this process... it should only take a few minutes.
9pm	5 min Exposure exercise (see email explanation notes)	
		- Breathing Exercise (x 10)
10pm		- Thank you thank you thank you for my abundance (x 10)
		- I love and accept myself unconditionally, exactly the way I am, right here, right now (x 10)
11pm	ER	
		- Mirror Work - If you can get to a mirror, if not, no biggie
12am		- Remember, JUST DO IT, practice practice practice
		READ, READ, READ (See Explanation Notes)

Figure 4: Daily Planner Explanation Notes

MR – Morning Rituals
Don't get out of bed until: - You have done 10 x deep breaths (See pages 161 on Deep Breathing). - You have said 'thank you thank you thank you for my abundance (think about all the things you ought to be grateful for)' for at least two minutes… it doesn't matter whether you drift off into other thoughts, that's fine, when you notice you have drifted off, focus your attention back onto gratitude (See rule 2 for my morning gratitude mantra). - Do not get out of bed until you are grateful for waking up today, millions around the world didn't, you have another shot at the title, another opportunity to do/be better. - Now focus on 'I am learning to love and accept myself exactly the way I am.' Say this at least 10 times. - Maintain Deep breathing throughout… Do your mirror work as per normal. **Visualisation Exercise** Use the short version in the morning… (visit attackpanic.co.nz to download free audio file)
AR – Afternoon Rituals
Rinse and repeat MR. ***Meaningful Vision Of The Future.*** - Think of something that you want to do in the future, in your case it might be just being yourself again, or going back to work or helping others. - You must see yourself doing that thing, don't worry about all the negatives that this vision will be bringing up, you can expect this so it's no big deal, this is only an exercise so it shouldn't be a biggie. - What are some of the other traits, conditions, things you need to have/do in order to get you to that place or thing? - Now, see yourself being that person, see yourself doing all those things that you need to do… see yourself having/doing the goal/vision - When you are visualising your meaningful vision of the future, repeat 'thank you thank you thank you for my abundance.' - Anything can be achieved when we are willing to chunk whatever it is that we want down and take consistent action on a daily basis… NO MATTER WHAT IT IS, BIG OR SMALL!!

ER – Evening Rituals (before bed)

Rinse and repeat MR

Visualisation Exercise.

Use the long version in the evenings.. (visit attackpanic.co.nz to download free audio file)

Whenever You Are Reminded During The Day

Whenever you are reminded too, whether you are feeling good or bad, say to yourself this following mantra - **'I am learning to love and accept myself exactly the way I am, thank you thank you thank you for my abundance.'** Say this 5-10 times, and then get on with your day.

Your mind will most likely drift off, that's fine, let it, accept it and move on. Rinse and repeat whenever you are reminded to repeat this mantra.

You can CHOOSE to say this no matter how you are feeling. As you are saying thank you thank you thank you.... Think of your vision of the future.

Acknowledging

Sit down and contemplate on all your achievements. Write down at least 15 achievements that you can be proud of, if you can think of more, fine write them down. Now spend 10 minutes (I have scheduled this for 5pm, but you can fit it in wherever you want) thinking about this list, and pat yourself on the back, really feel the sense of achievement, feel proud, you deserve it!

Remember your mind will wonder off from time to time. You can't stop this, so whenever you have noticed that you have drifted off somewhere else, gently bring yourself back to that list.

Use your 'thank you thank you thank you for my abundance' mantra.

Read, read, read

Get some new perspectives, go and read biographies, auto-biographies of some amazing people who have overcome far worse than what you and I have had to endure. Get inspiration, perspective from them.

Read and learn more about our mind, our universe. Open your mind, challenge your beliefs, challenge your point of view, really delve into why you think a certain way. Read, read, read. Don't read anymore about anxiety conditions, you are now an expert, so there is nothing else to know.

> Below are some suggested readings:
> 1. Viktor Frankl - Man's search for meaning
> 2. Louise Hay - You can heal yourself
> 3. Eckhart Tolle - The Power of Now & A New Earth
> 4. Joseph Murphy - The Power of your subconscious mind
> 5. John Kehoe - Mind Powers
> 6. Napoleon Hill - Think and grow rich
> 7. Tich Nhat Hanh - Living Buddha living christ
> 8. Ryan Holiday - The obstacle is the way
> 9. Johann Hari - Lost Connections
> 10. Dr Reid Wilson - Don't Panic
> 11. Dr Harry Barry - Anxiety & Panic
> 12. Mark Manson - The subtle art of not giving a F*ck

Breathe

Don't forget to practice deep breathing, whenever you are reminded to. It's free, there are no side effects, and it is good for you in so many ways. You can do this anywhere, anytime.

Chime Watch

Maybe even invest in a watch that can chime on the hour, and use this to remind you to breath deeply, and practice acceptance and gratitude..... and keep practicing until other thoughts occupy your mind.

Your only Job

Remember, your only job is to start practicing acceptance and gratitude CORRECTLY, it is not to do anything else; especially to try and stop your sensations and intrusive thoughts! That's what you have been trying to do for years probably without success, now it is time to do the exact opposite.

So this means that you may or may not feel even more anxious and overwhelmed at the start. And this is perfectly normal because you are new at this game, therefore you will probably suck at it! You may be focusing on your sensations and thoughts more now, which means you will probably get more of what you focus on. So, you may find yourself fumbling around a bit, not really sure of whether you are doing the right thing or not, and whether this stuff will actually work, hoping like hell that this stuff works. But just keep practicing the CORRECT use of acceptance with trust and courage.

Remember, your job is NOT to stop your anxious thoughts and sensations, especially if they are turning up automatically at the moment as a side effect of an underlying anxiety condition, or even as a result of just being highly stressed for whatever reason! Your job is to just start practicing not giving a shit! There's nothing you can do about them yet anyway, they will turn up whenever they turn up, but they will also fade away too. Your non-resistant accepting attitude will allow them to fade quicker!

Just keep practicing being ok with not being ok!! Some days you might feel good about it, some days you might not, but you are not trying to control this, you can't, and you don't have to, all you need to do is practice in this moment not giving a shit and accepting whatever happens. This attitude will allow you to pass through the anxious thoughts and sensations quickly.

You will then be free in the moment to direct your focus on whatever you want. For me, I always choose no matter what is going on around me to breath, and focus on gratitude and unconditional love and acceptance, here, now. You can choose to focus on whatever you want that inspires and lifts you!

Now the anxious thoughts and sensations will still be cropping up from out of nowhere, and you will still be feeling a bit nervous, but this will not come as any surprise to you now, even at this early stage of the programme. But I reiterate, it is irrelevant what and when they pop up, as you have the conscious power in the moment of how you want to react.

If you react with the correct attitude of acceptance and gratitude, the initial sensations and/or thoughts will not amount to anything - every single time.

The power is in this very moment. You no longer have to worry about the next bout of sensations and thoughts turning up, as you know that they will surely arrive sooner or later, but you also know that you don't have to stop them or get rid of them.

With the correct use of acceptance, they will fade away as fast as they appeared! You will then notice other non-anxious thoughts. Remember to bask in these moments with gratitude and acceptance. When you notice anxious thoughts streaming in again, practice letting them be, practice giving them permission to exist through the correct use of acceptance and gratitude - using your mantras!

Do this every single time. This is a conscious choice that you can make in the moment. The correct use of acceptance will take away all the resistance, fear and anticipation; the very fuel that anxiety needs in the moment to thrive. This attitude won't take away or stop the initial anxious thoughts, but it doesn't matter. What it will do however is completely disempower the panic cycle!

Go back and review The Problem Solving Process (page 236).

When Will I get Better?

The answer to this question is it doesn't matter when or even if you get better! Well, that has to be your attitude at least. Let me explain.

I'm guessing that to date, everything you are doing is based around trying to stop your anxious thoughts and sensations, trying to push them aside. Practicing being ok with not being ok is all you are to do. It is pointless to try and push them out. You have been doing that for years and it hasn't worked. When you stop resisting, they will fade away of their own accord.

Unconditional love and acceptance is about embracing and being at peace with you, warts and all exactly the way you are, here, now! It is as much about not resisting 'what is', not wishing, hoping you were somewhere else. It's also about loving and accepting your obstacles, your suffering, your challenges. Your anxiety is 'what is' for you at this moment. This is your journey and accepting this right now is part the deal, it's part of the healing process.

'Ok, so I am having a shit day, I'm ok with that, I accept that', and then get on with your day or task as best as you can. This means that you stop wanting to be healed, wishing you were healed! Accept who you are right now, 100%. Don't wish, want or try to be anything else!

All you are doing here of course is practicing being a non-anxious person, of course your future desired state is to be anxiety free, but you get there by practicing being non-anxious in this moment without expectation to be any different.

Maybe you will be well again soon, maybe you won't. Whatever the case your attitude is – 'So what!' You are not giving up, you are simply letting go of any fearful and resistant attitude that keeps adding fuel to the fire.

So here, now, in the moment you no longer need to concern yourself with when, how, or even if you will get better, you can now let go of all the hoping and longing to be well in the future. With the correct attitude you can be just fine, right now, in any given moment. Whether you get better, whether you don't, your attitude must be 'Fuck it, so what, whatever happens I will handle it!'

Remember Acceptance and Gratitude (Golden Rules 1 & 2) will not change anything in the 'now', but neither will *choosing* to allow yourself to be constantly stuck in a negative and anxious state. These two opposing attitudes will result in correspondingly different state of minds, actions and results.

So while I believe it is very important to have goals, or as Viktor Frankl would say, 'a meaningful vision of the future', it's also important that we accept what is in this very moment 100%. That means accepting who you are, loving yourself exactly the way you are now! That means everything about you…… including your anxious habitual behaviour.

Maybe you will get better, maybe you won't. You should most definitely ALWAYS have that vision. Maybe you will be 'normal' again next week, next month, next year! But whatever the case, learn to love and accept yourself, here, now!

Remove any and all expectation and hope of being well. Expectation and hope used for the wrong reasons can cause frustration, disappointment, dis-illusion, resulting in perceived setbacks. This mindset is based on fear and resistance.

Be sure that if you do have an expectation, it is not born out of desperation and fear, for that will surely slow down the process of healing.

Your ONLY job, day in and day out is to practice 'being ok with not being ok', giving yourself permission to be anxious! Take positive action on what you can control 'now', and accept everything else that has popped up today that you cannot control. *Choose* to be grateful, *choose* to look for things in your life to be grateful for. *Choose* to do things that support and nourish you when you can.

Use Only One Method

There are many programmes out there that may work. But whatever method you use, stick with it; do not try and implement more than one method. It just confuses the subconscious, and you will end up even more anxious.

I know my Building Blocks™ work because I healed myself, and I am healing others. All the healing principles contained in my Building

Blocks™ are the same rules that *all* ex-anxiety sufferers used to destroy their condition.

The main thing is that you get well so that you can live the life that you naturally deserve, whether it's through my method or someone else's. Just choose *one* only and go for it.

Dealing With Family & Friends

If you choose to tell friends and family about what you are going through (some sufferers won't want to discuss their suffering), knowing how to talk to them, and what to focus on when you are discussing your condition, along with instructions for them on how you want them to treat you, is what we are going to discuss here.

And just like there is the right and wrong way to practice the attitude of acceptance, there is also the right and wrong way in seeking support from family and friends.

The wrong Support

Friends and family, who have your best interests at heart, will naturally want to sympathise with you, thinking that they are doing the right thing. However, this is exactly what you *have* to avoid. Sympathy is the wrong kind of support you need; it is the breeding ground for anxiety. Sympathy will have the same effect as therapy and counselling. It will make you feel better, but it won't make you better!

When you have a sympathetic ear, you tend to talk about the effects of your condition; the intrusive thoughts, negative emotions, how it's affecting your life, how it's ruining your life, why me, if only (you know, the usual suspects), but never the actual the cause of your condition (underlying high anxiety). Spending time talking about this stuff just makes you focus more on the ugly sensations and thoughts, and all you are doing here is strengthening your condition.

- Your own experience will validate this.

The more you talk about your anxiety condition in this way while you're healing yourself, the more you give it power. All the anxious emotions and memories will come flooding up to the surface, and all that will do is activate an anxious response. It's a vicious feedback loop; the more you talk about it, the more power you give it.

The other wrong type of support that family and friends can give you, as well meaning as they maybe is advice like "harden up," "mind over matter," "it's all in the mind," "just get over it."

While there might be some truth in that advice, it is completely the wrong thing to say to you the sufferer. You're already well aware that it's all in the head, and that it's mind over matter. However, this advice coming from a non-sufferer just makes you feel even worse and inadequate.

The Right Support

The right type of support is reassurance and encouragement. What you want your friends and family to do is to provide reassuring and encouraging support whilst you are practicing your new attitude, practicing your new behaviour. Reassurance is completely different from giving advice, and it's certainly not sympathizing.

For those friends and family members that you do want to discuss your anxiety with, I want you to follow this approach:

Be ok with bringing it out into the open

This is an important step towards your healing. You are now learning (or re-learning) to unconditionally love and accept yourself, warts and all, as is, right here, right now. And not being ashamed of who you are, right here, right now is a big part of the deal.

Fronting up and letting family and friends know what you are going through is an important step towards your healing! This may or may not be a hard thing to do, you may be worried about feeling embarrassed perhaps if your family and friends see you in difficulty and maybe even judging you!

Who gives a shit!

No really, who gives a shit! That must be your new attitude as you begin your journey of healing. To help you with this, let's put a few things into perspective:

- You have nothing more than a bad habit; you have taught yourself to be anxious at inappropriate times. It's nothing more than a learnt pattern of behaviour, that you can unlearn!;
- No one is completely squared away. We are all having to deal with our own challenges or issues from time to time. We all have good days and shitty days! Keep your suffering in perspective;
- There is always someone worse off than you who has managed to transcend their own adversity or suffering.

So, when you're in a situation with family and friends and you are having difficulty, don't be embarrassed, love yourself unconditionally. It is what it is. Be committed to your practice, be committed to your new attitude. Remember, we are all fighting our own wee demons to some extent.

Tell your Friends and family what's going on

In your own words, explain to family and friends that you have an anxiety condition, a learnt pattern of behaviour that you are now addressing through a structured programme, and that you are on the road to recovery, and you are taking steps to develop new non-anxious behaviour, and you do need their support, but the right support.

Give them instructions

The right support therefore is what they say to you and how they treat you. Let them know that:

- You do not want them to mollycoddle you;
- You certainly don't want any sympathy;
- You do not want them to treat you any different;
- You want to get on with your practice, so you will no doubt have periods of difficulty. If they notice you having difficulty, let them know you don't need them to ask if you are ok, because you won't be! But that's okay;
- You don't need them to point that out. You don't point out their problems, so you don't want them to point out yours;
- You want them to reassure you that you are doing a great job. Instruct them to say things like "You can do this," "no matter what happens, you're going to be fine," "you're doing a great job," "this too shall pass" "Feel the fear and do it anyway";
- This is the sort of reassuring and encouraging support you need from them;
- Even if they can see that you're having difficulty, you don't want to be treated any different; just tell them to get on with the task at hand and stop asking if you're okay;
- Most importantly, instruct them to stop giving you advice. Their advice, as well meaning as it may be, will be completely counterproductive; it will just make you feel bad, because it'll come across as quite condescending.

CHAPTER 10

FINAL THOUGHTS

The answers to ending your suffering are contained in this book. There is no doubt, no argument. The question is, do you believe it? Do you have trust in the Building Blocks™ or don't you? The answer to this will depend on whether I have been able to connect with you through my own journey of suffering, discovery, and healing.

The information contained within the Building Blocks™ is nothing new. The healing principles are the same principles that all ex-sufferers have used to heal themselves and all successful teachers use to heal others.

Is this book going to spell the end to your searching for an answer, or will it just end up on the pile of all the other 'how to' books? Decide to do this or not; there is no in-between. If you do decide to go for it, do not look back; burn all your bridges and commit to doing whatever it takes to end your suffering. Practice and persevere with the Building Blocks™, no matter what setbacks and challenges are presented to you.

Build discipline around your daily routine. Use the tools that I have taught you in BB3 & 4, especially The Panic Attack Eliminator, your mantras, The Problem Solving Process, The Journal and the Daily Planner.

There is no magic bullet or 'secret sauce' that is going to miraculously take away your anxiety condition. As you are well aware by now, you developed your anxiety condition through behaviour overtime, and only behaviour overtime can make you better. Having said that, if there were only two things that you could take away from this book and adopt into your life, it would be the following:

- Become Aware: Before you react to your initial anxious sensations with fear and resistance, before your fears spiral out of control, step back just for a moment and be 'aware'. Notice, observe that you are about to react in your normal fearful way, and interrupt this feedback loop by asking 'what's the problem here?' Use the Problem Solving Process to answer the question.

  No matter how shit you feel, no matter how you are about to habitually react, you always have the present moment ability to choose how you want to respond, you can make this choice in the moment, and being aware and asking the question interrupts your normal habitual destructive pattern just enough to empower you to choose how you want to consciously respond.

  You don't have to react with fear, with resistance, you can be aware, interrupt your anxious cycle and choose to respond in any given moment with unconditional love, acceptance, compassion, empathy, forgiveness; no matter what thought, sensation or emotion pops up from out of the blue.

- Your Mantras: Commit to either using my mantras, or develop your own. Implement BB3 & BB4 (whichever applies to you) into your daily life through mantras. For example, trying to think of all the steps in the Panic Attack Eliminator (BB3) during the heat of battle will most likely just cause more anxiety and panic as you won't be able to think straight in that moment because your brain has just turned to mush (the technical terms are depersonalisation and derealisation). But through planning and preparation you can commit your mantras to memory, you can practice and practice reciting your mantras so the next time you find yourself in a hot moment you can just start reciting your mantras, and your mantras will trigger the correct attitude.

If you can become good at stepping back and being aware of your anxious thoughts and sensations before you go flying off the handle, and then consciously choose how you want to react through your well practiced mantras, you will be well on the way to getting your life back and becoming a non-anxious person again. If there was a secret sauce, this combo would be the closest thing to it!

The truth is, the problem is not the anxious thoughts and sensations that pop up either out of nowhere or as a result of a trigger from your environment, the problem is how you *choose* to respond. How you respond in the moment determines whether you fuel or extinguish the panic cycle. Master your mantras, master the art of being present, being 'aware', and your whole world will open up again and you will reignite a meaningful vision of the future. It's a beautiful thing.

The attackpanic Ethos

> *'Love yourself unconditionally, accept your life exactly the way 'it is' in this present moment; 'now' is all you will ever have, there can be no other way, there is no such thing as 'coulda', 'shoulda', 'if only' – 'now' is all there 'is'. Be grateful for everything and everyone in your life in this moment - you woke up today when millions around the world didn't, you get another opportunity to be the best you can be. Forgive yourself and others, no matter what you or they have done. Put all your effort into that which you can control, let go of everything that you can't control. Lighten up and don't take yourself too seriously. Discover your purpose or passion, follow it and reignite a meaningful vision of the future. You will find peace; you will find healing'*

Keep in touch. Let me know how things are going. If you need support or further advice, you can reach out to me at www.attackpanic.co.nz.

CHAPTER 11

FURTHER READING

All you need to know to heal yourself is contained in my Building Blocks™. If I have made that critical connection with you, you will have acquired the necessary belief, trust, and courage to do what you have to do to get better, and you do not have to look any further for answers.

However, I know that I won't be able to make that connection with *everyone* who reads my book, for whatever reason. If you are one of those readers, don't despair, below is a list of great teachers in the areas of anxiety conditions and behaviourism that you may wish to study and connect with.

- Charles Linden – The Linden Method
- Reid Wilson – Don't Panic
- Barry McDonagh – Panic Away
- David Burns – When Panic Attacks
- Harry Barry – Anxiety & Panic
- Uell S Anderson – Three Magic Words
- Viktor Frankl - Man's Search for Meaning
- Louise Hay - You Can Heal Yourself
- Eckhart Tolle - The Power of Now & A New Earth
- Joseph Murphy - The Power of Your Subconscious Mind
- John Kehoe - Mind Powers

Napoleon Hill - Think and Grow Rich
Tich Nhat Hanh - Living Buddha Living Christ
Ryan Holiday - The Obstacle is the Way
Johann Hari - Lost Connections
Mark Manson - The Subtle Art of Not Giving a F*ck

www.ingramcontent.com/pod-product-compliance
Lightning Source LLC
LaVergne TN
LVHW091721070526
838199LV00050B/2489